Western Horse Behavior and Training

ROBERT W. MILLER

Western Horse Behavior and Training

DOLPHIN BOOKS

Doubleday & Company, Inc., Garden City, New York

Dolphin Books Edition: 1975
Originally published by Big Sky Books
(The Endowment and Research Foundation,
Montana State University, Bozeman, Montana)
in 1974.

Library of Congress Cataloging in Publication Data

Miller, Robert William, 1923–1974.
    Western horse behavior and training.

    Original ed. published under title: Horse behavior and training.
    1. Horse-training   2. Horses—Behavior.   I. Title.
SF287.M6   1975   636.1′08′8
ISBN 0-385-08181-2
Library of Congress Catalog Card Number 75–19285

Foreword

This material has been prepared for students of horse behavior and training. It is for anyone who wants to learn more about horses, regardless of their age and regardless of their experience. The information presented involves not only detailed techniques for training horses but also an extensive discussion of the behavior of horses. An understanding of behavior gives the horseman insight into why a horse reacts the way it does. Experience teaches one how a horse will probably react under certain conditions. Thus a combination of using proper techniques and of understanding how and why a horse reacts should make your horse training more successful and certainly more interesting.

Although I have had a lifetime of experience with horses, I do not claim to know all there is to know about them. Neither do I claim to know all there is about teaching students, although I have spent half a lifetime doing that. A part of my job as a teacher has been to teach students to train horses. The techniques taught are necessarily different than a professional trainer would use, since he is concerned only with teaching the horse. Over the years we have developed techniques which do a reasonably good job of teaching students to understand the behavior and training of horses. In addition, the horses they train also learn but not as rapidly as if an experienced trainer were working them.

Of necessity my methods must give safety the number one priority. We never forget that horse breaking and training can be dangerous, and, therefore, we place considerable emphasis on developing a gentle, trustworthy horse. Second on the priority list is that students learn techniques that have been commonly and successfully used by horsemen for many years. This involves using equipment such as the snaffle and hackamore for early training and proper use of legs, weight and voice cues. In addition, we stress the development of good hands and a light, soft mouth on the horse.

My students are encouraged to use our extensive library collection of training books which present a wide variety of techniques. They are taught to understand there are many acceptable ways to train horses. What works for one person and one horse may not work for another. We hope the readers of this material will also keep this in mind, because the methods described here are certainly not the only way to train horses.

If you'll read this material with an open mind, as any good student should, I believe you'll find it interesting. Maybe you'll get some new ideas, maybe you'll only reinforce what you already know. In any event, here's hoping you'll always ride a good horse.

Starting first in old California and later in Texas, what is known as western horsemanship gradually spread across our nation and into Canada as well. Although the days of the open range are gone, the traditions live on in rodeos, horse shows, pleasure riding and cow ranches.

So wear your big hat with confidence and ride your good horse with pride; you belong to this great tradition!

RWM

Acknowledgments to

My Family

Three Student Artists

Margie Schultz
Anne Aller
Nina Ewing

and

All the horsemen who have been personal
friends and all acquaintances or authors from
whom I have learned what I know about horses.

Contents

CONTENTS

List of Illustrations

Western Horse Behavior and Training

CHAPTER I

Horse Behavior

Man has been fascinated by the behavior of animals for as long as he has existed on earth. This fascination resulted in a thorough understanding of the natural behavior of all the animals which primitive man depended upon for food, clothing, and religious rites. For many thousand years, primitive man used horses for these purposes and thus he must have had an excellent understanding of the behavior of the wild horse. He knew where to find him, how to get close enough to kill him, where he would run when frightened and all the other actions of the hunted animal.

Man's interest in the behavior of horses increased considerably when the horse was domesticated some 5,000 years ago. It became very important to understand not only its behavior in respect to feeding, breeding and care but also the relationship between training and behavior. After 5,000 years of such study, horsemen now have a good understanding of how horses behave or react to the conditions and demands of their domestication. Experience with horses provides an understanding of how they eat, rest, reproduce, and respond to training. Depending upon your own experience and knowledge of the horse, you will have an understanding of how a horse reacts but you may have little understanding of why he reacts the way he does. Only recently has the new science of animal behavior begun to answer these questions about the horse's reactions. In this chapter we will discuss how a horse behaves as well as why.

The evolution of the behavior of horses began over 58 million years ago when the primitive horse known as Eohippus (Greek for "Dawn horse"), first appeared on earth. At that time, the horse was a small dog-like animal living in swamps with little intelligence and ability. The drying of the earth eventually forced the Eohippus horse to adapt to a drier terrain. He gradually evolved the skeleton, physiology, size and intelligence which allowed him to survive. As these physical characteristics changed with the environment, so did his behavior. From a small, shy, swamp-dwelling animal, dependent upon brush cover and swamps for security, the horse adapted to dry ground and open country. Here survival depended upon keen senses and great speed.

The basic behavior of the horse today reflects the millions of years he lived on the open plains areas of the world. Here he ate the grass-like plants and raced for miles away from the slightest threat to his life. As we discuss the behavior of modern domesticated horses, we will be constantly referring back to his behavior as a wild animal. We will also occasionally refer to another member of the horse family, the donkey, and the result of its hybrid cross with the horse—the mule. Although we will not discuss them, the zebra, onager, and przewalski horse are also close relatives (Illus. 1–5).

SELF-PROTECTIVE BEHAVIOR

As the horse evolved through millions of years, his existence on earth was constantly threatened by climatic changes, disease, and predatory animals. It is an interesting fact that, although the primitive Eohippus horse evolved on the North American continent, he eventually became extinct here and the horse was nonexistent in this hemisphere when Columbus arrived. The cause of his disappearance is unknown but apparently his self-protective behavior failed or at least he was unable to adapt to the changing conditions. In this section we will discuss two aspects of self-protective behavior: how a horse protects himself from the elements and from predators. In later sections, we will learn that other behavior patterns of the horse, such as social, ingestive and eliminative, are involved to some degree in protection of the horse. Basically, all aspects of horse behavior are related in some way to protection of the individual and perpetuation of the species.

Protection from the Elements

The principal element that all horses seek to protect themselves from is the wind, particularly in cold weather. Wind increases the chill factor considerably. Horses will readily seek protection from it in cold weather by using trees, natural wind breaks and buildings. When grazing in wind, the horse will always prefer to have his tail towards it, in other words, graze with the wind. It is difficult to ride a horse into a driving rain or snowstorm because they want to turn their tail to the storm to protect their eyes and ears. However, when it is raining or snowing, some horses will not voluntarily go into a barn or shed. They prefer to stand outside as long as they are protected from the wind.

Not only do horses protect themselves from the elements but they also

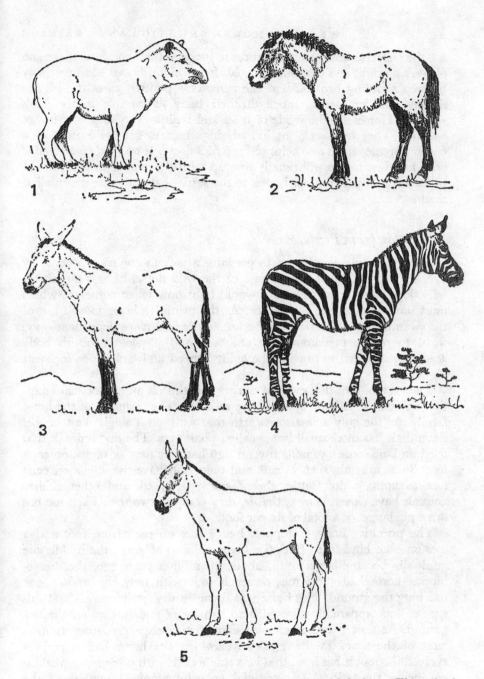

Illus. 1–5. The tapir (1) is a distant and primitive relative of the horse. This animal has four toes in front and three behind. It lives in swamps much as Eohippus did. Apparently widespread around the world at one time, it is now found only in Central America and Malay. The przewalski horse (2) is the only true living wild horse. (3) Donkey, (4) zebra, (5) onager, the wild ass of Asia.

use the elements and natural features to increase their comfort. If the sun comes up bright and clear after a cold, frosty night, horses will invariably be seen standing broadside to the sun. This position casts the biggest shadow and exposes as much of their body as possible to the sun's warmth. Horses use the shade of trees and buildings to keep cool in hot weather. They may seek out hill or ridge tops to get the benefit of a cooling breeze which also helps to keep flies away. If no shade is available on a hot day, horses will usually line up with the sun. This position exposes the least part of their bodies to the sun's heat and casts the smallest shadow.

Protection from Predators

Most wild animals respond to predator attack in one of two ways, by fighting or by running. In the case of the wild horse, he was almost totally dependent upon flight and would fight only when cornered, which must have been a rare occurrence. As the primitive horse moved out of the swamps onto drier land, he became more and more dependent upon flight to escape predators. The anatomy and physiology of his body gradually changed to provide the agility, speed and endurance for swift flight.

The type of foot that evolved during this time is an anatomical adaption unique to the horse and its close relatives. The members of the horse family are the only animals on earth that walk on a single digit or toe. Each digit has three small bones called phalanges. The first animals that lived on land some 350 million years ago had five toes, or digits, on each foot. Some animals, such as cats and dogs, still have five digits on each foot as humans do. Cattle, sheep, goats, deer, elk and other similar animals have cloven hooves, that is, they walk on two toes. Each toe has three phalanges or a total of six per foot.

The primitive horse, Eohippus, had 4 toes on each front foot and 3 toes on each hind foot (Illus. 6). Over millions of years, the middle toe gradually became larger until, about 28 million years ago, the merychippus horse had three toes on each foot with only the middle one touching the ground. This horse was living in dry, prairie areas and this type of foot apparently allowed it to run faster and further on the dry ground. At least it could run well enough to escape predatory animals most of the time. Twelve million years ago the horse had essentially evolved the foot it has now, that is, a single digit with 3 bones, or phalanges, below the fetlock. The vestigial (non-functioning) remains of the other two digits are the splint bones which can be found at the back of each cannon bone.

Flight was the principal protective behavior of the horse for millions of years after he moved out of the ancient swamps to dry hard ground. The

Pre Horse
75 million years

Pliohippus
12 million years

Eohippus
58 million years

Equus
1 million years

Mesophippus
38 million years

Merychippus
28 million years

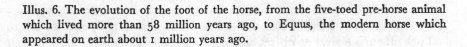

Illus. 6. The evolution of the foot of the horse, from the five-toed pre-horse animal which lived more than 58 million years ago, to Equus, the modern horse which appeared on earth about 1 million years ago.

fact that the horse was almost totally dependent upon flight to escape predators explains much of his behavior. For example, he has a strong urge to eat more or less continuously whenever possible because it might be necessary to run for long distances with no opportunity to eat. He has well-developed senses of hearing, sight and smell to give him warning of the approach of danger. He is very fearful of any type of confinement or restraint because this meant death to the wild horse. This basic fear of being trapped is why unbroken horses may fight so hard against being restrained with halters, foot ropes, or hobbles. Horses are especially fearful of having their feet caught and held. Even gentle horses may become extremely frightened if a foot is caught unexpectedly in a wire fence or a rope. The untrained horse is usually fearful of entering a small, tight space. This explains the difficulty that is usually encountered in attempting to load a horse in a trailer for the first time. It is not unusual for range horses to be very reluctant to enter a barn.

In addition to all of these fears, the wild horse was extremely fearful of something on its back. This is certainly understandable because anything that jumped onto his back was there to kill him (Illus. 7). In the early days in the west, it was not uncommon for mountain lions to kill horses, particularly colts, in this manner. Therefore, with this background and this innate fear of something on its back, it is entirely understandable why horses try to buck off a rider. Even after 5,000 years of domestication and almost constant association with man, any young horse may suddenly revert to the wild type and try to dislodge a rider. In later chapters we will spend considerable time discussing methods of preventing young horses from becoming frightened and trying to buck off their rider.

Considering the millions and millions of years involved in the evolution of the horse, it is not surprising that man has not been able to breed completely gentle horses. As a matter of fact, domesticated horses will return to wild state very rapidly if given the opportunity. This opportunity is provided when they are raised without any contact with man. As recently as the 1930's there were thousands of wild horses running in the range country of the west. These were all descendants of domesticated horses which had gone back to the wild state. There are several protected areas in the west where a few essentially wild horses still exist today. On some of the ranches of the west where colts seldom see a man and are never handled until they are to be broken to ride, they are very close to being wild horses. In later chapters we will refer to these as range horses and discuss breaking them. It is considerably different from breaking a barn-raised horse.

Old timers used to say that if a range horse didn't buck the first time it was ridden, it would never make a good horse. This, no doubt, was correct. If the wild range horse did not have enough intelligence to try to buck off such a strange object as a man and saddle, he must have been a very dumb horse. This is not true today, however, because almost all horse breakers try to never let a horse buck. Today it is very important to have dependable, trustworthy horses that are safe for any type of rider. No horse should be allowed to buck if it can be prevented. It must be remembered, however, that almost any young horse might buck if the conditions are just right, even the gentle barn-raised colt. As a matter of fact, there are some gentle barn-raised colts that are among the top bucking horses on the rodeo circuit.

Illus. 7. A mortal enemy of the horse, the lion, has preyed on horses for untold millions of years.

Horses are stimulated to buck in two ways, by the nerves in their back and by their eyes. Some colts, from the time they are born, will hump up and try to buck if they feel pressure on their back. Others may not feel this pressure until they have been ridden several times. Suddenly they re-

Illus. 8. It is not surprising that a spooky horse will think the rider on his back is a lion. Like the wild horse, he may believe his only chance for survival is to buck off or run out from under this threat to his life.

alize something is on their back and then they try to buck the rider off. Other colts may not be bothered by pressure on their back but will try to buck or run when they look back and see the rider. This type of horse can be very dangerous if they run. They may continue to watch the rider even while running at full speed and could run into fences or fall into ditches because they are not watching where they are going. Fortunately, most horses today will not buck or run if properly handled. If they do, they will soon learn not to. The fact that even completely wild horses can be broken to drive and ride is why the horse has been domesticated and has been so useful to man.

INGESTIVE (EATING) BEHAVIOR

Anatomy and Eating

The horse evolved from a swamp dweller living on soft water plants to a prairie horse living on dry ground and eating drier food. During this time several anatomical changes occurred which are related to his eating behavior. One of these changes was in the teeth. The Eohippus horse had what are called low crowned teeth, which were suitable for chewing or masticating soft foods. As he adjusted to drier, harder plants, his teeth gradually developed high crowns and became suitable for grinding range grasses. The modern horse has excellent teeth for eating the common feeds used today.

As the earth began to dry, the primitive horse began to depend more and more upon speed to elude predators. To increase speed, his legs gradually became longer. As his legs elongated, his head and neck had to become longer to enable him to continue grazing on low-growing plants. This process of mutual elongation of the parts is not always perfect. It is interesting to note the difficulty a young foal may have getting his head to the ground to eat. His legs may be too long in proportion to his head and neck, and he has to spread his front legs out to get his mouth to the ground. As the foal grows, his head and neck will grow faster than his legs. The problem of longer legs than the head and neck is soon solved. Even in adult horses, there is usually no excess length of neck and head. This is one reason they prefer to graze uphill rather than down.

One bit of evidence to indicate the gradual lengthening of the head is the space between the incisors (nippers), bridle teeth, and the molars (grinders). In animals like the dog, there is no space between the teeth because their head has not changed much from their more primitive ancestors. This lengthening of the horse's head was not only essential in order for him to continue grazing, but also proved to be a very useful characteristic upon domestication. The space between the bridle teeth and molars is the perfect place for a bit to hang in a horse's mouth. He cannot easily chew on it and soon learns to carry it in this position with no concern. Without this particular feature, it is very doubtful whether the horse would have proven so useful to man. It would have been much more difficult to control him if he could not carry a bit.

Another interesting anatomical feature of the horse involved with eating is his method of ingesting or getting food into his mouth. He uses his upper lip in a manner somewhat similar to the way an elephant uses its trunk. The upper lip of the horse is not nearly as long, obviously, as the elephant's trunk but it is strong, mobile and sensitive. It can be moved out and around food easily. The horse never uses its tongue as a cow does to get food into its mouth but depends upon the upper lip. Veterinarians often use the sensitivity of the upper lip to restrain a horse. A twitch, which is a string or chain tightened around the upper lip, hurts the horse enough that he does not feel pain in other areas where a veterinarian may be working.

Another aspect of food ingestion that is unique to the horse, among American farm animals, is its behavior in the wintertime when snow covers the grass. Horses will paw through the snow and clear an area where they can reach the grass. This instinct allows horses to winter out without supplementary feed in the northern range areas, providing the snow does not get too deep or crusted. Wild animals such as elk and buffalo also feed in this manner.

A dominant horse may allow a subservient horse to clear an area and then move him out of it if the grass appears particularly good. In observations on pawing, it is interesting to note that horses appear to paw equally with the right and left foot. In other words, they apparently are not right- or left-handed as are humans. Which foot they paw with is determined by how they are standing and in which direction they think grass can be found. There is no definite tendency to alternate feet consistently. For example, they may paw several different times with the same foot before changing to the other foot.

It is understandable why horses are not right- or left-handed if one examines the evolutionary significance. It would be a distinct disadvantage if a horse developed the muscles and strength of one leg more than another. At the walk and the trot, he must use the legs equally to support weight and to provide locomotion. At the run, he would tire more easily if he were dependent upon only one lead foot and could not change to the other one.

Eating Behavior

It is an interesting fact that although the horse has excellent vision, he cannot see what he eats. He has a blind spot that extends out in front of his nose (Illus. 22). Actually, the grazing horse does see the grass as he moves up to it but not as it enters his mouth. This apparently is no particular problem to the horse, or you, since you have a similar blind spot and cannot see food as it goes into your mouth.

Horse owners are more concerned with what a horse will eat than how he eats. In general, horses are very selective about what they eat providing they have a choice and are not forced to eat unusual or undesirable feed. Horses lived for millions of years on grass-type plants growing in

Illus. 9. If the length of leg is greater than the length of neck and head, it makes it a little difficult to graze. This foal must stand with its front legs spread apart to get its head to the ground.

drier areas of the earth. They still prefer this type of feed to broad-leafed herbs, forbs, weeds or other types of plants. It is rare for a horse to browse, that is, eat the leaves of trees or shrubs. However, they will browse on such plants as sage brush if no grass is available. Because he evolved on grass-like plants, not only does he prefer the grass plants, but they are the safest food for him. When other plants are fed, such as legume hays or the seeds of plants such as oats, corn or barley, caution must be used. All good horsemen know that too much grain can cause founder or death in horses. Also unlimited access to leafy green legumes may cause digestive disturbances. This is not at all surprising when we realize these are unnatural feeds for a horse.

Strange as it may seem, a horse is one of the few animals that can injure itself eating a natural feed. It is not uncommon for some horses to actually founder themselves on grass. This occurs in areas where grass is particularly lush and the horses are confined to small areas. They tend to overeat and under exercise. Shetlands as well as horses are quite susceptible to founder under these conditions.

Horses prefer grazing in open areas where they can watch for enemies. They also prefer young tender grass to coarse heavy-stemmed plants. If they crop an area in a pasture quite close, they may tend to overgraze this area because of their preference for young tender plants. On many horse farms, pastures are regularly mowed, this keeps all of the grass growing at about the same stage and helps prevent horses overgrazing some areas and undergrazing others.

Horses grazing in pastures do not establish a regular schedule for eating at certain times and resting at other times. Animals like cattle, sheep, deer and elk have a regular schedule. Horses graze and rest intermittently, with more time spent grazing than resting. Even when horses should not be hungry, they will graze along being very selective and taking only small amounts of the most tasty plants. As stated earlier, apparently the horse evolved with a basic urge to always keep his digestive tract full of feed in the event that he would be pursued by predators for many hours and have no opportunity to graze. Also, the digestive tract of the horse evolved to utilize feed most efficiently when the horse is eating more or less continuously. Recent research has proved what good horsemen have long observed—the horse does better if fed small amounts often rather than larger amounts infrequently. This is understandable when we realize how the horse evolved.

Although we have said the grazing horse does not establish a regular schedule, horses that are confined and hand-fed definitely do. They become very time conscious. If they are in the habit of being fed at, say, 7:00 A.M., they become restless and uneasy if their feed is not available when expected. For this reason, hand-fed horses should be fed at a regular time, or times, each day. It is better for the horse if he is fed at least twice a day, although this may not be feasible in some situations. Obviously, horses that are confined and fed by hand cannot feed exactly as would the free horse. However, an understanding of ingestive behavior allows the horse owner to approach natural feeding. Irregular and inadequate hand feeding is directly related to a number of aberrant or unnatural behavior patterns such as wood chewing, stall weaving, pawing and kicking. It also can be the cause of digestive disturbances.

One ingestive behavior pattern in new-born foals that sometimes causes concern is their habit of nibbling at the horse feces or droppings which they find in a corral or pasture. This would appear to be a very unsanitary habit that should be prevented. However, this urge of the foal to nibble on feces of older horses may have evolved as a method of inoculating the digestive tract of the foal with microorganisms. The horse is dependent upon microorganisms to digest grass. The feces of older horses have billions of bacteria and other microorganisms which, upon ingestion by a foal, would insure ample microorganisms in the digestive tract. Apparently there is little or no danger of spreading disease in this manner nor of infecting the foal with parasites. Parasite eggs must go through an incubation period on the ground for about two weeks before they would be infective. Foals usually will nibble only feces that are a few days old.

Practical Significance of Ingestive Behavior

We should recognize the horse's basic urge to keep its stomach full and try to feed confined horses accordingly. Ideally, the horse should be fed small amounts often, although usually it is not practical to feed more than two or three times a day. We should also be well acquainted with natural and unnatural feeds for a horse and the amounts of each that are safe to feed. In a later section, we will discuss the use of grain to reward a horse.

Drinking Behavior

In areas where water and feed are scarce, wild horses will usually come to water every other night. They will spend the night near the water, graze away from it for about a day, and return the second evening after making a big circle. At the farthest point, they may be 6 to 10 miles from water, depending upon how far they must go to find enough feed. If feed is plentiful, they may water each night during hot weather. The preferred time to come to drink is the evening, although occasionally the horses will come in just before dawn. In Nevada where water was scarce and the springs were small, it was observed by Pellegrini (1971) that the horses watered one at a time. The lead mare and her foal would drink first and the stud last. If the stud tried to drink out of turn, the boss mare drove him back.

Horses prefer to drink clean, clear water out of deep pools. If a horse is quite thirsty, it may lower its head deep enough to cover the nostrils. However, there is no danger of it drowning because it will not draw water into the lungs, only into the stomach. Cows prefer to sip from a shallow spot and are not as particular as the horse as to how clean the water is.

Grazing horses readily meet their water needs by eating snow in the winter time. As they graze along, they will ingest the snow with the grass. It is desirable for horses who are fed hay to have access to open water because they are standing in one place and cannot ingest snow as they eat. They will consume some snow when they are not eating but it may not be enough to meet their needs. Where water must be supplied artificially to horses, it is best to use troughs or fountains which have fresh water available at all times. If horses are watered by hand in buckets, they should be given water at least twice daily.

Eliminative Behavior

The grazing horse tends to defecate and urinate in certain areas and graze in others. This is particularly noticeable in small pastures where some areas may be grazed quite close with little evidence of droppings, while other areas have tall, rank grass with a greater concentration of droppings. Stallions are much more pronounced in this behavior than mares or geldings. In stallion corrals, droppings will be concentrated in a small area. The stallion is usually careful to deposit fresh droppings on the old mound of droppings. Thus there is little scattering. Mares and geldings, on the other hand, may walk to a defecating area in a pasture and stop at the edge, thus, each time they may be enlarging the defecating area.

Such a behavior pattern probably evolved in horses for one or two reasons. Most likely it evolved as a method for a stallion to mark his grazing area or territory much as dogs mark theirs with urine scent posts. Marking apparently served to warn rival stallions they were entering the territory of a certain stallion. The other reason for the evolution of this behavior might have been to provide some protection for horses from infestation by internal parasites. Many internal parasites are spread from one horse to another by grazing pastures contaminated with parasite eggs from the droppings of infested horses. Wild horses may have reduced this opportunity for the spread of parasites by defecating in certain areas and grazing in others.

Practical Significance of Eliminative Behavior

Internal parasites are a common and often serious problem in horses today. Domesticated horses cannot effectively utilize the protective mechanism described above because of confinement. Horse owners must use other methods to keep parasites under control. Regular worming of all horses is important. Harrowing of pastures to spread the droppings and destroy the parasite eggs by exposure to sunlight is beneficial. Pastures should not be overgrazed. Horses should be fed in mangers rather than on the ground to reduce the chances of the feed being contaminated with parasite eggs from manure.

SEXUAL BEHAVIOR

We will discuss this subject, first, as it applies to the reproductive process and, second, as it applies to training. The physiological control of sexual behavior lies in the endocrine (hormone) system. Certain hormones bring a mare into heat, or estrus, others keep her out. Still others maintain pregnancy and eventually terminate gestation. Sexual activities of the stallion are also controlled by hormones. Hormone levels are influenced by the length of day, thus horses tend to be seasonal breeders. Stallions are sexually more active in the spring and early summer although they will breed and are fertile any time of the year. Mares exhibit even a stronger tendency to be sexually active in the spring and early summer. They are much less active and less fertile the remainder of the year. There is a considerable amount of variation in the sexual behavior between mares and even within the same mare. Because of this variation, some mares can be difficult to successfully breed.

The gradual lengthening of the day in the spring months stimulates the master endocrine gland, the pituitary, to secrete hormones which will bring the mare into estrus and prepare her body for conception. The same pituitary hormones stimulate increased sexual activity in the stallion. As the days start to shorten after June 22, sexual activity gradually decreases. In many mares it will cease completely in the fall and winter months. Thus, the most fertile time for the mare and the peak of the sexual activity of both mares and stallions will be in May, June, and July when the days are the longest. During this period, mares will be most regular in their estral cycle and will be most apt to conceive. Other factors also affect the estral cycle such as nutrition, disease, parasites, lameness, and age.

Apparently, the true wild horse was even more restricted than domesticated horses in its breeding season. Most wild animals also have a short breeding season. There is a definite evolutionary advantage to a restricted season for breeding and thus for foaling. The nutritional requirements of a mammal are much higher during lactation (milk production) than any other time. The fact that the wild horses bred at the time of year which would allow them to foal at the start of the green grass is no accident, but a biological necessity. Foaling at this time provided the wild mare with the most nutritious feed at the time of her greatest need. Exactly the same phenomena can be observed in such wild herbivorous animals as deer, elk, antelope, moose and buffalo. All of them give birth to their young at the beginning of the green grass season. Another factor important for survival of the young is the mild weather which would come at this time of year in the northern climates. Since the mare's gestation period is approximately eleven months, she would also be on the best feed of the year for breeding back after foaling. Thus mares foaling in the spring on green grass will have the highest level of nutrition for lactation as well as for breeding. As proof of this theory, mares on the Pryor Mountain Wild Horse Range on the Montana, Wyoming border produce most of their foals in May and June. These are months when the grass is the most nutritious.

Five thousand years of domestication has allowed some variation to develop in the seasonal breeding pattern of the horse. Most likely this variation has developed because man has provided the feed and care needed by the mare to foal either earlier or later in the year. In other words, man has supplied the environment needed to foal at other times and thus horses have gradually adapted to this change. Foals are born any time of the year to domesticated mares, but by far the largest number are born in the spring. Perhaps in another 5,000 years, horses will not be seasonal breeders but will breed with equal ease year around as do pigs and dairy cattle.

Several major horse breeds, notably Thoroughbred, Standardbred and Quarter Horses, have a rather strange rule regarding birth dates. The rule, for some unknown and certainly biologically unsound reason, states a foal will be considered one year old on the first day of January following the year he was born. Thus, a foal born in January would be 12 months old the following January. It would have a great advantage in size and development over one born in July. This advantage would carry over into their first racing year as two-year-olds. The January colt would be two years old on his second January birthday, while the July colt would be only 18 months. All of this encourages the breeder to attempt to breed mares earlier in the season than is natural. As a result, these attempts often are unsuccessful. The entire matter could have been solved by starting the year on the first of March or April. Man's ingenuity being what it is, he would rather try something more complex than simply changing dates. Recently some breeders have begun artificially lengthening the day with lighted box stalls during the winter months in an attempt to start a mare's estral cycle earlier. Results have been encouraging and it will be interesting to observe what long range biological changes this may produce in the mare.

Mating Behavior of the Stallion

The stallion is the only farm male in which courtship is an important part of the mating behavior. Courtship, or teasing, prepares the stallion physically and mentally for mating and involves the senses of sound, sight, smell and feel. Courtship also allows the stallion to determine if the mare is at a stage of her estral cycle when she will be receptive of breeding. If teasing is done on a regular basis or if a stallion is turned loose with the mares, his presence may be an aid to establishing a regular estral cycle and conception in the mare.

In hand mating where the stallion is led to the mare, he almost invariably sounds the mating call when he is brought in sight of the mare. As he is brought up to the side of the mare, he will nip her and also smell her body. After smelling, he may raise his head high with the upper lip curled up as he attempts to define the odor of the mare. The urine and possibly the body of a mare in estrus has an odor which communicates her estral condition to the stallion. Experienced stallions can determine immediately by the odor and attitude of the mare if she is ready to breed. He will often strike with the front feet and some stallions may attempt to kick the mare. There is usually a considerable amount of squealing by the stallion and sometimes by the mare depending on the stage of her estral period.

Illus. 10. Range stallions approach mares carefully to avoid being kicked or struck.

Illus. 11. Typical head and upper lip position of a stallion as he attempts to detect an odor indicating estral stage of a mare.

Courtship by the range stallion is very similar to that of the wild horse. The range stallion will always approach the mare carefully from the front to avoid being kicked or struck. As they stand facing each other, he will be slightly off to one side to be clear of her front feet should she strike. He will usually strike the air several times as he smells her flanks, nips and squeals. The wise range stud takes no chances of being kicked and will not attempt to mount the mare unless she is in full estrus. In this matter, the range mare is unquestionably the dominant individual. As a matter of fact, she initiates and terminates the courtship of the stallion by her actions as we shall discuss in the next section. A stallion may be pasture bred to as many as thirty or even forty mares, although the average is ten to twenty. In recent studies on wild horses, breeding groups were found to be quite small. The average size of a group was two to three mares and a stallion. Occasionally a young stallion was included in the breeding group but he was dominated by the older stallion and did not breed mares.

Mating Behavior of the Mare

As we pointed out earlier, mares show considerable variability in their sexual behavior. The average length of time that a mare is in heat is about six days. Some mares will be in heat only one or two days while others may be in for two weeks and a few for two months or longer. In the six-day heat period, the average mare may be coming into heat for one or two days and will respond to the teasing of a stallion but would not be receptive to breeding. She may then stand for breeding up to the fifth day and be going out on the sixth day. She may object to breeding on this last day but often can be bred. The seventh day she would be out of heat and could not be bred. Most mares will go out of estrus more rapidly than they came in. Ovulation usually occurs at the end of the estral period. The average mare will start a new estral cycle every 19 to 21 days.

In hand breeding, the teasing by the stallion determines if a mare is in heat and if she is receptive to breeding. When the mare is out of heat, she will fight the stallion vigorously showing all the signs of considerable anger. Her ears will be laid back and with a very angry look she will kick viciously and squeal loudly. Such obvious lack of interest in the advances of the stallion usually cools his ardor rapidly and he loses interest in her.

All of this behavior changes when the mare starts coming into heat. In the early stages, she will become interested in other horses, particularly stallions if one is in the vicinity, or geldings if there is no stallion. She will approach the male with ears up and in a friendly manner. If there are no males available, she will be more friendly with other mares, even ones which are subservient to her. If she is isolated from horses, she will spend considerable time walking the fence and looking for other horses. If she is teased by a stallion, she will keep her ears up but may kick, strike and squeal. In a day or two, she will cease kicking and will urinate when teased. There may be a slight discharge from the vulva and rhythmic contraction or winking of the clitoris and vulva. At the height of estrus, there is also a slight enlargement of the vulva. All of these symptoms of estrus can be detected by careful observation. However, from a practical standpoint the most accurate and effective method of determining estrus is teasing with a stallion.

We have discussed the symptoms and duration of estrus in average mares. Remember though, there is considerable variation with some mares showing estrus for the entire breeding season and some not showing any. Such mares could be physiologically fertile but difficult to fertilize because of their behavior. The mare with the unusually long estral period is difficult to fertilize because it is difficult to predict accurately when she would ovulate. The mare not showing estrus could not be bred unless restrained and again it is difficult to determine ovulation time. Only skilled veterinarians or stud farm managers with considerable experience can obtain high conception rates in these kinds of mares.

Sexual Behavior and Training

STALLIONS

The sexual behavior of a stallion creates special problems if he is to be ridden. The stallion must be taught that he is to be a saddle horse at certain times. At such times he cannot make any of the sounds or moves of a stallion. Obviously, this is not easy to do because it is contrary to the basic behavior of the horse. Since it is not easy to do and because it can also be dangerous, I believe that only experienced horsemen should attempt to train a stallion. Although a few women can handle stallions properly, in general, it requires a man because of the strength and firmness which must be used. Even after a stallion is well trained, he can never be considered completely trustworthy. For this reason, amateurs and children should not ride and handle stallions.

In training a stallion to be used as a saddle horse, the horse must be absolutely convinced of the proper time to be a saddle horse and the proper time to be a stallion. The equipment used and location of the two types of uses should be separate and distinct. For teasing and breeding, a certain type of headgear should be used. He should be brought to a mare in an area set aside for that purpose only. Under these conditions, he is free to act as a stallion. In other areas and with riding equipment, he is to be a saddle horse and no sounds or moves of a stallion can be tolerated.

One of the very important features in training a stallion as a saddle horse is the method used to discipline him. Whatever method is used, it must be used immediately following the misbehavior and it must be used with enough authority to impress the horse. Some trainers carry a whip when they are on the ground and if the horse starts to act like a stallion, he is whipped on the front legs and forced to back up. If the whip is not available, the bridle reins can be used. It is important, in my opinion, not to discipline the horse by jerking on a bit because it may injure his mouth. A heavy halter or bosal can be jerked down without injuring his mouth.

If the horse misbehaves with the trainer mounted, the temptation to jerk on the bit should be avoided. One of the best methods is to spin the horse in a tight circle several times one way and several times the other direction. All horses dislike to be spun and it will almost always divert a stallion's mind away from whatever caused him to act like a stallion. As the horse is being spun, he can be whipped or spurred to further discipline him if necessary. This may sound like rough treatment but it is necessary to be a little tougher than the stallion if the trainer is going to maintain the upper hand. If this method of discipline is to be used, the horse must be taught to spin as a part of his regular training.

The handling of stallions while teasing and breeding is primarily a matter of controlling the horse in a manner that is safe to the handler, the mare and the stallion himself. Undisciplined stallions can seriously injure the handler, by striking, sometimes by biting and even by kicking, if the stallion should be allowed to turn away from the handler. An unruly stallion which runs uncontrolled to the mare and attempts to mount a mare not ready to be bred may be kicked and crippled or made sterile. Some stallions may strike, bite or kick mares and serious injury could result to the mare.

Some handlers use a whip on the front legs to control the stallion. Most commonly used is some type of headgear that will control the horse without injuring his mouth (Illus. 12–15). Some stallions can be handled in a halter, others in a snaffle bit. A lead strap with a chain run through the halter and under or over the nose or through the mouth may be necessary on some horses. A light chain run under the upper lip and through the halter is very severe and would be used on the rank kind of horse that could not be handled any other way. There are also a variety of so-called war bridles that can inflict considerable pain. These should be used only by an expert, on studs impossible to handle by more conventional methods.

MARES

The behavior of the mare when she is in heat almost invariably creates a problem in training. The problem is basically one of her losing interest

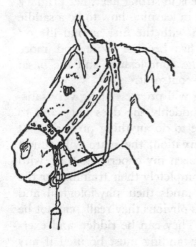

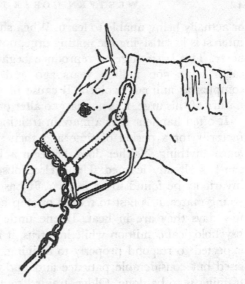

12. Lead chain under jaw.

13. Chain over nose.

14. Chain through mouth.

15. Chain under upper lip.

Illus. 12–15. Headgear for handling stallions. (Not pictured are various bits and bosals which may be used.)

or actually being unable to learn. When she is in strong heat, her primary interest is in satisfying the mating urge, not in learning how to be a saddle horse. This basic urge to reproduce began with the first animal life on earth some 500 million years ago and has become more and more complex as animals evolved. Because of the complexities and the basic nature of this urge, it is not easy to alter or control it.

It often happens that a mare in training will progress along very satisfactorily for a period of time and then suddenly she does not want to learn anything. Neither does she seem able to do anything properly that she has already learned. Upon close observation, the mare will almost invariably be found to be in heat. It has been my experience that, with young mares, it is best to reduce or stop completely their training for the few days they are in heat. If one understands their physiological and psychological condition while in estrus, it is obvious they really cannot be expected to respond properly to training. They can be ridden and exercised but considerable patience and understanding must be used if any training is to be done. Older, trained mares can be expected to perform somewhat more satisfactorily when in heat but even they will probably not do as well as when they are out of heat.

SOCIAL BEHAVIOR

Throughout millions of years of evolution, horses have developed a very strong need for the company of each other. Basically, this need is involved with self protection, because the wild horse did not feel secure unless he was with other horses. A group of horses have that many more eyes, ears and nostrils to detect danger and to warn each other. Thus, a group of horses feels secure, whereas an individual by itself will feel insecure. As this basic phenomenon evolved, horses have developed many interesting behavior patterns related to living as a group. In the following sections we will discuss need for company, social order, leadership, agonistic behavior, communications and play of horses.

Need for Company

The social behavior involved with a horse's desire for horse company is a very basic need that may create many problems in the training and handling of horses. The first time a horse is separated from other horses is a very traumatic experience. The horse almost always becomes very nervous and uneasy. It may not eat and certainly cannot concentrate on learning. Basically, it is afraid for its life. Fortunately, most horses learn they have nothing to fear by being alone. However, it takes time and careful planning to change this basic behavior pattern.

Modern horses, just like their ancestors for millions of years, have a strong preference to be with a group of horses because of the security provided by the group. In wild horses, the groups range in size from 3 or 4 horses, up to 6 or 7. The basic group is a stallion with his mares and foals, although an extra stallion might be included. Bachelor stallions also form groups of 3–5 head, while some old stallions may stay by themselves. Domestic mares and geldings on ranches may run in somewhat larger bunches. Within a group of domesticated horses, certain individuals may develop very strong attachments for each other. In other words they form small sub-groups of two or three horses. When separated, the partners of a small sub-group may display considerable distress, whinnying loudly and racing back and forth in a corral or pasture trying to locate the missing partner. This attachment among mature horses may be as strong as the mother-foal relationship and verge on being true love affairs. It certainly appears to be more than a need for group security.

Horses are very selective about who they will accept as a partner. However, they will, when no horses are available, accept other animals as their friends. For example, they will develop real affection for such animals as mules, goats, dogs, cows and even sheep. One Montana rancher reported that an old stallion who had been fought away from his mares by a younger rival made friends with a buck antelope who was

Illus. 16. Horses have a basic need for horse company. Here two massage each other over the withers. Horses often develop very strong attachments for their special friends.

alone for the same reason. The two were nearly always in sight of each other, although they would graze at some distance apart. When a horse must be kept alone for some reason, which is usually the case with a stallion, it may be helpful to have an animal like a dog or goat in the corral for company.

We have said that horses exhibit fear when left alone for the first time. However, they may also have such a strong attachment for a partner who is absent that they actually are lonesome, just as humans who are close friends might be when separated. For example, a horse might be kept in the corral while a group of horses, including his best partner, is turned out. The horse in the corral could be expected to show concern about being left alone but often his partner does too. The partner will be torn between the desire to stay with the bunch, which probably is basically fear of being alone, and the desire to stay with its friend in the corral, which may be basically friendship.

Although horses have a very basic need for horse company, they will replace this source of security with the security of the barn. Their feeling of security and safety in and around the barn may become an obsession which is commonly called being "barn sour." We will discuss the practical significance of this in the next section.

PRACTICAL SIGNIFICANCE OF NEED FOR COMPANY

As we have discussed, horses have a very basic need for horse company and until horses learn that they can be safe without horse company, it will be difficult to teach them anything. There are several methods used by horsemen to teach a young horse he can survive and his life is not in danger when he is alone. One method is to feed and water the colt in a box stall where he cannot see other horses and, except for being turned out for exercise, keep him there until he quiets down. Usually this would be done at weaning time, and most weanlings will adjust, within a few days to being alone. Older horses placed by themselves for the first time may take considerably longer. An occasional older horse may never really settle down when alone.

Another method is to move the young horse to another location where everything is new and different and his attention may be diverted from his need for old friends. Working a horse in a building or solid boarded corral where he can see or hear nothing but the trainer is helpful in teaching the colt to concentrate on the trainer and forget about his friends. When a young horse is first being ridden, he should not be taken out alone until the rider has him well under control. Being alone may increase his fear to the point that he would become uncontrollable if anything frightened him.

One of the problems in teaching a horse that he can survive without

horse company is that he most likely will learn that he is safe and protected in the barn or home pasture even without other horses. Thus, he
replaces the need for horse security with barn or home security. In other
words, as we have already mentioned, he becomes "barn sour." This is a
real problem with many horses. Once this attachment to the barn is established, it is difficult to overcome because it is satisfying the basic need
of the horse for security. With some horses, it appears they associate the
barn with the end of the ride and they hurry back or are reluctant to
leave because they know it means work.

Riding away from the barn with other horses will help but certainly
will not solve the problem because you may not always have someone to
ride with. Whenever possible while riding young horses, it is best to return to the barn by a different route than the one by which you left. Obviously, it would be very undesirable to let a horse run back toward the
barn, not only because of this problem, but because you would be bringing your horse to the barn hot and sweaty. In the long run, it takes much
time, patience, and firmness to overcome this problem. In some older
horses who have firmly established the pattern of being barn sour, it is
very difficult, if not impossible, to completely break them of the habit.
However, a good horseman should be able to control and discipline the
horse enough to make him physically, if not mentally, leave the barn.

Riding groups should take special precautions not to create situations
where the horse's need for company will be dangerous to a rider. For example, the group should not move until all riders are mounted. If the
group moves while someone is on the ground, this person might have
difficulty getting on safely because his horse gets excited at the prospect of
being left alone. For the same reason, the group should wait while a rider
gets off to open and close a gate, or to pick up something off the ground.

Illus. 17. Riding etiquette and good horsemanship require waiting for all riders to
be mounted before the group moves.

If the group is large, it may not be feasible or necessary for all of them to wait, but one or two riders should always stay with the one who stops. Not only is this the polite thing to do but it is also a very important safety feature.

A young horse which has never been by itself should not be taken from its group and put in a separate area unless that area is properly fenced. By properly fenced, I mean a fence which is high enough so that the horse could not jump it. It also should be constructed of material in which a horse could not catch a leg while pawing. It is obviously best to confine such a horse in a well built corral or paddock for a few days until he settles down.

Social Order

Many species of animals which live in groups establish what is called a "social order," or an order of dominance. You may have noticed that one horse in a bunch seems to be the boss and will bite and kick others, sometimes with considerable ferocity. If you made a study of the group, you could probably work out the social order for all of the horses in the bunch. You could arrange them in a numerical order, say from 1 to 10, if you had that many horses. Number one is dominant over all the horses, number two is dominant over all horses from 3 to 10, and so on down the line until number 10 is not dominant over any horse. Some horses, depending upon their disposition, are very strict enforcers of the social strata. They try to really hurt any horse below them in the order which gets out of line. This might be the number one horse or it might be number 9 who would have only number 10 to pick on, but who would do so very energetically. Another horse may maintain dominance by only laying back its ears and pushing a lower horse out of a feed box with its nose.

Each year my students work out the social order of about 20 head of young horses. They do this by placing a tub with a small amount of grain in the corral and removing the horses one by one as they determine which eats from the tub first. The position of some will be very easy to detect, while others will require close observation. The groups consist of both mares and geldings, the ages are two-, three- and four-year-olds, although we occasionally have an older horse or two. Usually an older mare (4-year-old or older) will be dominant, but geldings may also be dominant. A 2-year-old has never been dominant over an entire bunch.

It is not unusual to have a horse high in the dominance order paired with a horse that is near the bottom. As long as the dominant horse is in the corral, other horses will not be aggressive towards its partner. However, if the dominant horse is removed, then its partner will be put in its proper place in the social order.

It required millions of years for wild horses to evolve this type of behavior. The basic unit of the social structure was the breeding group consisting of a stallion and several mares. The mares established and maintained a social order among themselves. Bachelor stallions, who did not have mares, also stayed together in small groups and were organized in a similar manner. In 1965, I observed the behavior of approximately 100 range stallions that had been gathered off a large Montana ranch and put together in corrals. These studs definitely had a social order with certain mature, battle-scarred individuals obviously dominant over others. It has been reported that in the few remaining wild horse herds in the West this same phenomena of an order of dominance has been observed among bachelor stallions. Pellegrini (1971) reported in his study of wild horses in Nevada there was an order of dominance among breeding groups. When a dominant stallion and his group came to water, he would chase a subservient group away while he and his group drank.

Geldings, the result of man's alteration of the stallion, exhibit a somewhat confused social behavior when with mares. Some geldings in the presence of mares, assume the characteristics of a stallion and will become quite possessive of certain mares. They will actually herd the mares and try to keep other geldings or mares away. This behavior will be most pronounced in the spring months which corresponds to the natural breeding season of horses. Other geldings have no real interest in the mares and will fight them away from feed or certain desirable spots, such as in the shade of a tree or building. Still others are definitely subservient to mares and are at the bottom of the social order in a mixed group. One of the main reasons many early day western riders would not ride anything but geldings was because the gelding is less concerned about social order and fighting.

In general, the behavior of geldings is less erratic and more stable than mares because of the absence of sex hormones. As we pointed out earlier, mares in heat are not as responsive as when out of heat. Also mares coming into heat create disturbances when mixed with geldings. Even today it is common for ranchers to prefer geldings for saddle horses, and to not keep mares with the geldings. Although we have said geldings usually fight less than mares, an occasional one, who has more of the behavior of a stallion, will be very aggressive toward other horses. Apparently these aggressive geldings have a higher level of certain male hormones than do most geldings.

Another interesting fact about social dominance is that it is rare for any mature horse, be it mare, gelding or stallion, to fight a foal or short yearling to establish dominance. They appear to recognize that the foal is no threat to their position and therefore disregard them. The foal communicates its immaturity by approaching the adult very timidly, extending its head and opening and closing its mouth. As yearlings or coming two year olds they will lose the instinct to behave in this manner and become subject to attack by older horses.

LEADERSHIP AND SOCIAL ORDER

The study of the social structure of a group of horses is very interesting, particularly if one speculates on the reason for the evolution of such behavior. Apparently social order evolved in horses as basically a protective mechanism for the individual, as well as for the group with which it associated. As with many species, the horse found safety in numbers as we have already mentioned. However, for a group of horses to function most effectively, there must be some order among them and, in particular, there must be a leader.

In wild horses, the stallion was not the leader. He was the defender or protector of his group of mares from rival stallions and predators. He herded his mares, kept them together, fought off other studs and chased other breeding groups out of his territory but was not the leader. Within his group of mares, there was a social order. The dominant one would be a mature mare in the prime of life, who was the most aggressive and who had special characteristics of leadership. These characteristics would include an intimate knowledge of the area in which the group lived as to the location of grass, water, areas protected from storms and areas least apt to subject the horse to predator attack. Also, the lead mare would know all the trails in the area and the best escape routes. The stallion would bring up the rear.

The mare would establish and maintain her leadership by ample use of her teeth and feet. When a new mare was added to the bunch, which must have happened occasionally, a test of dominance would be made. The leader could be moved down to second place in the order if the new mare proved the best fighter. In this event, the best fighter might be the leader rather than the one with the greatest ability to safely lead the group. However, it must be assumed that in the wild horse there was a positive relationship between aggressiveness and ability to lead. In addition to the occasional addition of a new mare into a group, some of the replacements were probably fillies born in the group. Older mares ordinarily would be dominant over the younger ones, and thus the older one would be expected to be the best leader by virtue of experience. Pellegrini (1971) reported that in the wild breeding groups he studied in Nevada, the stallion always brought up the rear when the group strung out to travel. The leader was the dominant mare.

Domesticated horses exhibit many of these same behavioral patterns. When domesticated horses string out to travel, the leader or most dominant individual is usually in the lead or near the lead with the others following in line behind. In some bunches, I have observed the leader to be one of the younger, more adventuresome mares and not the most dominant one. The horses following would not necessarily be arranged in an exact dominance order. Usually the least dominant would be to the rear where it would not be subject to discipline by more dominant individuals. In this position, the dominant horses appear to almost completely disregard the less dominant individual unless there is crowding. If the less dominant should try to pass, it would subject itself to a vigorous bite or kick. As the horses move along single file, head to tail, the less dominant feels safe, not only from discipline, but also from the danger of predator attack. They give the appearance of having complete faith in the leader. They follow along relaxed and secure, although if the leader signals danger, they can react very rapidly.

PRACTICAL SIGNIFICANCE OF LEADERSHIP

There is some evidence that a horse's natural inclination to be a leader or a follower is involved in its ability to win races. For example, a horse that is inclined to be dominant may be difficult to hold off the pace. He may have a real driving urge to take the lead as soon as the gate opens and if held back, uses up too much energy fighting the jockey. On the other hand, if he is allowed to take the lead, he may use up too much energy early in the race and fade in the stretch. If such a horse has an abundance of speed and endurance, and can be taught to stay off the lead at the start and save his energy for a drive to the front toward the end of the race, he may be a great race horse. Many of the champions apparently are this type of horse.

The opposite to this type would be the horse which is naturally a follower and, therefore, would be reluctant to pass horses. Such a horse might win races, assuming he has running ability, only if he were in the lead from the start. There have been a number of famous race horses who were known as front runners, that is, if they took the lead right from the start they stayed there and won the race. If they were beat out of the gate and were behind horses, they would lose the race.

When riding young horses outside for the first time, it is wise to use their natural inclination to follow a leader by having a rider on a gentle horse go along. The young horse will follow the older one and go along much easier, especially if there are any spooky objects to pass. After the colt has gone out a few times with another horse and the trainer has reasonably good control, he must be made to go alone. This is an essential part of his training.

AGONISTIC BEHAVIOR AND SOCIAL ORDER

As we have been discussing, horses display agonistic, or fighting, behavior to establish a social order. In a group of mares, this will be done by body biting and kicking, with biting more commonly used to maintain dominance. Kicking is used more to establish dominance when strange mares are put together. However, particularly aggressive ones may kick others whenever the opportunity is presented. Stallions will keep their mares together and under control mostly by body biting, although they may occasionally kick at a mare. When gathering and moving his mares, a stallion will often lower his head almost to the ground, and with his ears laid back tight, move along in a weaving manner, swinging his head back and forth. This is a signal for his mares to bunch up and move. Some stallions will not accept new mares in their bunch. They fight them away mostly by biting and chasing.

When two stallions fight, it is a considerably more serious affair because they are fighting for a group of mares and the loser must be driven away. In the wild horse, there probably was considerable bluffing and threatening and serious fighting was held to a minimum. On the other hand, if domesticated stallions, who have never run with other stallions, get together, there is little bluffing. Mature stallions fight viciously and can do each other considerable damage. Much of the serious effects result because the vanquished one tries to escape but can't because of fences or obstructions. In desperation, he may jump a fence and get cut seriously in the wire. In any event, it is a very serious matter when two mature studs get together. All stud owners take considerable precautions to avoid this happening.

Stallions fight by biting, kicking and striking. Mostly they fight head to head and most of the biting is on the neck, shoulders and front legs. Front legs are used for striking as the stallions rear, although usually not much damage is caused by striking. Deadly damage can be done with the teeth if the windpipe or a jugular vein is severed; however this is rare. After a serious fight, stallions will be badly scarred by teeth as well as hoof marks. The horses are more afraid of being kicked than bitten because of severe pain and possible serious injuries from solidly placed hind feet. When horses whirl to kick, the one that lands the most solid blows will probably be the victor. A horse may be knocked off its feet if hit from the side by a charging adversary.

It has been reported that jacks are unusually vicious in fighting stallions or other jacks, and in the early days a jack would virtually clean the range of stallions in what it considered its territory. Apparently jacks did most of their damage with their teeth. They occasionally killed a rival by cutting the windpipe or jugular veins because of their tendency to bite in this area. The primitive Miohippus horse, which lived about 28 million years ago, had large canine teeth which may have been used for fighting, as boars use their tusks.

In wild horses, there was a more or less continuous battle between mature stallions with mares and those without. Those without mares were

AGONISTIC BEHAVIOR

Illus. 18. Dominant mare using her teeth to keep another mare at the proper distance.

Illus. 19. Stallions fight viciously with teeth and feet.

fighting to get them and the others were fighting to keep them. All of this activity was heightened during the spring mating season. When young stallions were chased out of their mother's groups, they formed small groups of their own and, no doubt, spent considerable time play-fighting with each other. As they matured, the stronger ones built up their own small herd of mares.

Geldings may fight as mares do, that is, mostly by biting and kicking. Young geldings often play-fight as if they were stallions, which involves staying head to head, rearing, striking and biting. If they are playing, hard kicking is usually not done. Some geldings with stallion tendencies will herd mares and fight away geldings or unwanted mares.

PRACTICAL SIGNIFICANCE OF AGONISTIC BEHAVIOR

The fact that horses do fight to establish a social order always creates the potential for trouble when strange horses are first put together. This is particularly true if a new horse is being added to an established group. It may reduce chances for injury if the horses are allowed to make initial contact over a good plank fence for a day or two. Allowing horses to become acquainted over a wire fence is, of course, very apt to result in a wire-cut horse. When strange horses are mixed, it is best to put them in a good-sized pasture where there is plenty of room to escape attacks. They should never be put in an area where a dominant horse can trap a stranger in a corner from which he can't escape without getting severely bitten or kicked. The trapped horse may try to escape the attack by jumping the fence and seriously injure himself in the attempt. It might help to put the new horse with one member of the group who is not aggressive for a few days. After a relationship is established between these two, the group might accept the new member with less commotion.

Agonistic behavior and social order may create a potentially dangerous situation for both horse and rider when riding groups get together for a ride. For example, an aggressive horse may kick at another one and kick the rider's leg or body instead. To reduce the chances of such accidents, all horses should be spaced well apart when standing about or moving as a group. When traveling single file, the following horse should not be allowed to crowd up on the horse in front. Faster moving horses should go to the front rather than crowding horses from behind. When passing, a horse should be taken well out to the side to avoid being kicked or bitten as it goes by. Remember, loose horses trail along more or less in dominant order, and the dominant one accepts the less dominant as long as it stays immediately behind. This same relationship is also apparent when horses are being ridden, and alterations in this arrangement must be done carefully.

Agonistic behavior may be a problem within a group if one of the individuals becomes the forceful protector of its close friends. Occasionally, a mare or gelding will assume this role and will fight other horses away from its partner. A gelding may cause the most problem by attempting to keep other geldings away from his special mare friends. This is a role he would have played with considerable vigor had he not been castrated. The danger here is injury by kicking or biting and the only solution may be to keep the protector by himself.

COMMUNICATION AND SOCIAL LIVING

As the horse evolved a social system, he also evolved a rather extensive communication system. Horses use vocal as well as a variety of visual signals to express their feelings to other horses and, as we shall see, to humans as well. Most of these signals are interrelated, that is, several of them will be used to communicate one idea.

Voice Signals

Snort–Warning Sound. This sound is used to warn a group of horses of impending danger and is made by blowing air out through the nostrils. A horse will snort when he sees something that is frightening. He will usually lose his fear if he can be persuaded to smell it and realize that it is not dangerous. Sight is the primary sense involved with snorting. Smelling and hearing are secondary and are generally used by the horse to determine if the object is really dangerous. In wild horses, the snort was apparently used primarily as a warning of the presence of predators. A snort probably resulted in a rapid departure from the area, particularly if the suspicious object moved or if the horse detected a dangerous odor.

Neigh or Whinny–Distress Call. According to Webster's dictionary, this sound is the cry of the horse. This is a most apt description. It is a loud piercing sound made when a horse finds himself unexpectedly alone. It is used to express great concern, anxiety and even terror. In brief, it is a distress call. The solitary horse is afraid for its life because it lacks the protecting eyes, ears and noses of the group. He neighs in hopes that his group will hear him and answer. Apparently wild horses did answer, however, domesticated horses may not. Many times I have seen one horse, separated visually from its group, making repeated distress calls. The group could easily hear it but they would continue to graze unconcerned while their lost friend called and ran about looking for them. The group gives the appearance that it does not care about the problems of the lost one, and might even appear to be hiding from him. If the lost horse has a close friend who has missed him and is also anxious and concerned, the friend may answer. By going toward the sound of each other, they will be reunited. As we will discuss later, if a mare and foal are separated, they will answer each other, although occasionally a foal will seem to tease its mother by going out of sight and not answering her calls.

Horses do learn to get along by themselves in barns, corrals or pastures. However, these lone horses will usually exhibit great interest when another horse does come into sight and will often neigh loudly and run about excitedly. The neigh or whinny is used when visual contact is lost or when it is about to be lost as when a horse is left alone in a barn or corral. It is never used to express pain or anger.

Nicker–Greeting. A horse will use a nicker to greet horses, other animal friends, its home and even humans. The sound implies that the horse is pleased to see an old friend. Perhaps it is also a sigh of relief that mutual friends are reunited. It is not unusual for a horse to nicker to its owner when he or she comes to feed it or to put it in the barn. It is a rather pleasant sound and indicates all is well.

Squeal–Anger. This is a sound of anger and is often heard when horses are fighting. An occasional horse will squeal in anger while trying to buck off a rider or any empty saddle. Stallions and mares will often squeal at each other during the breeding season, sometimes in real anger, other times in what appears to be mock anger. A squeal is not a pleasant sound and is obviously used to convey unpleasantness and anger.

Stallion or Mating Call. This sound, made only by the stallion, is loud, penetrating, shrill and threatening. It is a sound that can send shivers up and down your back. In the wild stallions, it is used as a challenge or a warning. The studs without mares used it as a challenge to those with mares who in turn used the same sound as warning to their rivals to keep away. When a wild stallion sees a strange horse, this piercing sound fills the air and, depending upon the situation, could lead to a battle. However, according to recent studies on wild horses, there is considerable more bluffing than actual fighting between stallions. In other words, it is mostly noise when stallions get together, not much fighting. Today, in domesticated horses where stallions are usually kept away from other horses, a stallion will use the call whenever he sees a horse or thinks he sees or hears one. In horses today, it could be considered a mating call.

Rolling Snort. This sound is made by blowing air out through the nostrils but it is not an indication of danger as is the snort. It is a soft rolling or vibrating noise similar to the sound you can make by blowing out through lightly closed lips. It is often heard when a bunch of horses are turned out of their corral into a pasture. Perhaps it is a method of blowing the corral dust out of their nostrils. It really sounds as if the horse is expressing pleasure and relief at being turned out where he can relax and graze. Occasionally saddle horses will make this sound as they start a trip. Maybe it is a sound to indicate pleasure at going to work.

Mare Sounds. A mare uses soft nickers to talk to her new-born foal. These sounds vary in length and intensity and probably are used to reassure the foal that all is well or to warn of approaching danger.

PRACTICAL SIGNIFICANCE OF VOCAL COMMUNICATIONS

In general, vocal signals are not involved in any important way with training horses except for the snort. In training, if the horse snorts, the trainer knows he is afraid of something and must proceed accordingly. A trainer does not expect a horse to squeal at him when he is mad or nicker at him when he is happy. Some horses do nicker when they see their owner coming, probably expecting to be fed. Vocal sounds are, however, of considerable value in the management and care of horses. A good horseman is always listening for sounds of what his horses are doing. For example, if you hear horses squealing you may want to investigate who is fighting and determine if there is any real danger of one being injured. If you hear a horse whinnying loudly, you know he is separated from his friends. If you hear a stallion calling, you know he has seen or heard other horses.

Ears as a Visual Signal

The ears of a horse are the most easily understood visual signal with which a horse communicates its feelings to humans. It is not entirely clear if this is true for horses communicating with horses, but it could well be. Horses are undoubtedly more astute observers than humans. A horse must consider all parts of the body as well as the general posture of other horses. The eyes and ears of the horse work together. He wishes to hear all that he sees, and thus the direction he is looking can be determined by the position of the ears. He can look and listen ahead with the right eye and ear and back with the other pair. The following feelings of the horse are clearly indicated by the position of its ears:

Anger. When a horse wishes to express anger at another horse or at a person, the ears are turned back and laid down on the top of the head. The more angry a horse is, the tighter the ears will be held against the head. This ear position may also be accompanied by an angry gleam in the eye, an extension of the head to bite and an opening of the mouth. All of this can make a horse look very ferocious. Even the complete novice can recognize the horse is not in a very pleasant mood. An angry horse will not have his ears pointed in the direction he is looking. During periods of great stress, a horse may lay its ears back. Race horses tend to do this in the heat of the race. It indicates a great determination to win.

Interest. If a horse has both ears pointing forward, obviously looking at something, but with the body relaxed, he is expressing interest but no fear. This is a very good characteristic for a horse to possess. You would prefer a horse to look at you when you walk into a stall or corral rather than stand there asleep. The same is true when you are riding him. You would want him to be interested and observant of where he is going and what he is doing.

A horse may also express interest in what is behind him or, more specifically, what is on his back. When first ridden, a colt would be expected to watch the rider quite closely unless he is an unusually gentle colt who has no interest in or fear of humans. The breaking process, if successful, will convince the spooky colt that he has nothing to fear by looking back and seeing the rider. Some spoiled horses who are looking for a chance to run or buck may cock one ear back and, with the eye on the same side, watch to catch the rider in a careless moment. The other eye and ear are looking for a good place to stampede or buck. Needless to say, this is the kind of horse that must be ridden with considerable caution.

It is interesting to watch the ears on a well-broke, responsive horse as he works. He may keep one ear and, therefore, one eye on the rider to watch and listen for any cues. The other eye and ear are focused where he is going. He may alternate as he looks ahead with the right eye and ear and then back with the same ones. These horses are usually a real pleasure to ride.

Fear. When a horse has both ears ahead, the body tense, the head high and the eyes concentrating hard, he is afraid of what he sees and will be ready to leave the country. Certainly the wild horse, whose life was constantly being threatened, would be ready for instant flight as he stood tensely watching a suspicious object. His alarm would be communicated to other horses who had observed his actions and heard his loud snort which would undoubtedly be part of his signal.

Relaxation. The relaxed, secure horse expresses his contentment with his ears as well as his entire body. The ears are relaxed, usually turned to the side or slightly back. The head is allowed to sag and invariably the horse will be standing on one hind leg, the other cocked up in a resting position. The entire attitude of the horse is one of complete relaxation. As a matter of fact, he may be asleep. He can, if startled or aroused, awake instantly and be prepared to run for his life. A startled horse will almost always jump away from the source of the fright but he may also kick before he jumps. This is why you must always be certain a horse is awake when you walk up to it. Even then, it is dangerous to approach a horse from the rear.

PRACTICAL SIGNIFICANCE OF EARS AS A VISUAL SIGNAL

As pointed out, the ears are the most easily recognized visual signal a horse uses to express his feelings. Good horsemen always have one eye on the ears of a horse with which they are working. As we discussed, the position of the ears will indicate fear, interest, anger or relaxation and it is essential that a horseman be aware of these moods.

The Tail as a Visual Signal

Kink. A kink in a horse's tail on a frosty morning is often accompanied by a hump in its back when the saddle is put on. There may be more of a hump when the rider gets on. The old timers always mounted that kind of a horse rather gingerly, expecting a big explosion. It is doubtful that many horses today would respond in the same manner, but it is always a possibility. It is difficult to understand what this signal could mean to other horses except that the horse is feeling good and may be ready to run and play. Horses often have a kink in their tail when they are excited and playful.

Tail Held High. Horses often raise their tails high as they run and play. No doubt it communicates the idea to other horses that it is time to play. They usually have their heads up high and toss them as they snort and run about, bucking and kicking happily into the air. For short distances, horses may trot or lope in a stiff-legged, bouncy manner which again indicates they are feeling especially good. In wild horses this stiff-legged gait may have been a signal to alert all horses in the vicinity of the presence of some very interesting and potentially dangerous intruder.

If a horse is difficult to catch in a small pasture, it may race away with its tail and head held high and its head turned to watch you as it goes by. At times like this, you could swear the horse is laughing at you. Really all he is doing is asking you to chase him some more, as horses often do with each other when playing. A high tail indicates the horse is feeling good. It has come to be a symbol of animation and high spirits in certain horse show classes. At least two breeds, American Saddle horses and Arabians, have been selected for high tail settings and a level croup to facilitate a high tail carriage. Sometimes a high tail carriage means the trainer has applied a small amount of ginger under the tail.

Interest

Watching ahead with one ear
and eye and back with the
other pair

Sleep

Anger

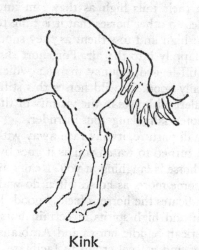

Kink

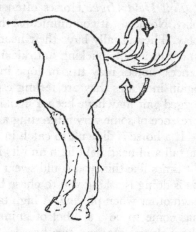

Warning or irritation

Illus. 20. Ears and tail as visual signals.

Tail Between Legs. A horse that is badly frightened or one that is preparing to kick may tuck its tail between its legs almost as a dog does. Colts that are tied up for the first time will generally have their tails tucked. Tucking the tail may serve as an indication of capitulation when two horses are fighting. This would prevent further injury to the loser as it tucks its tail tightly and runs away. Foals often walk up to strange horses with their tails tucked.

Tail Switching. A horse switches its tail when it's irritated about something such as fly bites or the actions of the rider. It is common for young horses when they are being broken to develop the habit of continually switching their tails as they are worked. Too much use of a whip on the rear quarters or spurs in the ribs would be obvious causes of tail switching. Also too much use of leg pressure or continual kicking will produce the same results. All of these would be similar to fly bites, that is, a continuous source of irritation. The horse might very likely develop a conditioned reflex of switching his tail as he moves along. Even though the primary source of irritation is removed, the horse would continue to switch its tail.

There are also more subtle ways a horse may be conditioned to tail switching. A young horse that is worked too hard and too long may develop such a distaste for work that he expresses his dislike by continuously switching his tail. Once a horse develops the habit it is very difficult to break. It is not a serious habit, but it does detract from the horse and is usually discounted in the show ring. It also may be a source of some irritation to the rider. As soon as switching is detected in the young horse, steps should be taken to eliminate the cause of irritation. This might mean reducing or stopping the training of the colt for a period of time.

A more extreme form of tail switching is tail ringing in which the tail is thrown around and around in a circle. Apparently, horses who develop this habit are expressing their irritation in a more extreme manner. It is also possible that a tendency for such a habit might be inherited.

PRACTICAL SIGNIFICANCE OF TAIL SIGNALS

If a young horse has a kink in his tail when you saddle him on a cold morning, he might test your riding ability. Tail switching probably has the most practical significance because it indicates you are annoying the horse in some way. Unless you want the young horse to perfect tail switching along with other aspects of his training, you should try to determine the reason for switching and make some changes. If caught early, the problem may likely be corrected; if not, it will become a fixed part of his behavior.

Mouth and Lips as Visual Signals

Lips. It is not clear what communicative value the lips have other than the expression of at least three emotions which reflect the feelings of an individual. Their expressions may be of value to the horse owner, but it is difficult to understand their meaning to other horses who tend to completely disregard them. If a horse eats something that is distasteful, he may raise his head and lift the upper lip to express his displeasure at the taste, although it is possible he is objecting to the odor. This often happens when some type of medicine is put in the grain. A horse may also give this same response if he is feeling mild discomfort or pain somewhere along the digestive tract. The early stages of colic may produce this evidence of discomfort.

Stallions appear to detect, or attempt to clarify, odors of other horses or droppings. A stallion will first smell, then lift his head high and turn his upper lip up as if he is trying to differentiate between minute traces of odor. It is common in many species of animals for the female to produce an odor indicating she is in estrus. This odor will attract the male. The urine of a mare in estrus is believed to contain such an odor. It is also common in certain species, such as the dog, for the males to mark their territories with small amounts of urine deposited at specific places. We mentioned earlier that stallions tend to deposit their droppings at certain locations. When they smell the droppings, they may be attempting to determine if there is an impostor in their area.

Mouth. We discussed earlier the fact that foals and yearlings appear to communicate their juvenile status to older horses by opening and closing their mouths. The young ones cautiously approach a stranger with their head extended and rapidly open and close their mouths. Usually they will not be attacked when they have thus communicated their immaturity. It is possible horses use their mouths to express anger. When horses fight, they pull their lips back slightly and open their mouths exposing their incisor teeth just prior to biting. This all happens very rapidly when horses are seriously fighting, and may have little communicative value.

Eyes as a Visual Signal

The eyes are rather limited as a means of communication because they cannot be altered nearly as much as other parts. The only visible change that can really be made is in the opening of the eyelids. A frightened horse will have his eyelids wide open and this could play a small part in communicating his fear to other horses. In some horses, the white sclerotic ring becomes more visible when the eyes are opened wide. Changes in the ears and general position of the head and body of the frightened horse are far more noticeable. No doubt they are of considerable more value in the communication between horses and between horses and humans than are the eyes.

Nostrils as a Visual Signal

The excited or frightened horse will flare the nostrils to allow a greater intake of air into the lungs. This may be accompanied by a snort. The same dilation of the nostrils occurs when a horse is breathing hard from exertion. The nostrils are flared by the contraction of small muscles. This could serve as a minor, visible signal to other horses. At least one breed association, Arabians, notes the desirability of a wide, flaring nostril for their horses. Presumably this would allow greater intake of air and therefore greater endurance.

Play

One of the social patterns of the horse is its interest in playing, particularly the younger ones. A few days after birth, foals are racing around their mothers kicking and bucking. If there are two foals, so much the better. It is not long before stud foals will be play-fighting with each other. This continues on until they are separated at an older age. Geldings participate in the same type of play but without as much intensity as the young studs. Fillies are more inclined to run races with each other but will play-fight a certain amount.

A group of horses may decide to run for no apparent reason, other than to play and exercise. If the area is large enough, they may run for

Illus. 21. Horses playing.

miles. While playing, horses easily make sudden turns, flying changes of lead, rearing, striking, bucking. Most spectacular of all, they can kick with both hind legs while the body is off the ground. The latter is said to have inspired an early teacher in the Lippizzan School to include this move, called the capriole, as part of the repertoire of these famous horses. He observed horses doing this in play and decided to teach them to do it on demand. Some experienced horsemen base part of their selection of potential reining horses on their actions as they play. If the young horse executes flying changes of lead, sudden stops and turns with considerable ease and grace, there is a good chance he can do the same with a rider.

INVESTIGATIVE BEHAVIOR

Investigative behavior or curiosity is very closely related to fear and thus to self-protective behavior. The young foals are the ones most apt to be curious about something. But they are usually prepared to run at the slightest evidence of real danger. Curiosity is a part of the learning process of the young and is found in many animals, as well as in children. It would appear that curiosity teaches a foal to be afraid. As he gets older, he may become less and less curious of new and different objects and more and more afraid of them without investigation. In other words, a curious foal will want to investigate something new and learn if it is dangerous. An old horse may take it for granted that anything strange is dangerous and will act accordingly.

Curiosity and fear are factors that must be considered in breaking horses to ride. However, by the time a colt is old enough to ride, he is usually well beyond the curious stage and is primarily fearful. This display of fear of strange objects is usually referred to as shying. Great care must be taken not to allow the young horse to shy and run away from a strange object when you are riding him. It must be remembered that basically a horse may be afraid of almost anything that moves or is an odd shape or color. As a matter of fact, a horse may be frightened by its own shadow and shy away from it. This is why shadow rolls are used on race horses. The shadow roll is a sheepskin-covered nose band which prevents the horse from looking down at its shadow.

To prevent a young horse from developing the highly undesirable habit of shying, several factors must be considered. First, until he is well under control, it is unwise to ride a young colt into an area where strange objects may cause him to shy. As we will discuss later, it may take at least 10 to 15 rides to get a colt under proper control. On the first rides outside in unfamiliar or spooky areas, it is a very good idea to have an older, gentle horse along. The colt will be much less apt to become frightened by a strange object if he has horse company. When a horse is under control and can be handled, he should be made to go up to a spooky object and be made to smell it. Usually after a horse smells something, he will lose his fear of it.

In my opinion, some curiosity and alertness, but not fear, is desirable in a horse. It makes them more interesting to ride. They will have their head up, their ears working and will really be watching and looking where they are going. Horses that go along with their heads down, their eyes half closed, and with the attitude they could care less where they go or what they do may satisfy some riders but not me.

Curiosity and fear are also involved when horses are first taken to horse shows and rodeos. They will be curious, but may be more afraid of all the new sights, sounds and commotions. They cannot be expected to perform up to capacity until they adjust to the new surroundings. It is a good idea to take new horses to two or three such affairs before they are entered in any competition.

MATERNAL BEHAVIOR

The termination of gestation brings about a marked change in the behavior of the pregnant mare. Prior to foaling, most mares are quiet, lethargic, slow moving and usually cranky with other horses and sometimes with people. A short time before foaling her behavior changes and immediately after foaling it changes even more, as we shall discuss in the following pages. Just prior to foaling, the most noticeable change is the mare's restlessness and general uneasiness. Mares in box stalls walk about the stall nervously as if looking for something. Actually the mare is trying to respond to a primitive urge to get away by herself to foal. Range mares will sneak away by themselves at foaling time. There are two interesting reasons for this urge for privacy we will discuss in the section on imprinting.

When the uterus begins to contract at foaling time, the behavior of the mare changes again. She may show considerable discomfort by kicking at her stomach, by lying down and getting up and by holding her tail up. When she gets up, she may turn and look at the area where she was lying, hoping to see her foal. Mares may break out in a sweat as the uterine contractions increase in strength. During labor, the mare's entire attention is devoted to the problem of giving birth to a foal. However, if a mare is startled or disturbed in the early stages of labor, she may cease all activity for a period of time. Some mares appear to be able to delay birth until human observers have tired of waiting and have gone.

Records show that a majority of foals are born at night. In wild horses there would be an evolutionary advantage in foaling at night when many predatory animals are less active. Darkness would give the mare added protection. If everything is normal, the foal should be born 15 to 30 minutes after uterine contractions begin. Cows and ewes are usually much slower about giving birth than the mare. As we said earlier, the mare will lie down and get up several times during labor but ordinarily she will be lying down when the foal is born.

The birth of the foal produces yet another change in the mare's behavior. The mare's discomfort and apparent concern for herself during foaling is replaced immediately by concern for the new-born foal. An experienced mare will stand up and turn to her foal immediately following birth and begin nuzzling it. She may nicker to it softly. She uses her lips to help dry the foal and perhaps to stimulate circulation. She may attempt to pull off the fetal membranes if they are around the foal.

In a matter of minutes the healthy foal will try to stand and the mare will watch anxiously as it struggles. Once on its feet it will soon be trying to nurse. Most mares show great patience as the foal attempts to find the udder. Within an hour the range mare and foal may move a short distance away from the place of birth and both lie down while the uterus of the mare goes through another series of contractions to expel the fetal membranes. After resting, the pair may move again. Within twenty-four hours the healthy new-born foal is strong enough to travel a mile or more.

After foaling, a mare may become very suspicious of anything which tries to approach her and the foal. This behavior is very noticeable in mares foaling out in a pasture. The day before foaling, a mare may be easy to approach and completely indifferent to the presence of people, other horses and animals. With the arrival of her foal, her behavior changes dramatically. As soon as something comes in sight, the mare will get her foal on its feet with a sharp, nervous nicker. The pair will move off as fast as the age of foal will allow. Most mares will lose their fear and suspicion within a few days, particularly if they are ordinarily gentle and quiet.

Imprinting

The preference of the mare to foal by itself away from other horses apparently evolved for two reasons first, to provide the foal with the opportunity to identify or imprint on its mother and second, as a protective measure against predators. Imprinting is an interesting phenomena which occurs in many species of animals. At the time of birth, the new-born foal will follow any moving object including humans. If other horses are near, it is possible the foal would imprint on a horse other than its own mother. It is not unusual for a dominant mare without her own foal to steal the foal of a less dominant mare who has just foaled. Unless this switch is detected in a short time, the new-born foal could get into a serious, if not fatal, condition from lack of milk. However, if the mare foals alone, the foal will imprint or learn to identify its mother in a short time. Within two or three days, the foal should be physically strong enough to stay with its mother even though another mare should try to separate them.

The other reason mares may instinctively prefer to foal by themselves is to reduce the chances of being found by predators during and shortly after foaling. Similar behavior is common in many females such as cattle, pigs and most wild animals who ordinarily stay in groups except when giving birth to their young. Apparently there was less chance a predator would find a single mare off by herself in a secluded spot than if she stayed with her bunch.

Identification and Protection

The mare identifies its foal at birth, partly by odor, but as the foal grows, recognition by sight and sound appears to be more important. If a mare and foal are separated for a time, they do not smell each other when reunited but recognize each other's appearance and sound. Cows and ewes definitely use odor to positively identify their young throughout the nursing period. Sight and sound are used by them when mother and offspring are not close enough to detect odor.

Ordinarily the mare and foal will never willingly lose sight of each other. If they do, they both become severely agitated. The mare does not leave her foal sleeping while she grazes away out of sight as do cattle and wild animals such as deer and elk. The reason she does not leave her foal is that no effective means for reuniting the two after a separation has evolved in horses. If the mare was out of sight and the foal was disturbed by a predator and ran off, they would not find each other again except by chance. They have no instinct to return to the last place they saw each other as do many animals. Domesticated mares and foals in fenced pastures will eventually find each other. They race about making considerable noise until, by chance, they hear or see each other. The chance of a wild mare ever finding her foal if they were separated by any distance was very remote.

We pointed out earlier that the horse's principal protection from predators was flight. The mare ran each time danger threatened and her foal had to run by her side if it was to survive. The mare would stand and fight only to protect her new-born foal or if cornered and could not run. As soon as the foal was strong enough to travel, she would run rather than fight. All healthy foals exhibit an amazing ability to get on their feet and travel within a short time after birth. No other farm animal and probably few wild animals are as precocious.

Mares will fight away any animal which threatens a new-born foal.

Most domesticated mares will allow humans to approach and handle their new foals. A few will show signs of anger and will attempt to scare away a person. Although very rare, it has been reported that a mare did fight and kill its own foal. In the case cited, it was thought the mare's udder had become very sensitive and she fought her foal when it tried to nurse and eventually she killed it. Such behavior is most unusual in the mare. In cattle, where this type of behavior is occasionally observed, it appears that the cow believes that the new-born calf is a predatory animal. When the calf tries to get to its feet, it is knocked down and trampled by the confused mother. Some sows will kill and eat their young. Such aberrant behavior is very likely associated with domestication. It certainly could not have been common in the wild ancestors of these domesticated animals or the species would not have evolved.

FOAL BEHAVIOR

The most remarkable behavior pattern of the new-born foal is its very strong urge to get on its feet as soon as possible. In a matter of minutes after birth, a healthy foal will be attempting to stand. It will attempt to raise the front end first, which is the normal way for a horse to get on its feet. Cattle, sheep, deer, elk and most other ruminants raise the back end first. First, the foal will raise its head and after a short time roll upright on its chest with the front legs extended and the hind legs under its body. Then the struggle to get on its feet begins. It may fall down several times but keeps trying until eventually it is standing on all four shaking legs. The mother will watch anxiously but is helpless to assist in any way except by encouraging nickers and a nuzzling with her nose.

Soon after standing, the new foal will attempt to nurse. It instinctively associates the warmth and bulk of its mother's body as the source of nourishment. The foal also knows that it must turn its nose up and under the body of the mare to locate the teats. It may attempt to nurse between the front legs, as well as the back ones, until it successfully locates the udder. It instinctively knows that it should press its body against the body of the mare to be in the proper position. After nursing and moving around for a time the foal will look for a suitable place to lie down. Because it had such a struggle to stand, it will appear somewhat reluctant to get off its feet but eventually will be forced to do so by fatigue.

The new-born foal nurses frequently, usually once or twice each hour. If the mare is not giving enough milk to satisfy the foal, it may try to nurse more often. As the hours pass and the foal becomes stronger, the mare may move a short distance each time the foal is on its feet. Within twenty-four hours or less from birth, most foals can lope if their mothers feel it is necessary to move rapidly. If another horse or person attempts to approach the mare, the foal will move to the side of the mare away from the approaching object. The wild foal would have greater protection from predatory animals in this position.

In the previous section on maternal behavior, we discussed why the mare has such a great fear of being separated from its foal. The new-born foal has this same fear and makes every effort to stay with its mother. However, the foal may forget about this matter occasionally as it gets older. For example, it may become interested in playing and running with other foals and stray away from its mother, or the foal may decide to investigate some strange object at some distance away. Eventually the mare or the foal or both of them will realize they are separated and there will be some frantic moments until they are reunited. With domestic horses, such separations almost always have a happy ending. With wild horses, this probably was not true because of the presence of predators who were always waiting to catch a foolish foal. It is interesting to watch foals who apparently enjoy teasing their mothers by deliberately disappearing behind a building or tree. After the mare has become properly concerned, the foal calmly walks out into sight and appears to say, "What is all the excitement about?"

Foals, particularly the young ones, spend a good part of their time sleeping. They do not sleep standing up as older horses usually do but flat on their side with legs and head extended. They prefer to lie down in a dry place and will seek out such a location if one is available. In the section on maternal behavior we discussed the imprinting behavior of the foal. We discussed the method foals use to communicate their age to older horses in the section on Social Behavior.

SPECIAL SENSES OF THE HORSE
AND BEHAVIOR

Sense of Sight

Horses have what is called monocular vision, that is, each eye is independent of the other and can see different pictures. Humans have binocular vision and see the same picture with both eyes. The position of the eye on the horse's head allows it to see a broad area on each side as well as behind and in front. When a horse wants to see an object clearly, it will turn to face the object and use both eyes in a binocular manner. As indicated in Illus. 22 and 23, the height and position of the horse's head determines if it is focusing on a near or far object. A horse with a high head carriage and with its nose high can see at a distance but is dangerous to ride because it cannot see where it is placing its feet. The danger increases considerably as the speed of the horse or roughness of the terrain increases. In later sections, we will discuss techniques that can be used to teach a horse to carry its head in a position which allows it to see properly while being ridden.

It is difficult for a horse to judge distance accurately because it has essentially monocular vision. In the evolution of the horse, it was more important that he see a wide area around him as he watched for predator animals than to judge distance accurately. Predator animals such as wolves, coyotes and lions all have binocular vision and excellent depth perception which is essential in chasing and catching prey. With certain types of use, it has become important that a domesticated horse have the ability to judge distance. For example, a rope horse must run up to, then follow at a certain distance, the animal which is to be roped. This is called rating and requires the horse to accurately judge the distance between himself and the animal he is following. If he is too far back, the

VISION AND HEAD SET

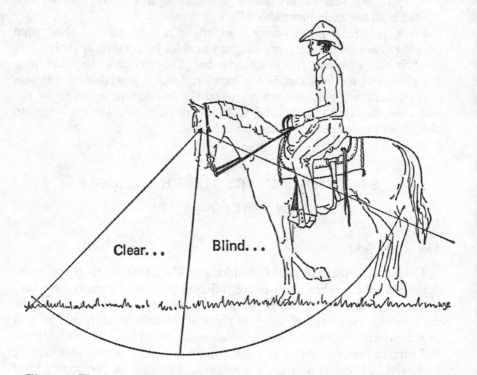

Clear. . .   Blind. . .

Illus. 22. The horse with a perpendicular head set can see clearly the ground in front where it will be placing its feet at a walk, trot or collected lope. At the gallop or run, the horse will extend its nose forward to see at a greater distance. Note method of holding reins which is conducive to this type of head set.

rider's rope would not be long enough; if he is too close, it is difficult to see around the horse's head to rope. Essentially the same rating phenomena applies to barrel racing horses who must accurately judge the distance to the barrel as they prepare for the turn. Jumping horses also must accurately determine distance to the jump to select their take off point. In addition, they must determine the height and spread of the jump.

Some horses have considerably more ability in judging distance than others. Two factors are apparently involved in this difference among horses. According to Smyth (1966), the eyes of some horses are placed more toward the front of the head giving them better binocular vision. In measurements Smyth made on horses, he found the eye of the thoroughbred horse set further to the front than the shire draft horse. Although he did not find much variation among thoroughbreds, there apparently is a small amount and some variation could also be expected in other breeds. If there is variation, this could be a factor in selecting horses

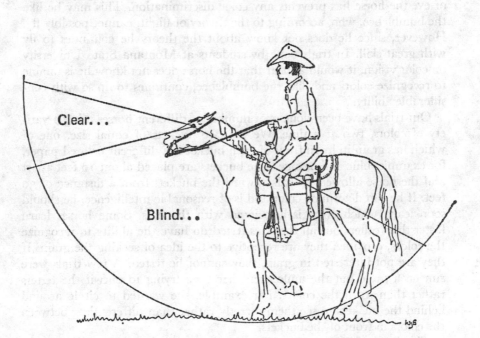

Illus. 23. This high-headed horse would be dangerous to ride because it cannot see the ground. Reins coming out of the top of the hands and hands held high produce this type of head set.

for rodeo or jumping. Other factors involved in judging distance are the ability of the horse to learn and the ability of the trainer to train. These two are probably more important than eye position.

Anyone who has ridden horses at night knows that the horse has good vision in the dark. It is not as acute as a cat's but considerably better than your own. The large pupil of the eye of the horse lets in enough light to give him good night vision. Undoubtedly the horse also uses other senses, such as smell, hearing and feel through his feet, as an aid to traveling at night. Thus horses can be ridden at night with reasonable safety, particularly if the horse is familiar with the area. However, it could be dangerous to ride a horse on a very dark night in an unfamiliar area. They may step into holes or walk into wire or other unsafe objects. Also, a horse does not consider low tree limbs or clotheslines as any problem to him as long as he can get under them. Such obstructions could be a considerable problem to a rider on a dark night.

COLOR VISION

Most authorities maintain the horse is color blind. They claim the type of eye the horse has prevents any color discrimination. This may be like the bumblebee, who, according to the theory of flight, cannot possibly fly. However, since he does not know about the theory he continues to fly with great skill. In trials done by students at Montana State University on color vision, it would appear that the horse does not know he is unable to recognize colors and, like the bumblebee, continues to do so with considerable ability.

Our trials have been done on a number of different horses using a variety of colors, two at a time. We use two buckets of equal size, one of which has grain in it. In front of each bucket is a different colored paper, for example, blue and orange. The buckets are placed about 10 feet apart and the horse allowed to walk toward the buckets from a distance of 30 feet. If he can determine color and is of reasonable intelligence, he should soon learn which color is associated with the oats. Some horses learn faster than others but all the ones tested do have the ability to recognize the colors, provided they are receptive to the idea of seeking the grain. If they are not interested in grain, they cannot be tested. A few trials were run on a mule but the mule spent her time trying to outwit the testers rather than learn the colors. For example, she wanted to circle around behind the buckets to see them directly rather than differentiate between the colors in front of the buckets.

The horse does not see colors in the same way humans do. It is difficult, if not impossible, for the horse to differentiate between colors when they are subjected to very intense light. However, the horse may recognize colors in semi-darkness more readily than humans. Tests have shown that the horse probably can recognize a color with different saturation. For example, the horses tested could recognize that dark yellow and light yellow were the same basic color. Colors which have been tested in pairs and which a horse can distinguish between are black and white; blue and orange; dark purple and dark yellow; light purple and light yellow; and red and green.

Although some people may not agree that the horse can recognize color, all would agree that the horse has excellent vision. The acute vision of the horse can be used effectively in training, particularly during ground work. Trainers who spend a considerable amount of time longeing, or driving their horses around them in a circle, can teach a horse to respond to very slight visual cues. Horses will learn to cue on very slight movements of the trainer's hands, feet, body or whip. Circus horses which work at liberty, that is without direct control from the trainer, respond to the slightest visual signal from the trainer.

Probably the most unusual example of the ability of a horse to visually detect slight cues involved a horse called Clever Hans. This horse, owned by a well known German horseman who lived around 1900, was said to possess the ability to tell time, work simple mathematical problems and do other amazing feats. The problems could be given in writing as well as verbally. The horse would tap out his replies using one front leg for tens and the other for the numbers one through nine. Apparently, Clever Hans had powers of reasoning and understanding similar to humans and far superior to any ordinary horse. After considerable study by the leading scientist of the time, it was finally determined that the horse was actually responding to very slight and unconscious cues from the trainer. These cues were so slight as to be all but invisible to other humans but easily understood by the horse. One report stated the horse was responding to the pulsations of a vein in the neck of the trainer who was himself subconsciously counting for the horse. As he counted, the tiny vein pulsed in a manner understandable to the horse.

Sense of Hearing

It is known that Eohippus lived in swampy, brushy areas where a highly developed sense of hearing would be more essential than exceptional vision. In thick brush, it would be impossible to see far enough for this sense to provide adequate protection. Sound and odor would both indicate the presence of predators more effectively. However, as conditions changed, the relative importance of these three senses changed. The fossil evidence indicates that the primitive horse gradually became adapted to dry, open, prairie lands where the sense of hearing would not be as essential as the sense of sight. Even though its importance in survival may have been reduced, the horse continued to use its hearing enough to prevent any appreciable evolutionary loss of this sense. Perhaps there were periods when the horse was forced to live in, or at least pass through, timbered or brushy areas where hearing would be essential for safety. In any event, the modern horse has excellent hearing, which undoubtedly evolved millions of years ago as an important part of the protective mechanism of the primitive Eohippus.

Today the acute hearing of the horse is very useful in training. The horse can be taught to respond to a number of very soft voice commands. If you wish, you can teach a horse the meaning of the words walk, trot and lope, as well as the conventional start and stop cues. None of these voice cues need to be spoken loudly. In some areas where horses are used for hunting in timber or brush, their sense of hearing is very useful in locating wild animals. The rider, whose hearing is much inferior to his mount, need only to watch the ears of his horse to determine the location of game that have been disturbed. The horse will point its ears toward the source of the sound, in part to hear better and in part to attempt to see the animal. The horse will hear animals move at a much greater distance than he can see them in brush or timber country.

Sense of Smell

One of the important protective mechanisms which evolved with the horse was the sense of smell. This well-developed sense must have been very useful in detecting the presence of predators. It is not, however, as well developed in the horse as it is in the predators themselves who depend upon it to find food. Such common predators as bears and coyotes can detect the slightest odor at considerable distances. In addition to protection, the wild horse used smell to identify companions who may have been separated from the group. Also, this sense was used to help identify the home range. It is common for horses, particularly stallions, to smell fecal deposits. Apparently they do this to determine if they are on their home range and if there are any trespassers.

Modern horses today use the sense of smell in a number of ways. As did their wild ancestors they use odor to identify each other. When new horses are put together or old friends reunited, the first thing they do is smell each other, nose to nose. They appear to remember and recognize old friends or enemies immediately. This recognition is possible because of a keen sense of smell, together with an excellent memory for the odor of other horses. Horses also very likely recognize humans by odor. A horse may want to smell you when you walk up to catch it.

There is some evidence horses can detect fear in humans by a change in body odor. If a person is frightened, the hormone levels in the body change. This change could result in a slightly different odor from the sweat glands of the skin. Dogs may be even more adept than horses at determining such changes. If a person is afraid of a horse, he will also be nervous, tense and inclined to make sudden, jerky movements. All of this will communicate his fear to the horse and almost invariably makes the horse nervous, tense and fearful.

We have already mentioned that stallions probably detect a change in odor when a mare comes into heat. We also pointed out that horses may refuse to eat certain foods if drugs have been added. They may be objecting to the odor as well as the taste. Mares apparently use odor to identify their new-born foals.

Sense of Touch

The horse, like all higher animals, has a well-developed sense of touch. Certain areas of its body are more sensitive to touch than others, possibly because these areas are more essential or more vulnerable to injury. For example, the horse is particularly sensitive about the nose, eyes and ears, all of which are very essential parts. Injury to these parts would greatly reduce the horse's chance for survival because they involve smelling, breathing, seeing and hearing. Unhandled horses are always very fearful of anything touching or holding their legs. Such a reaction is understandable when we realize that if the legs of a wild horse were caught or held in any way, it would have meant death to the horse. Horses are also very sensitive in the flank. This area has no skeletal protection for the digestive tract and even a small injury here could be fatal.

One area on the horse which is sensitive to touch but is not really vital or vulnerable is the withers. It is difficult to explain why this area became sensitive unless it was to provide a location for a pleasant exchange of massaging between two horses. Two horses often stand alongside of each other massaging each other's withers with their lips and teeth. They apparently enjoy this mutual back scratching. Usually, but not always, the pair are social partners. See Illus. 16.

Another sensitive part of the horse is the frog which serves as an organ of touch. Normally, the frog touches the ground each time the foot does and thus the horse feels the ground. The horse can determine from the feel of the ground if it is safe terrain to walk on. For example, if the ground is getting soft, it may indicate the horse is approaching a swamp and should not proceed. The horse prefers dry, firm soil to swamps or rock. It is possible horses feel ground vibration through the sensitive frog. If this is true, wild horses could have detected the approach of a heavy, big-footed predator. More likely the horse felt the movement of a group of animals which had been disturbed and were running. Such movement would alert the horse to possible danger.

Sense of Touch and Training

The sense of touch plays an essential role in training horses. In the early stages of training, the young ones must be taught not to fear the touching of its nose, eyes and ears. Considerable care must be taken to convince the horse that you do not intend to injure these vital organs. So-called head-shy horses may have been mistreated in some way in the early stages of their handling. The most critical area seems to be the ears. A few horses are unusually sensitive about the ears and may refuse to allow a headstall to be slipped on over the ears. The horse might be this way the first time it is bridled or, more likely, it may develop this sensitivity at some later time. Unusual sensitivity of the ears may be caused by an infection. Horses develop warts or fungus growth on the inside of their ears that causes considerable pain if the ear is handled in any way. If this is the problem, it is best to use a headstall with a buckle on the side that can be unbuckled and slipped on behind the ears without touching them. In other words, bridle the horse in the same way you would put on a halter. Once a horse is spoiled, it is very difficult to convince it that you will not hurt its ears by bridling.

Touch is the most important sense used in cueing horses. Sight and sound are used but not nearly as extensively as touch. We touch the horse with our hands through its mouth and neck. We touch the horse with our legs in the rib area and with our weight at its withers. Unfortunately, the areas that are most extensively and commonly used in training and riding are not very sensitive to light touch but instead respond more to pain. These areas are the mouth and ribs, both of which lack a system of nerve endings which could respond easily to light pressure. Because the untrained horse will respond in these two areas to pain, there is a temptation by some riders to get results by pulling hard, jerking, kicking or spurring. This gets temporary results but invariably leads to a hard mouth and dead ribs. It may also produce head throwing, tail switching and other bad habits.

The withers is the one useful area on a horse which does respond naturally to light pressure. In the early stages of training, a horse will learn to start, stop and turn with slight shifts of the rider's weight. Of course, these weight cues must be reinforced with the hands and legs until the horse learns what is expected of him. Unfortunately, many riders do not realize the usefulness of weight. They do not use it at all, use it inconsistently, or use more exaggerated weight shifts than necessary. Excess use of weight may throw the horse out of balance and cause poor stops and disunited leads. Inconsistent use only confuses the horse and he will eventually not respond at all to the cues.

Almost all horses will learn to respond to lighter and lighter weight cues. Most, but not all, will learn to respond to light pressure on the mouth and ribs. It takes a great deal of skill, patience and understanding to develop lightness, but, in my opinion, the results are well worth the effort. Once you have ridden a light, responsive horse, you will never want to ride the other kind. In later sections we discuss some techniques which can be used to develop lightness.

Some horses become so light and responsive that it is almost impossible to detect the cues to which they are responding. It appears that the horse is responding to the thoughts of the rider rather than any perceptible cues. The rider thinks he wants to turn and the horse turns. The rider thinks he wants to lope and the horse lopes. At least one author, Smyth (1966), believes there may be an exchange of thoughts between horse and rider, in other words, mental telepathy. More likely, the horse is

Illus. 24. The big whip and spur will not produce performance in this horse. He is taking a snooze.

Illus. 25. Mental telepathy. A responsive horse may appear to read the rider's mind. Note how one ear and eye are back watching for cues from the rider while the other ear and eye are looking ahead. Such a horse is a real pleasure to ride.

responding to cues of the hands, legs or weight that are so slight that even the rider is unaware of what he is doing. Such lightness is the ultimate in horsemanship.

HOME RANGE AND HOMING INSTINCT

Home Range

During the millions of years the horse has existed on earth, it has evolved a strong instinct to stay in a certain home range. Horses probably evolved a home range behavior as part of the self-protective mechanism.

There apparently was an advantage to staying in an area where they were well acquainted with the best sources of feed and water and the most likely routes to avoid or escape predators.

Within the home range, each breeding group of wild horses had a specific territory which it considered its own. Stallions vigorously defended their territory against invading stallions or groups of horses. According to Pellegrini's (1971) study of wild horses in Nevada, there was more bluffing and threatening by the defending stallion than actual fighting when he was being threatened by invasion. However, the home stallion would fight when necessary to defend his home and his mares. Their behavior was most pronounced during the breeding season and much less during the winter.

Home ranges on the Nevada Wild Horse range were found to be about 12 square miles per band of horses. The bands were small, consisting of 3 to 4 horses. Lone bachelor stallions had smaller ranges. The boundaries of each home range were clearly defined by well-traveled trails. Occasionally a group would stray up to half a mile into a neighboring territory in search of feed. When sighted and challenged by the home stud, the invading group would hastily depart for its own range. The defending stud rarely pursued the invaders beyond his boundary trail.

In Nevada where water was not plentiful, there was an overlapping of home ranges at water holes. Each stud did not attempt to defend a territory at the water hole but instead depended on a social order to maintain his integrity. In other words, there was a social order established between the bands. While the dominant band drank and grazed around the water, the less dominant group waited at a respectable distance.

As we pointed out earlier, eyesight is the principal protective sense of the horse. Therefore, horses prefer to establish their home range in an area where they can effectively use their eyes. This means open country and also means that some altitude is desirable because the horse can see further. The ideal wild horse range is mostly open country with hills and ridges where the horses can graze and keep a careful watch for enemies.

Domestic horses display this same basic home range behavior if they are allowed enough freedom. In big pastures, or on open range, the horses will have favorite areas where they prefer to spend most of their time. If available, these preferred areas will usually be open, grass covered ridges or hills. In mountain country, horses, if given the opportunity, will invariably seek out the high open ridges.

There is no evidence that wild horses had extensive seasonal migrations as do many wild animals. The horses did move short distances at certain seasons because of the changes in feed and water. On the Nevada Wild Horse Range the horses winter on the higher ridges because snow is available for water. In the summer, they are forced to stay in the lower sagebrush flats where water is located. Although the winter and summer home ranges of a band are not physically connected, they are in the same general area. Similar winter and summer ranges also exist in the Pryor Mountain Wild Horse Range in Montana.

Homing or Back Tracking Instinct

The homing pigeon is not the only animal that can find its way home from great distances. Many animals exhibit this type of behavior and the horse is one of them. As wild horses evolved territorial behavior, they also evolved the ability to return to the home range if they were forced to leave. We have said that the wild horse's best defense from predators was flight. Apparently it was necessary to run for miles to escape certain types of predators and often such flight would necessitate the horse leaving its home range. If the home range had some definite survival advantages as we mentioned above, it would be to the horse's advantage to return, thus the necessity of a homing instinct.

Land managers at the Pryor Mountain Wild Horse Range have attempted to relocate some bands of horses from overgrazed areas to areas where feed was more plentiful. Such attempts have not met with much success because of the strong homing behavior of the horses. This behavior is most pronounced in the lead mare, who is the one that is the most determined to return to her home range.

There are many stories told about the remarkable ability of horses in the open range days to find their way back after being sold and trailed away from the home range. Occasionally some of these horses would escape from their new owner and travel several hundred miles back to the home area. Today, with most of the country fenced, it is impossible for a loose horse to make its way back any distance. Anyway, most horses are trucked or trailered to new locations and thus have no way of knowing which way is home.

As all experienced riders know, horses will exhibit homing behavior while being ridden. This behavior might also be called barn sour as we discussed in an earlier section. The horse is displaying a strong urge to return to the home range, in this case the barn, where he will feel safe and secure. There is an interesting way in which you can test the ability of your own horse to return to his barn or home area.

To test your horse's homing or back tracking behavior, you will need to go for a ride in a new area which is unfamiliar to your horse. Plan a route which will require considerable change of direction to reach the point farthest away from the origin of the rider. The more winding the route you choose and the longer the ride, the better the test will be. Avoid riding on distinct trails as much as possible. When it is time to start back, give your horse its head and observe his ability to find his way to the starting point. Most horses will know the general direction they have come and will try to head directly back. If there are not too many natural and unnatural barriers, this technique will get them back to the starting point. A few horses and mules have the ability to backtrack themselves step for step and thus avoid the barriers.

Many years ago while on a pack trip in the remote northwest corner of Yellowstone National Park, I rode a horse who displayed this backtracking ability to an unusual degree. We were camped on the headwaters of the Gallatin river and decided to ride to a lake some 16 miles away which drained into the Yellowstone River. At that time very few people visited this part of the Park and there were only a few faint trails used by wild animals. There were no trails between where we were camped and the lake we wanted to visit. To reach the lake we followed the natural drainages and passes. We passed through thick timber, open grassy meadows, creeks, swamps and hard, rocky areas, with much turning and twisting to avoid the natural barriers. Most of the way our tracks were all but invisible because of the hard, rocky ground, the heavy grass or the thick pine needles in the timbered areas. Although we were lucky and found a good way to the lake, I was not certain that I could backtrack myself the same way back to camp. As we started back, I soon realized my horse was doing a much better job of finding his way to camp than I was. He backtracked himself perfectly, step for step, the entire 16 miles. Much of the way our track was invisible and how he managed to follow it was a mystery to me at that time.

Since that time, I have ridden a few other horses with the same backtracking ability. They do not appear to follow the trail by its odor as would a dog. Some horses can follow a back trail which is several weeks old and where all odor has disappeared. They cannot depend entirely upon visible tracks because they can follow a completely invisible trail through water or rocks. It would appear these horses have a photographic memory of the trail and use this mental picture to backtrack themselves. In any event, it is a very interesting and amazing display of homing instinct.

MEMORY

The elephant is famous for its memory, probably because it lives so long and thus has ample opportunity to demonstrate its ability in this respect. Although not usually given credit for it, the horse also has an excellent memory. It was essential for the wild horse to remember through-out its life its accumulated experiences. In particular, it needed to remember places, situations and animals which threatened its existence. Also, it needed to remember the best locations for feed, water and shelter.

Sometimes, it seems that domestic horses only remember the bad, scary things that have happened to them. For example, if a young horse gets frightened by a rope around its legs or under its tail and is allowed to fight and kick until it is free, it will remember this all of its life. Each time it gets into a similar situation, it will react in the same way. Obviously, such behavior can be dangerous to the horse and the handler.

If a horse is frightened by some object such as a piece of paper or an odd shaped rock and is allowed to shy and run away, it will remember this for a long time too. Not only does the horse remember the object which scared it but also the location. I remember having a horse shy and get very frightened by a bright piece of light metal which moved as the wind blew. Although I made the horse go up and smell the object, it was still not certain this wasn't some kind of a deadly animal ready to eat it alive. About a month later, I chanced to ride by the same place on the same horse. As I approached the location where the metal had been, the horse began to act very suspicious and was obviously expecting to be frightened by that same spooky piece of metal. As it happened, the metal had been removed in the meantime but the horse still remembered the location and was all ready to be frightened again. Such behavior is un-derstandable when we realize how essential it was for the wild horse to remember any threats to its life.

In the previous section we discussed the homing instinct of horses and how it may involve remembering each step of a route followed away from home. This instinct may also involve remembering over a consid-erable period of time. On a hunting trip in Wyoming some years ago, our old pack mules turned off the main trail to a campsite where they had been about five years before. The mules were getting tired and had remembered the campsite and thought it was time to be unloaded.

A friend of mine had a horse which he frequently hauled in a trailer to take rides away from his home place. Each time he returned from a trip the horse would nicker as he turned off the main road into his driveway. It was the horse's way of greeting his home corral and saying he was glad to be home. This friend moved to another state and, of course, took his horse. Upon his return three years later, he wondered if the horse would recognize the home place. Sure enough, as he turned in the driveway, the horse nickered.

Not only do horses remember scary happenings and the way home but fortunately, they also remember what we teach them. Sometimes it may be necessary to refresh their memory a little but if they have learned something they won't forget it. For example, if a new-born foal is broke to lead shortly after birth, he will remember this training when he is caught at weaning time. It will take a minute or two but he will soon be leading as well as he did at the end of his earlier training. It is the same for everything else we teach a horse. If a horse learns to stop, turn, take leads, chase cattle, run the barrels and all the other things we teach, he will not forget.

Sometimes we may think a horse has forgotten something because he does not respond as expected. If, after a few minutes, he still does not respond, then either we are using the wrong cues or we never taught the horse properly in the first place. In general his memory will be much better than ours. Most of what a horse learns he will remember all of his life. Of course, older horses could not be expected to properly perform difficult athletic feats which they learned as young horses.

SLEEPING AND RESTING

Horses sleep soundly very much as humans do. They sleep more than we realize because the adults usually sleep on their feet and it is sometimes difficult to determine if they are sleeping or merely resting. When asleep, the head droops, the eyes are closed and they are invariably standing on three legs. One hind leg will be cocked up while the other three carry the weight. Horses will alternate the use of the hind leg while resting unless they are lame and cannot use one. A horse always supports weight equally on the front feet except in the case of lameness. In one study, it was found that horses may sleep up to seven hours per 24 hours, almost as much as humans sleep.

Foals sleep lying flat on their side and spend a large percent of their time sleeping. As they grow older, they lie down less and also sleep less. Most mature horses do not lie down regularly although a few will sleep and rest in this position. It has been reported that some horses have not lain down for years except to roll. Any time you see a mature horse lying in a pasture while all the other horses are grazing, it is cause for some concern. The horse may have colic or some other problem. If two or more horses in a bunch are down, they undoubtedly are sleeping or resting. Apparently it is uncomfortable for most older horses to lie down for any length of time because of the crowding and pressure on the internal organs. This does not appear to be a problem for foals. In a wild bunch, all horses will not sleep at one time. At least one or more horses will be watching for dangerous intruders. In the Nevada study, the mares appeared to be the most watchful, although the stallion also was alert.

At night horses alternate between sleeping and eating. They do not do this on any set time schedule, according to Williams, who studied horses in box stalls. Horses turned out to graze at night after being used during the day will eat more or less steadily for the early part of the night. After they satisfy their initial hunger, they will alternate between sleeping and grazing until daylight when they will again graze steadily for a period of time. A group of domestic horses apparently all eat at the same time and sleep at the same time. As we pointed out above, wild horses do not all sleep at the same time during the day and, although not studied, probably not at night either.

The above remarks about the behavior of grazing horses at night are the result of personal experience on many pack trips into the mountains, where part of my responsibility has always been to know what the horses are doing at night. On these trips, the horses are hobbled and turned loose to graze, hopefully near camp. Cowbells are hung around the necks of one or two of the horses as an aid to locating the horses in the morning should they stray from camp. The music of the bells lulls the horse wrangler to sleep because, as long as he can hear them, he knows he won't have trouble finding the horses in the morning. Most horse wranglers sleep light and wake up if they do not sometimes hear the bells. Sometimes the bells are not ringing because the horses are sleeping. They sleep for a time without making a sound and then, start grazing, the bells ring and all is well. The horse wrangler can go back to sleep, at least until dawn. Daybreak is a critical time because if the horses have been restless during the night, this is the time they will often decide to head back to the home ranch.

GROOMING

The horse grooms itself by rolling in the dirt. Certain members of the bird family, domestic chickens for example, have dust baths as do buffalo. Pigs and elk have wallows of mud. Pigs use their wallow mostly as a means of keeping cool in hot weather. Elk apparently use theirs to coat the body with mud to discourage summer insects. Perhaps the mud has some grooming effect also. Horses usually prefer to roll in dry, soft dirt, the dustier the better. After rolling, the horse shakes itself vigorously to remove as much dust as possible. The horse always seems to feel better after he has been sweating from hard work and is tired if he can have his dusty bath.

This method of grooming probably evolved as a type of control on external parasites. It may have also been used as an aid to removing winter hair. Inasmuch as the tongue of the horse is not suited to grooming, as it is with cats and cows, this is about the only method which could be used by the horse. Its greatest value with modern horses may be in relaxing a tired horse after a hard day's work. For other horses, it may be just a pleasant experience.

CHAPTER II

The Learning Process in the Horse

The learning process in the horse is basically the same as in other animals and humans. As we will use the term, learning means a modification or change in the behavior of the horse as a result of previous experience. We would hope the modification in behavior is desirable and permanent. For example, we hope the horse learns not to fight when he is tied up with a halter. The experience here is in being tied and with a little practice, that is, being tied up several times, he should learn not to pull back. With enough practice the learning should be relatively permanent. Thus in horses we hope to modify their behavior in a desirable manner by training and we hope that the change is permanent. The behavior of the horse has also been modified by its own experiences from the time it was born. Some of these experiences have been purely personal and some as a result of association with other horses. For example, the natural curiosity of a foal should have taught it what scary items are really dangerous and what ones are not. It would have learned by personal experience. Many of its experiences and its learning are a result of its association with its mother and other horses. For example, if its mother was a wild one and ran every time she saw a man then the foal soon learned that it should run too.

In addition to the learned behavior, the foal is born with a certain amount of innate or instinctive behavior which produces behavioral responses without previous experience or learning. For example, the newborn foal struggles to get to its feet within a few minutes of its birth. Almost as soon as it is on its feet it attempts to nurse. It is obvious that the horse is born with certain behavior patterns already fixed. This innate behavior plus what he learns by himself, from other horses and from man gives him his total behavior.

The training of the horse involves changing some of the basic behavior which a horse is born with or learns prior to being handled by man. It also involves teaching the horse to respond to the rider's commands and perform certain useful functions. Changing some of the basic behavioral patterns such as fear and need for company may be difficult. We will discuss methods for doing this in later chapters.

HOW A HORSE LEARNS

Most of the learning of the horse which comes with training can be explained by the stimuli-response theory. Stated simply this theory means that if the horse is given a certain stimuli or cue he will respond in a certain manner, providing he has learned what he is supposed to do. For example, it usually does not take long for a young horse to learn to respond to the stimuli of oats in a bucket. When he is shown the bucket and hears the grain being shaken in it, he responds by coming to eat. The stimuli is the bucket with oats; the response is coming to the bucket to eat.

There are two types of stimuli used in the training of the horse, primary and secondary. As we will use the terms, a primary stimulus is one which the horse is born with; a secondary stimulus is one which he acquires by learning. In the example of the horse coming for oats, both types of stimuli are involved. Hunger, a primary stimulus makes the horse want the oats. The sight and sound of the bucket with the oats serves as a secondary stimulus or cue which the horse learns to associate with eating oats.

Primary Stimuli

Primary stimuli are more of a problem in breaking than finishing horses. The most difficult part of the breaking of many horses is the process of overcoming the instinctive urge of the horse to respond to the primary stimuli. The primary stimuli which we are most concerned about in breaking horses are fear, need for company and sexual behavior. In previous sections we have briefly discussed some techniques which can be used to help solve the problems involved with these primary stimuli. In later chapters we will discuss fear and need for company in more detail. Hunger is a primary stimulus which can be used, successfully to reward a horse for some desirable behavior, such as allowing itself to be caught. Oats or grain mixtures are the most common reward used although some people use sugar cubes, carrots, apples and other similar food. We will discuss the use of this primary stimulus as an aid to catching, loading in trailers and rewarding horses.

Secondary Stimuli from the Trainer

There are numerous secondary stimuli or cues to which a horse learns to respond. The list includes those used by the trainer while on the ground as well as while riding. In addition the horse also learns to cue on such things as cattle, barrels, stakes and jumps. In the normal process of breaking horses, the first cues a horse learns are those used while the trainer is on the ground. When a colt is being broke to lead, he learns to respond to the pull of the rope. If he is well broke to lead he moves when the handler moves and speaks to him without a pull on the rope. He learns to stop when the handler stops and says "whoa." Thus he has learned to respond to voice cues and the movement of the handler's body.

As the horse proceeds in its ground training, it can be taught to respond to the pull of driving or longe lines. It may learn further voice cues such as walk, trot and lope. Some trainers teach a horse to watch and respond to the position in which a long whip is held.

The most commonly used cues are the so-called natural ones which the trainer uses while mounted. These cues are the hands, legs, weight and voice. The hands communicate the rider's commands to the horse's mouth and to a lesser degree to its neck. Horses may also learn to watch with

HANDS AND CUES

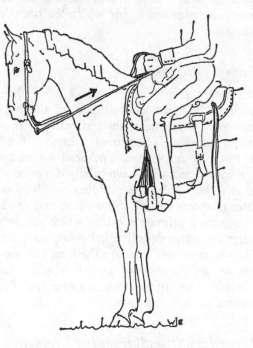

Illus. 26. Leading rein pulls nose out and leads horse around.

Illus. 27. Direct rein. Note horse flexing at poll and reins held low and coming in through bottom of hand.

their eye for movements of the hands. For example, in the early stages of breaking, a hackamore colt will learn to turn when he sees the rider's rein hand move out to the side. Leg and weight cues are received through nerve endings in the ribs and withers and voice cues through the sensitive ears.

Hands. As we pointed out earlier, light hands may produce a light soft mouth; hard hands will produce a hard mouth. Hands held high will produce a high head set; low hands most likely will produce a low one. At least three different types of rein cues are usually learned by horses. Most riders use a leading rein on green horses ridden in a snaffle or hackamore. The cue is several pulls to the side, each pull followed by slack. The desired response is the turning of the head, the bending of the neck and the following with the body in a circular turn. Riders also use a direct rein cue on green horses which means the reins pull directly back. The desired response to this cue is flexing at the poll, in other words, giv-

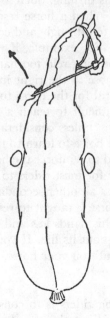

Illus. 28. Indirect or neck rein with incorrect results. Nose tipped the wrong way because of too much indirect pressure.

Illus. 29. Correct neck reining. Horse's nose in line with neck. Note how reins can be held on a green horse to give slight leading rein in direction of turn.

ing the head to the pull, and stopping or slowing down. The pull should be as light as possible, never a jerk, and each pull should be followed by slack. Thus there is an alternating pull and slack on the direct rein the same as on a leading rein. In the early stages of training, the pulls will be strong and gradually diminish in strength as the colt learns to respond to lighter pulls. The pull serves as the cue, the slack serves as the reward for giving the head. Giving slack is an essential part of producing a light responsive mouth.

The third type of rein cue is used on finished horses and is commonly called neck reining or more technically an indirect or bearing rein. This is the most difficult of the three reins for a horse to learn. The horse must respond to the opposite of a leading rein pull combined with a direct pull. If this sounds confusing to you, think how it must be to the horse. Because it is confusing to many riders, many horses never learn to respond correctly. The correct response is for the head, neck and shoulders to turn as a unit, without lateral flexation of the head and neck in either direction and without head throwing, stargazing or opening of the mouth.

The most common incorrect response to indirect reining is for the horse to tip its nose away from the direction it is turning. Such a response is always the fault of the rider not the horse. When a horse responds in this manner, the rider is using the bearing rein too strongly and causes the horse to respond as if it were a leading rein. For example, if the rider wishes to turn to the left and pulls the right bearing rein too hard across the neck of the horse, it will pull the horse's nose to the right instead of toward the direction it is turning. It is unnatural for the horse to turn its head the opposite direction of a turn. It is difficult to teach a horse to respond properly to the stimulus of neck reining unless considerable time is allowed. It is also virtually impossible for the horse to learn to neck rein correctly unless the leg and weight cues are used to reinforce the hands.

As a matter of fact, it is virtually impossible for most riders to develop a light, soft, responsive mouth on a horse unless all other secondary stimuli are used as extensively as possible. If the horse is taught to respond to legs, weight and voice cues, the rider can use his hands less and less and thus keep the horse's mouth responsive throughout its life. If you are interested in developing and keeping a light mouth on your horse, you will want to give this idea careful consideration.

Legs. A common mistake of many beginning riders is to consider the legs as only a cue for moving the horse ahead. When they want the horse to start or to go faster, they kick him in the ribs. Actually the legs can serve a much broader function because they also can be used to control the lateral or sideways movement of the rear hand. This lateral control is essential for many basic moves the finished horse should do, such as pivots, taking leads, side passing, correct stops and backing.

As we pointed out earlier, a horse does not respond naturally to light pressure on the ribs, but he does respond to pain. However, pain cannot be used as a secondary stimulus because the horse soon becomes numb and will require more and more pain to produce a response. Fortunately, a horse can be taught to move away from, or yield to, light pressure on his ribs. He must be taught this because, first, he is not by nature responsive to light pressure in this area and second, his instinctive reaction is to move into rib pressure to maintain his balance. If you have tried to move a young horse sideways by pressing on his ribs, you have found that most horses will resist the pressure because of their fear of being pushed over. This fear reaction is particularly noticeable when loose horses are crowded into a tight place such as a truck or small corral. As the horses crowd together, they lean into and push against each other to maintain their balance. Some horses do not ride well in trailers because of their fear of losing their balance on turns. They fight this insecurity by exaggerated leaning away from the turn and may even attempt to brace themselves by placing their feet on the wall or divider of the trailer.

You may have noticed we have referred to teaching the horse to respond to leg pressure not to pain from kicking or spurring. Actually, kicking will not usually cause any pain to the horse but it does tend to have a deadening effect on the nerve ends in the rib area. Continual kicking invariably leads to less and less feelings in the ribs. Spurs, if properly used, can restore some of the feeling. However, in general, spurs should be thought of as a device for disciplining the horse rather than as a tool for teaching response to light leg pressure. When a horse which should know better refuses to respond to leg pressure, then spurs can be used to refresh his memory.

If the horse is to learn to respond to leg pressure, he must be rewarded for his response. The reward is in releasing the pressure, which means that the legs squeeze and release, squeeze and release. This is essentially the same technique as is used with the hands where the rider pulls and slacks, pulls and slacks. As with the hands, the horse can be taught to respond to lighter and lighter leg pressure. A well-trained horse will respond to pressure so light that the movement of the rider's leg can hardly be observed. Notice we are talking about leg, not heel pressure. Except for short-legged riders on big horses, it is difficult if not impossible to squeeze with the heel. Specifically, it is the calf of the rider's leg that teaches the horse.

The legs may be used together or singly. In general when both legs are squeezed, it is a cue for the horse to move ahead or increase speed. Some riders squeeze with both legs as a cue to stop. If one leg is used, it is a cue for the horse to move away from the leg or not to move into the leg. For example, in a slidepass to the right, the horse is moving away from the pressure of the rider's left leg. In a rear hand pivot to the right, the rider's left leg prevents the horse from moving the rear quarters to the left. In general, leg pressure is used only when the rider is sitting in the saddle. It is difficult to use it while standing in the stirrups, although a rider can kick his horse while standing if he is leaning ahead in the saddle.

A rider may apply leg pressure at different locations along the side of

LEGS AS CUES

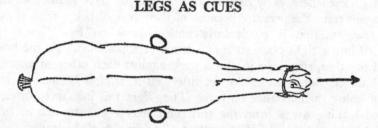

Illus. 30. Equal pressure from the calves of both legs to move a horse ahead.

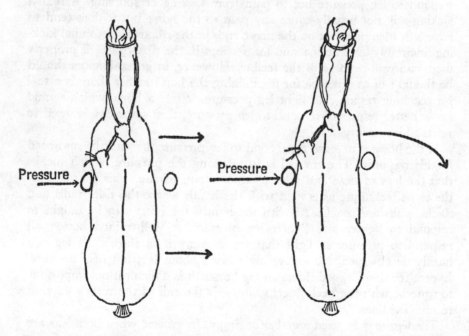

Illus. 31. (Left). Left leg pressure moves horse to the right in a side pass.
Illus. 32. (Right). Left leg pressure prevents the rear quarters from moving left in a pivot to the right.

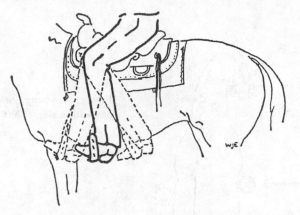

Illus. 33. Pressure can be applied at different positions for different results. The one natural position is all that is needed for western horses. *Remember* squeeze and release leg pressure. Do not kick. As training progresses, use lighter and lighter pressure.

the horse with each location being a slightly different cue to the horse. Most commonly, riders squeeze with the calf of their leg where it naturally hangs about over the cinch. If the leg is moved slightly forward of the cinch and squeezed, it can serve as an aid to the hands for moving the forehand sideways, away from the pressure of the leg. Conversely, some riders touch the horse on the shoulder with their foot as a cue for extending the horse's leg into a lead at the lope. When leg pressure is applied several inches behind the cinch it can be used as a cue for a pivot on the rear hand. Thus a horse can be taught to respond differently to leg pressure at different locations. Such refinements are not necessary, however, for training good western horses. Unless a rider has had considerable experience in using leg cues, it may be best to use the one position where the leg hangs naturally.

Weight. Although the horse does not naturally respond to light pressure on the mouth and ribs, it does respond to slight shifts of the rider's weight. As a matter of fact, a young horse will learn to respond to the stimulus of weight shifts easier than any other rider cue. There are two reasons for this. First, we have said that the withers of the horse are a naturally sensitive area with extensive nerve endings which can feel light pressure. Second, it is natural for the horse to balance itself as it turns, stops, and starts. When the free, riderless horse turns, it will lean in the direction it turns. If it didn't, it would fall over. Try it yourself and see what would happen as you turn at the run if you did not lean in the di-

WEIGHT AS A CUE

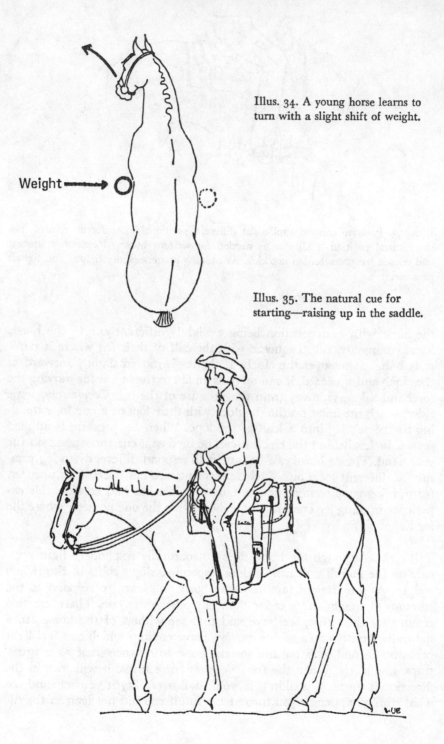

Illus. 34. A young horse learns to turn with a slight shift of weight.

Weight ⟶

Illus. 35. The natural cue for starting—raising up in the saddle.

Illus. 36. The natural cue for stopping—sitting down.

Illus. 37. An unnatural stop—the rider's weight too far back, prevents a natural stop.

Remember—*do not exaggerate weight cues—excess weight throws the horse out of balance.*

rection you turn. The horse balances itself by changing its head and neck position as it stops and starts.

Since it is natural for the horse to balance its own weight, it will instinctively attempt to adjust for the rider's weight. After a colt has been ridden four or five times and is accustomed to the rider's weight in the middle of him, he will almost automatically attempt to compensate for a weight shift to the side. If the rider shifts his weight slightly to the left stirrup, most colts will turn slightly to the left to compensate for the weight shift. It may be necessary to use the leading rein on the same side to get the initial response, but after a few lessons most colts will turn with only a slight weight cue. This is the beginning of teaching lightness and responsiveness and reduces the need for using the hands for turning.

Weight cues also serve as very important secondary stimuli for starting and stopping. It is natural for the rider to lean ahead slightly and raise the body out of the saddle just a bit to start a horse forward. Young horses learn to respond to this cue easily. Conversely, sitting down in the saddle can be used to stop the horse. To make this cue obvious for the green horse, the rider must have his weight out of the saddle and sit down firmly when the horse is to stop. Naturally the hands and voice must be used to reinforce this cue in the early training. Eventually most young horses will learn to stop quite well at the walk and trot with just the weight and voice cues and an occasional reminder from the hands. Later on during the finishing stages when more speed is used, weight will be an important cue to use in conjunction with the voice, hands and possibly the legs for stopping.

Interestingly enough, some trainers use their weight just the opposite to that described above. They stand up to stop and shift their weight to the left when they want to turn right. This does not seem quite as natural a way to ride but some riders get good results with these methods. In any event, it is obvious that the horse will readily learn to respond to weight cues and the cue does not need to be excessive. Remember the withers are naturally sensitive to light pressures and horses can feel very slight shifts of weight. Remember, too, the horse must balance its own weight as well as yours. Excessive leaning to the side or back can seriously hinder the performance of the horse because it throws him out of balance.

Voice. Although a horse has never been known to talk a human language, they certainly learn to respond to one. With care a trainer can teach a horse to come when called, recognize its name, start, stop, turn, back up, get over and walk, trot and lope, all with word cues. The most important voice cue, and one we will spend considerable time discussing in Chapter VI, is the sound "whoa" or "ho." This sound has apparently been used for hundreds, perhaps thousands, of years as the standard voice cue for stopping and quieting a horse. Other ancient and still widely used cues are the clucking and smacking sound. The clucking sound is made with the tongue against the roof of the mouth and smacking sound with the lips as in kissing. These sounds are commonly used to start to increase the speed of the moving horse. Zenophon, a Greek horseman writing before 300 B.C., describes the use of these two sounds.

Voice cues are taught over a period of time by repetitious use of a sound at an appropriate time and with proper reinforcement by other secondary stimuli. The sound must be made in exactly the same way each time it is used, until eventually the horse responds to it with little or no other cues needed. For example, in teaching a horse to move ahead with the clucking sound, the rider will need to use his legs, raise his weight slightly in the saddle and, on some colts, tap him lightly with a whip. As soon as the colt begins to learn to respond to all of these stimuli, the cues are reduced or discontinued one at a time until only the voice is needed to get the desired response. Teaching a horse to respond to voice cues is an essential part of developing lightness and responsiveness in the horse.

Other Secondary Stimuli

Wherever horses are used to handle cattle, the cow itself serves as a cue to the horse to turn, stop or increase speed as needed. Once the horse gets the idea what is expected, and providing he has enough natural ability, the rider is just there for the ride. He has little to do on the well-trained cow horse except stay on. The modern cutting horse shows this ability to cue on the cow to perfection.

Almost any horse of any breed can learn to work cattle but some are born with what is called "natural cow sense." The first time such horses are used around cattle, it is obvious they are watching the cow and wanting to work it. When following a gentle cow at the walk, these natural cow horses will instinctively turn each time the cow does. It is a very interesting ability bred into the horse. More emphasis has been placed on cow sense in the selection and mating of Quarter Horses than any other breed. As a result, a higher percentage of Quarter Horses exhibit natural cow sense than any other breed.

Roping and steer wrestling horses must also learn to cue on cattle. The rope horse must learn to catch cattle very rapidly and then rate the animal, that is, stay at the correct distance to allow the roper to throw his rope. Calf roping horses must follow directly behind the calf while horses used for catching steers by the head are usually taught to follow slightly to the side. Steer roping horses ridden by the heeler must learn to turn and come up on the left side of the steer as it is turned to give the roper a throw at the hind legs. Each of these three types of rope horses, the calf roping horse, the steer heading and steer heeling horse are all specialized and must learn to cue on the calf or steer in a slightly different manner.

Since it would be confusing to a horse to follow one animal directly behind and another one slightly to the side, good calf roping horses are seldom used to head steers or vice versa. However, some calf roping horses are used for heeling. Steer roping horses are often used for either heading and heeling since there is enough difference between these two catches so that the horse would not be confused.

Steer wrestling horses must cue on cattle in an entirely different manner than rope horses. As the steer leaves the chute, the horse must catch and then pass, close by on the left side of the steer. The horse must continue to run straight ahead to be clear of the rider after he gets down on the steer. Horses used to pickup cowboys, after they have completed rides on rodeo bucking horses, must run alongside of the bucking horse and stay in that position until the bucking horse rider has been taken off. Both the steer wrestling and pickup horses perform difficult jobs which cannot be done properly unless they cue on the animal they are chasing.

The earliest recorded use of the horse for chasing animals is found in ancient Egyptian drawings. These drawings show horses being used by hunters to kill wild cattle and even lions, with spears. Amazingly enough, the hunters are shown standing in a chariot pulled by two or more horses. Apparently they were doing this in quite level, smooth country. However, it must have taken tremendous horsemanship to drive a chariot close enough to a wild animal so that it could be killed with a spear. Undoubtedly, the horses learned to cue on the wild animals and become adept at putting their master in the proper position for the kill.

Probably the most skillful equestrian hunters of all time were the American Indians who hunted buffalo, antelope and deer on horseback. These wild animals were chased and killed in their natural habitat which was no picnic ground. The buffalo horse had to carry the rider close to the side of the animal where an arrow could be properly placed just ahead of the hip bone into the paunch and lungs. The horses were ridden with a rawhide rope half hitched to the jaw and with no saddle. The young buffalo horse was trained to get in the proper position by use of the rein and rider's weight and legs. However, his most important training was learning to cue on the buffalo. When this was perfected, the rider was free to concentrate on shooting the arrow. Considering the terrain, the wildness of the animals and the hunter's weapon, this booked tremendous skill for both horse and rider. It certainly took a horse which had learned to respond instantly to the secondary stimulus received from the buffalo and the rider.

The Plains Indian valued his buffalo horse more highly than any other possession. Not only did the horse provide him a relatively easy method of obtaining food but also the excitement and thrill of the chase. Apparently, the horses learned to enjoy the chase too, at least according to a report filed by the explorers, Lewis and Clark. In their trip up the Missouri

River to its headwaters and thence to the Pacific Ocean, they purchased horses from the Indians of the Rocky Mountains. In their return down the Yellowstone River in 1806, these horses displayed a keen interest in chasing buffalo. At that time the explorers had about 50 head of horses, considerably more than they needed to ride or pack. The extra horses were driven ahead and each time they approached a bunch of buffalo the horses would take after and circle them as if they were carrying a hunter to the kill. Naturally this created some problems and loss of time in getting the horses gathered up. The explorers solved the problem by sending two riders ahead of the loose horses to scare the buffalo out of their path and thus remove the source of the secondary stimulus for the buffalo horse.

Inanimate Stimuli. Horses also learn to respond to the visual stimuli of a number of inanimate objects such as barrels, poles and jumps. The well-trained barrel horse looks for the barrels as soon as it enters the arena. As the horse approaches each barrel, it must decrease its speed slightly, then turn and begin looking for the next barrel. All of this must be done with a minimum of rider cues if the horse is to win, because rider cues tend to slow the horse. Of course, the horse is taught to cue on the barrel by the use of the hands, legs and weight. These cues are used less and less as the horse learns to respond to the barrel.

The good stake racing horse must learn to cue on the stakes and the jumping horse on the jumps. The latter must learn to estimate rather accurately the height of jumps and the proper take off point. Horses also learn to cue on such objects as trailers or gates. Some horses, who are hauled frequently, will want to jump in a trailer if they see the doors open. They associate the open door with loading. If the gates on a ranch or at stockyards are made to open on horseback, horses soon learn to side

Illus. 38. Barrel racing horse looking for the barrel—the stimulus to run and turn.

pass up to the gate every time they approach one. The side pass is the response to the visual stimuli of the gate.

GENERAL RULES FOR TEACHING CUES

Successful horse trainers invariably have a system which they follow in training horses. The system involves, in part, a set of basic rules which they use in teaching cues. Some of the horsemen have thought out these rules very carefully and can explain them in some detail. Other equally proficient horsemen have instinctively developed a system which works well for them but which they cannot explain. The following suggestions for teaching cues would have general acceptance from most horsemen because they are based on the natural behavior and responses of the horse. As a student of horsemanship, you should consider each rule very carefully and adapt the basic idea to your own system.

RULE ONE—TEACH THE SIMPLEST AND MOST OBVIOUS EXERCISES FIRST.

It does not take much thinking to realize that it is best to teach a horse to lead at the walk before he is taught to lead at the trot. This same basic rule applies to everything else we teach the horse. Sometimes, however, it is not so obvious which is the simplest move and therefore where to start. Careful thought will be required to work out a training program which progresses logically from simple to more complex moves.

For example, in teaching a horse to make flying changes of lead, some horsemen begin with the initial ground training of the horse. The trainers teach the horse to pivot on the forehand while they are on the ground and then while mounted. Next they teach a side pass and a two-track. After these moves are learned, the horse is taught to take a lead on demand, then to make a simple change of leads and eventually a flying change.

A less complicated and more obvious series of steps from simple to more complex is used in teaching a horse to stop. It is best to teach a horse to stop at the walk, then the trot, then the lope and finally the run. In later chapters we will discuss in detail how to proceed from the simple training-exercise to the more complex.

RULE TWO—TEACHING MORE THAN ONE EXERCISE AT A TIME.

During the training of a horse, the trainer will be working on several different subjects at any one time. It would be far too time consuming to teach and perfect one move before beginning the training on another. After the first few initial training sessions, almost all trainers will begin to work on several subjects during the same session. This will not confuse the colt as long as one move is not dependent upon the correct execution of another one. For example, a colt could be worked on making easy stops at the trot and also rounding turns during the same session. The cues for stopping are different from those used for turning and there should be no chance of confusing the colt. On the other hand, if one were trying to teach a colt to side pass before he was taught to yield to leg pressure, there could be a problem.

RULE THREE—STRIVE FOR PERFECTION BEFORE SPEED.

With only a few exceptions, most moves we want to teach a horse should be taught at a slow speed. The speed should not be increased until the horse has mastered the move at the slower rate. Teaching moves at a slow speed has several advantages. First, it gives the horse time to think about and then respond to, your cues. This slight delay between receiving and responding to a cue is characteristic of all initial learning in horses as well as in humans. As a first grader, you learned to write very slowly and only after practice were you able to write with speed. It is the same with a young horse learning to stop, for example. When stopped at the walk, he will have time to think about and respond to the voice, hand, leg and weight cues you would use. As his reflexes improve with practice, he will learn to respond more rapidly to the cues and eventually to stop at faster and faster speeds.

Another important reason for teaching most moves at a slow speed is to allow the horse time to place its feet properly. Correct foot position is essential if a horse is to stop, turn, side pass and perform various other moves required of a western horse. As the training of a horse continues, foot position becomes more or less automatic. In the early stages, he must be given adequate time to place his feet.

A third reason for doing things slowly at first is to allow the inexperienced trainer time to give the cues in the correct manner and sequence. In moves where all four natural aids are used in a certain sequence, only experienced trainers can give them correctly without thinking about each one. Until you can do this, it is certainly best to go slowly.

Many young horses are spoiled by using too much speed too early in their training. They do not know what is expected, their feet are out of position and the rider may be confusing them with cues that are wrong or out of sequence. More young barrel racing prospects are spoiled by running the barrels too fast too soon than for any other reason.

Although most training should be done at a slow speed, there are some exceptions. If it is more difficult for a horse to do something slow than fast, then by all means, speed should be used. One exercise which horses can do easier with speed is a flying change of lead. Loose horses naturally make a flying change when they are running with some speed. If they are going at a slow gallop, they will often drop to a trot to change leads. It takes a well-trained, collected horse to make flying changes at a slow lope. Therefore, when teaching this move to young horses, running them at a

Illus. 39. Trotting the barrels. The early training of the barrel horse should involve much slow work; first, a few days at the walk, then several weeks at the trot, then several weeks or even months at the slow lope and gallop. Too much speed too early can ruin a good prospect.

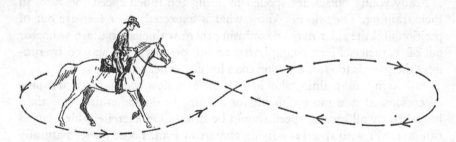

Illus. 40. Running the figure 8. One of the few moves taught a horse where speed is useful. After the basics of taking leads and making simple changes are well learned, most horses will learn a flying change easier if they are run rather than loped.

good gallop will usually make it easier for them to learn to change leads. As they learn what is wanted, they can be expected to make a change at a slower and slower lope.

RULE FOUR—THE CUE MUST BE REPEATED IN EXACTLY THE SAME MAN-NER EACH TIME IT IS USED.

It is obvious that if you said "whoa" one time to stop and "giddup" the next time to stop, it would be impossible for the horse to learn what you want. The same principle applies to all other cues. If you use pressure from the right leg as a cue to turn left, the pressure must be applied at the same place each time. Inexperienced trainers must be very careful to use their cues in exactly the same way each time. With experience, all of this becomes natural and the trainer does not consciously think about how to use each cue.

Although the cues we are discussing are standard and widely used, there may be slight differences between riders in their actual use. This is why it is best for only one rider to train a horse. There is less chance that the young horse will be confused because, assuming the one trainer is consistent, the cues will always be the same. Fortunately, once a horse is well trained, it will respond to basic cues which are slightly different. Thus more than one person can obtain satisfactory performance from the horse. However, there cannot be too many differences or even the best trained horse will become confused. One of the saddest sights to see is a well-trained horse trying desperately to respond to the confused and illog-ical cues of a poor rider who thinks he is an expert. In time, a confused horse may develop undesirable behavior patterns such as tail switching, bit chewing, open mouth and extreme nervousness. Some develop the very dangerous behavior of rearing or running away. The horse certainly could not be blamed for such aberrant behavior if it has been confused by poor riding for too long a time.

Although cues should not vary in location of application nor intent, they may vary in intensity. In general, all cues must be used with more intensity or force on the green horse than on the horse further along in training. When a horse is first being taught to respond to leg pressure, the pressure must be applied with enough vigor to catch the horse's attention. As the horse learns to respond, less and less pressure should be used. This same principle applies to the use of the hands, weight and voice. The gradual reduction of the intensity of the cues as the training progresses should produce a lighter and more responsive horse. As we have pointed out earlier, this is a goal that is well worth striving for.

RULE FIVE—THE CUE MUST BE CLOSELY RELATED IN TIME TO THE EXPECTED RESPONSE.

This means that when you cue a horse to produce a certain response, the response, or attempted response in the case of a young horse, must immediately follow the cue. The horse has no capacity for a delayed response. You cannot give him a cue and have him respond sometime later. If you are teaching the horse to come to your call by rewarding him with grain when he responds, you must give him the grain immediately. He would not associate the reward with your call if there was any appreciable delay. We will discuss in a later section of this chapter the importance of no time delay when punishing or disciplining a horse.

RULE SIX—WARM-UP THE HORSE PHYSICALLY AND MENTALLY BEFORE STARTING A TRAINING SESSION.

There are a number of physiological changes in the body when the resting horse becomes a moving or working horse. These are essentially chemical changes which requires a certain amount of time to begin functioning. This time requirement is why horses should always be warmed

ENDING A TRAINING SESSION

Illus. 41. Stopping and patting the horse on the neck.

up before any serious exertion. The horse should be walked, trotted and loped a few minutes at each gait before a training session is started.

The usual method of warming up the horse mentally is to repeat something he has already learned or at least something he is in the process of learning. After a few minutes of this, the trainer can proceed to new material or work on the perfection of a move. Although it is necessary to repeat certain exercises to warm up a horse, a trainer must be careful not to repeat anything too much. In general, if a horse is doing a certain move correctly he should not be required to do it often. There is always a temptation to keep working the horse on a move he does well because it makes the trainer feel as if he is accomplishing something. The temptation should be avoided because very likely the horse will become bored and tired of doing the same thing repeatedly and may refuse to do it correctly.

RULE SEVEN—END EACH TRAINING PERIOD DISTINCTLY.

While a horse is being schooled, it should be mentally alert and physically ready to do whatever is asked as best it can. When training is not in progress, the horse should be calm and relaxed. The horse needs to learn

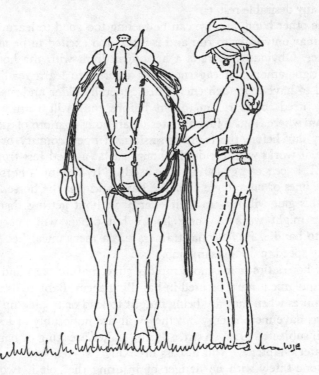

Illus. 42. Dismounting and adjusting cinch.

when he should be alert and when he can be relaxed. One way to teach the horse this is to end each training period distinctly. If the horse is being ridden in an arena the trainer can dismount in the middle of the arena, loosen his saddle and lead the horse out. All of this serves to tell the horse that the work is over and he can relax. If the horse is being worked outside, the rider can get off, adjust his saddle and then go on for a pleasure ride or return to the barn. A simpler method, although not as obvious to the horse, is to stop, pat the horse on the neck and then ride on.

Any type of distinct ending of a training session helps prevent the horse from becoming barn sour. He will learn not to spend all of his time thinking about returning to the barn, rather than paying attention to the trainer. Horses learn they must be alert and attentive until the signal is given for the end of the training session.

RULE EIGHT—KNOW THE STAMINA OF YOUR HORSE.

In general a horse must be alert and feeling good if he is to learn readily. A sick, weak or exhausted horse will learn very little. Some riders do not recognize this and try to use unnecessary force or punishment to improve the tired, sick horse's learning ability. Such techniques seldom produce any desirable results.

On the other hand, a horse can be feeling too good to learn. This kind of horse may only want to run and is really too excited to be attentive to the trainer. Obviously, there is a happy medium with the horse having just the right amount of eagerness and interest to learn readily. Horses that tend to have too much energy are generally older and more mature and they need to be ridden down before they will learn. This may require anywhere from a few minutes to an hour or more of steady exercise every day before the training session. If open country or trails are available, it works well to ride the horse out at a good fast trot until the edge is off. Excess energy can also be used up by driving a horse at a trot in double lines or on a longe line. We have said trot the horse because in general this gait will use up their energy without getting them excited. Galloping might work on some horses but others will only get more difficult to handle. Professional trainers use a mechanical hot walker set at trotting speed to do this same job.

Young horses tire much more rapidly than mature ones and thus considerable judgment must be used in handling them. Baby foals will tire in a few minutes when they are being taught to lead or to pick up their feet. Weanlings have more energy but they will tire noticeably in less than 10 minutes if subjected to much stress during halter breaking or handling.

In a later chapter we will discuss breaking two-year-olds to ride. This can be done safely with no danger of injuring the colt if two rules are followed. First, the colt must be well grown out, strong and feeling good and second, the trainer must not get the colt too tired. Not only will the colt be unable to learn if he is too tired, but it may actually cause permanent physical damage if he becomes exhausted. The training periods for two-year-olds should be short. Also, as soon as the colt is broke to ride and is reasonably gentle, he should be turned out until he is three years old. Two-year-olds should be given plenty of grain to supply energy for training as well as for growth.

Three-year-olds can definitely stand more work than a two-year-old but they can still be hurt if they are ridden to exhaustion. Four-year-olds can be ridden hard but some care must be used. Horses are considered mature at five and from then on up to 15 years of age they can do a tremendous amount of work if fed and cared for properly.

Each horse is different in the amount of energy it has and the work it can perform. Thus it becomes a matter of judgment for the trainer to decide just how much a horse should do, how much grain it needs or how much exercise it must have before it can learn. To make this judgment, the horse trainer must study each horse carefully.

RULE NINE—THINK WHILE YOU TRAIN.

Although all horses have common basic behavioral patterns, each one is an individual with its own characteristics. The stimuli used on one horse will not always produce exactly the same response on another one. Thus the good horse trainer must be constantly thinking about the responses he is obtaining and if these responses can be improved by using slightly different techniques. To those who are constantly striving for better and better training results, this provides a real challenge. It is a challenge to understand what is motivating a horse to do what he does, be it good or bad. It is also a challenge to think out a successful training program for each horse.

A good trainer must be resourceful and wherever possible take advantage of the natural behavior of the horse. For example, the first time a young horse is backed, he should have his tail, not his head, pointed in the direction he naturally wants to go, such as to the barn or toward other horses. Many similar situations arise which require careful thought to properly utilize the basic behavior of the young horse. As the behavior of the horse is modified by training, it is less and less necessary to be concerned about the horse's natural inclinations. The well-broke horse is trained to respond to the demands of the rider and to disregard its own basic impulses of fear, need for company, hunger, sexual needs and other conflicting behavioral patterns.

Patience is another essential attribute of the successful trainer. Cues must be patiently repeated in exactly the same way many times before some horses will learn the correct response. In concluding this section, we want to stress the importance of thinking while you train horses. Not only will you be more successful but it will be much more stimulating and interesting.

RATE OF LEARNING

Factors Affecting Rate of Learning

The rate of learning, which may vary considerably among horses, appears to be dependent upon four factors: intelligence, athletic ability, age of the horse, and the training techniques used.

The intelligence of the horse, as we use the term, would be measured by the ability of the horse to learn the responses expected. Some learn much easier than others, while a few never seem to learn anything. It is unfortunate that the intelligence of the horse cannot be determined until training actually begins. It would be most helpful in selecting young unbroke horses if one could measure their intelligence before the selection. The problem of spending money for a horse which lacked the intelligence to be successfully trained would be avoided. Perhaps some day a simple test of intelligence will be developed.

One possible method of testing the intelligence of a horse would be to measure its ability to learn to read. Now, you may not have been around too many horses that could read but we have had several on our campus who could. At least these college-educated horses have learned to recognize symbols. This can be considered a form of reading and is probably the manner in which you first learned to read. My students have taught horses to distinguish between such symbols as a cross, square, circle, rectangle, triangle and several other similar ones. Other research workers have taught horses to recognize up to 20 different symbols.

Anyway, some horses can be taught to recognize or "read" such things and furthermore some horses learn to do this faster and easier than others. Some horses will not or cannot learn to "read." Since there is a difference among horses in this respect, it should be possible to measure this difference. Perhaps such a measurement would be an indication of the horse's ability to learn other things we may try to teach, or in other words, a measurement of its intelligence.

You might wish to try to measure your own horse's ability in this respect. We have used grain as our inducement in the same way as we tested a horse's ability to determine color. A 6×8 inch card with a cross drawn on it is placed in front of a bucket with grain and a card with a circle is placed in front of another bucket about 10 feet away. The second bucket also contains grain but is covered with a screen. The horse is allowed to walk to the buckets and if he selects the correct one he is rewarded with a bite or two of feed. At first his choice will be at random but if he is intelligent he will soon learn to look for and "read" the cross.

Illus. 43. Reading a sign. A horse's ability to learn to read may be an indication of the ability to learn other things.

Of course, the position of the buckets must be rotated at random or the horse would go to the position and not look for the correct sign.

By recording the number of times it takes a horse to develop an accuracy of 80% or better, one can compare horses in their ability to learn to "read." This may be a measurement of their ability to learn other responses. If such a measurement could be taken on young horses before they were ridden, it might be useful. However, all of this is speculation because there is no evidence that such learning would be correlated with other types of learning. Neither is there any evidence that such a test would be practical. We have discussed it as an interesting possibility.

Athletic ability obviously affects the rate of learning of horses which are being taught to perform difficult athletic feats. For example, some horses have the natural ability to make flying changes of lead and seldom, if ever, cross up in their leads. These horses have the coordination and general athletic ability to maintain the correct position of both front and hind legs. Usually these horses rapidly learn to change leads or to take the correct lead on demand. In my experience, this kind of horse is not nearly as plentiful as the kind that has trouble with leads. The difference is in the natural athletic ability of the horse.

Fortunately, athletic ability of young horses can be measured to a certain extent before they are ridden. Careful observation of young ones, as they move about a corral or run in a pasture, can give the astute observer some idea of their potential. If a young horse can stop, turn and change leads easily as it plays, chances are it can do these things with a rider. On the other hand, if a loose horse crosses leads when he changes direction at the run or stumbles at the trot, he is almost a cinch to be a slow learner as far as athletic ability is concerned. In general though, it has been my experience that more horses learn slowly because of a lack of intelligence than a lack of athletic ability.

The age of the horse is related to the rapidity of learning. In general, horses under five learn faster than older horses. Horses from five to about ten years of age still have the capacity to learn rapidly but their rate of learning something new may be slowed by previous learning. In other words, these mature, broke horses may have learned to do something one way and you are trying to teach them to do it another way. Obviously, it will be a slow process to unteach something before something else can be taught.

I remember trying to teach a seven-year-old horse to side pass up to a gate so that it could be opened without dismounting. A former rider had always ridden straight up to a gate and dismounted and led the horse through. The horse had easily learned to side pass but it required a considerable amount of time and patience to get him to side pass up to the gate. Previous training had to be unlearned before the horse could learn something new. Attempting to correct bad habits of spoiled horses is in the same category.

Training techniques used is another factor affecting the rate of learning of horses. Correct techniques used consistently and accompanied by patience and careful thinking should produce rapid learning. Improper techniques used inconsistently with little patience or thought slow the rate of learning considerably. We have just been discussing general ideas on how to correctly use cues. In later chapters we will discuss in some detail the specific cues to use in training western horses. We hope that students of horse training will find this information useful in improving their training techniques and therefore the rate of learning of their horses.

Three Rates of Learning

Insight: Some horses learn some exercises quite rapidly or, as we use the term, by insight. The horse is shown what is the expected response and, with one or two tries, the correct response is learned. Much of the time this type of learning is closely associated with one or more primary stimuli, such as hunger or fear. Most horses learn quite rapidly that if they come to a bucket of grain there will be something good to eat. They also rapidly learn where to find the hay manger, water, shade and protected place. Horses also learn very rapidly anything that stimulates fear. If a horse becomes tangled in a rope and kicks its way out, it does not forget this experience. Every time a rope touches its legs it will kick and fight to get away. It has learned rapidly by fear. It will learn much slower not to fear a rope.

Although desirable responses can be learned by insight, it often happens that horses learn more undesirable responses in this manner than desirable ones. When one relates this type of rapid learning to the basic fear behavior of a horse, it becomes understandable. Only the wild horses which learned very rapidly what was dangerous and a threat to their life lived long enough to produce offspring. Learning by insight evolved in this manner and is still a basic part of the behavior of domestic horses.

Trial and Error: Most learning in horses occurs by trial and error. The trainer gives the horse a certain cue, for example pressure from the left leg, and the horse is expected to move its rearhand to the right. In several days of patiently applying the pressure and using the voice and hands to assist, the horse should learn the correct response. By trial and error he learns to yield to the leg and to move to the right, not to the left, not forward, not back. Because the horse learns slowly by trial and error over a period of time, it is essential we remember to use cues in exactly the same way each training session. It is equally important to have patience and to understand when the horse is trying to learn even though he is making errors.

Delayed or Latent Learning: Although horses are not supposed to be able to think and solve problems, they do exhibit a type of latent learning that makes one wonder. It sometimes happens that at the end of a particularly trying training session the horse does not seem to have learned anything, despite the best efforts of the trainer who may have been working on this exercise for several days. The trainer is discouraged and almost ready to give up. After a couple of days rest, the trainer begins the same lesson again and finds, to his surprise, the horse is responding exactly the way he should. In some inexplicable manner, the horse has learned during the two days rest what was expected of him.

Latent learning may occur overnight or after several weeks or even months. It is not clearly understood exactly what is happening in the mind of the horse but it is clear that this type of learning does occur. Therefore, the wise horse trainer should take advantage of this phenomena and if the horse is having trouble on a certain exercise, give him a chance to think it over for a time. The results may be surprising.

MOTIVATION AND LEARNING

Motivation is an important factor in learning in animals as well as in humans. Your motivation for reading this material is your desire to learn about horses. Some animals are easily motivated to learn through their desire to please their human masters. The dog is probably the best example of this type of motivation. Animals may be motivated to learn rather unusual exercises by their strong desire for food, others by their fear of punishment.

Motivation to please. A few horsemen believe a horse is motivated to learn by its desire to please them. This may be true under certain conditions where a particularly strong attachment has developed between the person and the horse. However, this type of learning must be considered rare and unusual and most trainers must have other motivational methods available.

Motivation by food can be used successfully in horse training but is limited in its practical application. In later sections we will discuss the use of grain to motivate a horse to come when called or to load in a trailer. Some trick horse trainers use grain to reward the horse after it has successfully executed a trick.

The big problem of using food comes while mounted. It is possible for a rider to feed a horse pellets by leaning around to the front and giving him some in his hand. However, this would not be practical on a finished western horse chasing cows, competing in the show ring or at a rodeo. To motivate a horse to learn to stop, turn, slow lope and all the other moves a western horse should do by feeding pellets and then discontinue the practice once training is completed could lead to considerable confusion for the horse. For this reason, grain is not ordinarily used in this way although it does have some interesting possibilities.

Motivation by fear. Many experienced horsemen use fear as an important motivating tool to teach a wide range of responses. They use the natural fear of the horse of anything that inflicts pain. In actual practice what this really amounts to is the horse is taught to develop a strong desire to escape punishment. He learns that if he does what is expected he will not be punished, and there is no pain.

Now, we need to make it clear that punishment is not used in the form of a big club, nor any real abuse of the horse, but in much more subtle ways. In many cases, this punishment really only involves making the horse uncomfortable. For example, when a baby foal is being broke to lead and a rump rope is used, most foals do not like the feel of the rope around their hindquarters. To escape the unpleasant feeling of the rope, they move ahead and soon are leading. The same is true of leg pressure on a horse's ribs. It does not like the feeling of being touched in the ribs and it learns to avoid this mild form of discomfort by moving away from the leg. The horse learns to give its head to the bit for the same basic reason. There is an almost endless number of examples of a horse being motivated to learn by avoiding some forms of mild punishment.

Forms of Punishment

Pain. As we have said, most of the punishment used on horses is really more a slight discomfort rather than any pain. There are, however, situations where something more than mild discomfort must be used to get the horse's attention and to motivate him to learn. A whip or spurs are commonly used by horsemen for this purpose. After a horse has learned that these devices can cause him considerable discomfort, they can be used mostly as a threat and little or no pain need be inflicted. This is particularly true of the whip or romel. The trainer may need only to show the whip to the horse, as old timers used to say, and the visual stimulus will produce the desired response. Once a horse learns to respect spurs, the rider can get the desired response most of the time by leg pressure with only a threat of using spurs. Horses vary considerably in their sensitivity to pain. Some horses will require only a slight touch of the whip or spur to produce a response; others need considerably more than a touch. The number and sensitivity of nerve endings in and just under the skin apparently account for the differences. Thoroughbred-type horses are usually more sensitive than the draft types. Mules, and particularly donkeys, are rather insensitive.

Some riders are tempted to discipline their horses with the bit by using sharp jerks to hurt the horse. As we pointed out earlier, the principal result of such punishment is a ruined mouth and improper head set. It is poor horsemanship to ever jerk a horse's mouth. The bit should not be considered a device to be used for punishment. Hard pulls with a snaffle or a hackamore are a different matter. They can be used as strong discipline without injuring the horse. Note we said pulls not jerks, because even with these mild head pieces, they should never be jerked.

Voice. Horses can be taught to regard the voice as a mild form of punishment or at least a warning. A sharply spoken word to an alert, responsive horse may be all that is needed to tell the horse he has done something wrong. The horse is not nearly as responsive to voice discipline as a dog but, nevertheless, it is always worth trying to use your voice because it may reduce the need for more severe forms of punishment.

One more thought about punishment. If it is going to be effective and meaningful to the horse, it must be used immediately after a disobedience. With even a slight delay, the horse may not connect the punishment with his error and thus the punishment only confuses and frightens the horse and serves no useful purpose. In some cases where punishment can coincide with the wrongdoing, it is particularly effective. A horse that has developed the bad habit of nipping or trying to bite, can be disciplined in this manner. You must anticipate his misbehavior and, as he reaches for you, meet him with a sharp slap of your hand or arm just above the mouth. A few lessons will usually break the habit or at least make the horse much more cautious about whom he bites.

Some horsemen believe slapping a horse in this manner will make him head shy. If the timing is correct it should not, because the horse learns he is being punished for doing something wrong. It is very interesting to watch the expression on a horse's face which has been disciplined in this manner but is tempted to try a bite. You can see him debating, "Should I or shouldn't I risk a good slap for the satisfaction of a little bite of my trainer?"

Forms of Reward

We have said that an important motivating factor in training horses appears to be their desire to escape punishment. A horse also learns to respond to a reward. We discussed how grain can be used in this respect but as we pointed out, this type of reward has certain practical limitations. It is unfortunate that other types of reward also have limitations, the principal limitation being the horse does not appear to recognize and respond to them.

If horses would respond to a kind word and a pat on the neck the way a dog does, their training would be much easier. But they don't. The horse shows very limited recognition of these rewards. However, they are apparently of some value so it is a good idea to routinely reward your horse with a pat on the neck and a kind word when he does what you have asked. These rewards can be used when the foal takes his first step in leading and from then on for everything he does properly.

Probably the most effective and practical method of rewarding a horse for doing a good job is to end the training session or at least stop working on a move he has done satisfactorily. Over a period of time, the horse will learn to associate proper execution with rest, or at least a change, and thus be motivated to perform his best. See Illus. 41 and 42. This takes advantage of the horse's natural inclination to prefer doing what he wants rather than what the trainer wants. Most horses prefer eating, sleeping and moving about freely to doing what a trainer wants. A few horses really appear to enjoy being trained but they are the exception in my experience. On the other hand, many horses enjoy doing something once it has been learned. Finished cow horses, barrel racers, jumpers, trail horses, race horses and many others learn to really enjoy their work but this is after the training is completed.

To use rest effectively as a reward for an accomplishment, the trainer must be certain the horse has performed the move as well as he is capable before he is rested. It would defeat the purpose if the horse were rewarded for doing something poorly. For example, in teaching a young horse to back for the first time, if the colt will freely back 2 or 3 steps, this could be enough. The backing lesson should be ended for that day although other work could continue. The next day the lesson should continue until he will back 4 or 5 steps and then the backing lesson should be ended. If however, after several lessons, the colt only wants to back 2 or 3 steps, the session should not be ended until he has backed as far as he is capable at the particular stage of his training. This same principle would apply to all other types of training. Work the horse until he has done as well as he can, then stop. There are some exceptions to this principle such as a filly being in heat or if a horse appears to be sick, but in general it should be adhered to rather closely.

HYPNOSIS IN HORSES

There is evidence that a few horsemen have the unusual ability to hypnotize horses. An article appearing in *American Heritage* described in detail a man who apparently had this ability. This man, John Rarey, was born in Ohio in 1827 and died in 1866. He spent his childhood on a lonely farm without playmates his own age and learned to make friends with the farm animals.

He developed the ability to handle all farm animals with ease and also some wild animals. Although he learned to use a leather strap, known as Rarey's strap, to tie up a front foot on a horse, he apparently used no other form of restraint and never any form of pain or punishment. His technique consisted of touching and talking to the animals. The purpose of the strap was to immobilize a wild or dangerous horse so that he could approach it safely. The strap held up the front foot and unruly horses were laid down by pulling their heads to the opposite side of the tied foot.

As a young man, he went to Texas and worked with the wild range horses with considerable success. At 30 years of age, he went to England and performed many amazing feats with spoiled and vicious horses. He became so well known, the Queen of England asked for a demonstration of his ability.

His most famous success came with an outlaw stallion called Cruiser. This horse, foaled in 1852, had been a Derby favorite in 1855, but the horse had gone bad and turned killer. He kicked two grooms to death and although he was a valuable breeding animal, he could not be handled in any manner. The owner bet Rarey 100 pounds he could not

Illus. 44. Hypnosis in horses? John Rarey's knee snap apparently was used to allow the famous horseman to touch and talk to vicious horses and in effect hypnotize the horse.

tame the horse in three months. Rarey went into the stall, apparently in some manner got his strap on the stallion, laid him down and in three hours time rode the horse out of the stall. He also had the owner ride the horse.

He beat a drum while sitting on another outlaw stallion and hooked the horse to a carriage with a mare and drove the pair about with no trouble. He became famous throughout England and much of Europe for his ability to handle any type of horse. His fame followed him back to America when he returned after three years abroad.

A modern psychologist, Dr. F. Dudley Klopfer, of Washington State University was asked to comment on Rarey's technique. The scientist concluded that Rarey had the unusual ability to hypnotize animals. Rarey himself apparently did not understand what he was doing and his contemporaries thought the technique of using the strap to lay the horse down was the secret that subdued the horse. However, as we pointed out earlier, the immobilization was to allow Rarey to talk to and touch the horse and it was this that hypnotized the animal, not the strap.

Although rare, other people with this unusual ability have been reported. An article published December 1, 1954 in the *Montana Farmer-Stockman* described a man by the name of Jack Healy, who apparently could hypnotize horses. Healy, born in 1870 at Helena, Montana, and who died in 1932, specialized in driving horses without lines. Not only could he drive broke horses in this manner but he also hooked up and drove for the first time wild range horses without lines.

According to eye witnesses, Healy touched, talked to and looked into the eye of the horses to hypnotize them. It was said he could go into a corral filled with the wildest of the range horses and there were some wild ones in those days, and after a short time of talking, crawl under and over them. He could slap the most unruly bronc on the hip, pull its tail and pick up its feet.

My father knew this man and had seen him perform several of his feats. He said one of Healy's favorite tricks was to walk up to a team that was pulling a load and stop them. Regardless of what the driver did, the team would not move until Healy gave them a signal to do so. It must be a remarkable experience to see such a performance.

CHAPTER III

Equipment

The riding equipment we use today to break and finish horses had its American origin in two separate and distinct areas, California and Texas. Spanish missions settled in Old California in the 1770's gave rise to our first range cattle and horse operations and therefore our first truly western equipment. It was here that the use of the hackamore for training cow horses was perfected and perhaps even invented. The use of the spade bit for reined cow horses also reached perfection here although the bit itself was handed down from Old Mexico and Spain. The center fire saddle, rawhide reins, riata for dally roping and hair mecates were all a part of the California tradition which slowly spread to the adjoining states of Nevada and Oregon and eventually into the northwest states. Charlie Russell, the famous Montana artist, describes this equipment as being used in Montana in the 1880's. The early Californians, who were themselves Spanish, used and perfected equipment brought up from Old Mexico and directly from Spain. Their training techniques can also be traced directly back to Spain and even to the Vienna Riding School, which was a gift from the rulers of Spain to Austria in the sixteenth century.

Somewhat later in the 1830's and 40's, the Texas range cattle and horse industry began and another source of western riding equipment developed. Although Texas was originally a part of Mexico, the equipment developed there does not show nearly as much Spanish influence as the California equipment. With the exception of the rim fire or full-rigged saddle, there is little Spanish influence apparent.

Although the range cattle industry in Texas started a half century or more later than in California, its influence on equipment and training spread much further and faster. This rapid spread northward across the great plains came with the expansion of the range cattle industry and trail herd era. It reached the Canadian border in Montana and North

Dakota by 1880. The distinguishing features of the Texas equipment were the rim fire saddles, low port bits, and short grass ropes tied hard and fast to the saddle horn. The use of snaffle bits for breaking horses in Texas may be of Spanish origin or more likely indicates eastern states or English influence. The first American settlers in Texas had come from Missouri, Louisiana and other states to the east where the snaffle was in common use. As the spade bit can be traced back to Spain, so the snaffle bit can be traced back to England and Europe. In recent years, pelham bits have been introduced in the west, again evidence of English or eastern influence.

It would appear that although the Texans were influenced slightly by the Spanish and eastern states, most of their equipment was of their own design. It was well suited to the type of horsemen, horses and work that was done in Texas at that time. Their training techniques reflect this same localized development and was distinct from both the Spanish and eastern United States and English styles.

SADDLES

The most expensive piece of equipment for the horse trainer is the saddle. Therefore, a saddle should be selected carefully because you will likely use it for many years. When selecting a saddle, it would be best to actually ride or use the one you are interested in to make sure it is suitable for you. Since this is not usually possible with new saddles, you should ride other people's saddles until you find one you like and try to get one similar to it.

The saddle you select should be designed for the type of use you intend for it. As a horse breaker, you will want a different saddle than a roper or barrel racer or pleasure rider. You'll want one that is safe, comfortable and useable. To be safe, the saddle must be made strong enough to stay together in one piece under your type of use. Ropers need the strongest saddles while pleasure riders are not greatly concerned with strength. To be comfortable, the saddle must fit your body for length of seat, width of fork and position of stirrups. It also must fit the horse properly and keep you in the proper position on the horse in relation to his center of balance. Depending somewhat on conformation, the center of balance of a horse is about 6 inches behind the elbow, in other words, just about where the cinch ordinarily goes. Because an understanding of the center of balance is rather important in selecting a saddle and, as we will see later on, in the way you ride and your horse performs, we will discuss it now in some detail.

CENTER OF BALANCE—ILLUS. 45–46.

To explain more about the center of balance of a horse, we might use a teeter-totter which most of you played with in your younger days. The center support of the teeter-totter is similar to the center of balance of the horse. If you sit directly over this center of support or balance on the teeter-totter, you feel very little movement even when the board is moved as high or as low as it can go on the ends. If you sit a foot away from the center you feel more movement and so on as you move further and further away from the center of balance. You will remember what happens if you're sitting on the high end and the kid on the low end gets off. All of this applies to the position you sit on the horse although it is not as exaggerated since you can't get as far away from the horse's center of balance. However, if the movements of the horse are exaggerated as they are when one bucks, then the effect of being away from the center of balance is magnified considerably. Rodeo contestants who ride bucking horses or bulls must stay over the center of balance. They will get thrown high in the air if they get back even 3 or 4 inches.

If you don't agree with what I'm saying or don't quite understand, get on a horse bareback and compare the feel of sitting over his center of bal-

Illus. 45. The center of balance of a teeter-totter is similar to that of a horse. If the rider sits over the center of balance it is much easier to ride the horse, because there is less up and down movement. It is also much easier for the horse to carry the weight and to run, stop and turn.

ance with sitting further and further back on his loin. I think you'll agree it is rather difficult to stay on a horse at any gait faster than a walk if you're sitting back very far on his loin. The only way you can ride bareback and stay on the horse is to stay over the center of balance. Young people who ride bareback a great deal become very good natural riders. They learn to stay in balance with the horse because, if they don't, they'll fall off. It seems to me then, that a saddle should simulate bareback riding as closely as possible, as far as keeping the rider in balance with the horse. We shall discuss this idea as we proceed with our discussion of saddles. Before we leave the matter of balance, we need to discuss two more aspects, first, what your added weight does to the performance of the horse if you are out of balance and second, what roping does to the horse's balance.

Going back to the teeter-totter, you will remember if you sit over the point of balance only the slightest bit of weight is needed to move the board up and down. If you move back on the board, it takes a little more weight on the other end to raise you and so on as you move back. This same principle applies to the horse. If you are over his point of balance, it is easier for him to lift your weight to run, stop, turn or do any other performance type moves. The further you are away from this center, the more energy the horse must use and the more difficult it is for him to maintain his balance to perform. You have noticed how jockeys ride, crouched over the withers. This position plus the fact that their stirrups are hung forward of the cinch puts them well over the center of balance. This position allows the race horse to carry the jockey's weight with the least expenditure of energy. The horse would use considerably more energy if the rider were back 2 or 3 inches. If your horse is going to perform with the least expenditure of energy and his maximum maneuverability, you cannot be behind his center of balance.

Roping presents a slightly different problem but, nevertheless, one that involves the horse's balance. If you were to attach a rope to the end of the teeter-totter, it would not take much pull to make it turn. As you move the rope closer and closer to the center of balance, it takes a little more pull and the board moves less and less distance. If the rope is attached directly over the center of balance, the pull is on the center stand and will not turn the board.

The same principle applies to roping, particularly when the rope is tied hard and fast to the horn. If the horn is over the center of balance, the horse takes the jerk on his legs without whipping his body. The further the horn is away from the center of the horse, the more sideways whip or pull there would be on the front or back of the horse. We are talking here about a pull more or less to the side of the horse. If the pull is straight ahead and the horn forward of the center, it tends to put the jerk mostly on the front legs. Whereas, if the pull is straight back, it tends to raise the front end. Because of all this, ropers have developed a preference for a saddle which puts the horn over the center of balance. This position of the horn makes it easiest for the horse to absorb the shock of a jerk or pull and to work the rope. We will discuss the characteristics of a good roping saddle in the following section.

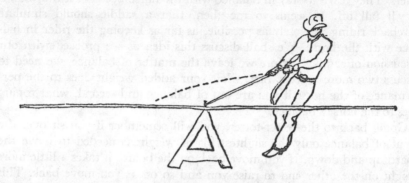

Illus. 46. The pull of the rope over the center of balance of the teeter-totter does not move the board. If the rope was attached a short distance away from the center, the board would move easily. The same principle applies to a rope horse. It is much easier for the horns to absorb a jerk or pull of the rope, if the horn of the saddle is over the center of balance.

Tree

Tree—Illus. 47.

The foundation of the saddle is the tree which consists of four pieces of wood, the two bars, the cantle and the fork. These pieces are carefully fitted together. Then the good saddle makers cover these wooden pieces with wet bull hide which is laced tightly together. Properly constructed trees made by reputable companies are almost indestructible under ordinary use. As a matter of fact, most good saddle makers give a lifetime guarantee that their saddles will not break or hurt a horse's back. Trees covered with canvas or plastic material would not have such a guarantee. A new process of making trees from poured fiber glass may eventually replace the rawhide covered trees, but as of now the rawhide tree is the best. Trees come in many sizes and shapes as we'll see in the following discussion.

Length of the Tree

The length of the tree of a saddle is determined by the distance from the inside of the fork to the inside of the cantle. This distance is normally from 12 to 16 inches. It has been my experience that many riders, particularly youngsters, often have a longer tree than is advisable. If the tree is too long, it is almost impossible for the rider to stay forward over the center of balance of the horse and sit down in the saddle. In a long saddle, the rider must stand in the stirrup to be over the center of balance. This is all right for ropers but certainly doesn't work in the equitation class or if you are riding a reining or cutting horse or riding all day in the range country. Most youngsters and slim built adults should be using 12 or 13 inch trees.

Some people say the longer trees are more comfortable because you have more room to move around. This may be true at the walk or slow lope on a gentle horse. However, it may be very uncomfortable on a horse that is really doing something because it is difficult to stay over the center of balance of the horse. At least for me, if I can't stay over the center of balance of the horse, I'm mighty uncomfortable because I feel very insecure sitting back on his loin.

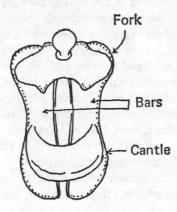

Illus. 47. The saddle tree.

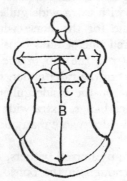

Illus. 48. The measurements of a saddle. Line A. Width of fork. Line B. Length of seat. Line C. Outside width of gullet.

TYPE OF FORK—ILLUS. 49–51.

There is considerable variation in the type of forks which a saddle may have. The extremes going from what is called an A or slick fork to the bear trap. The A fork is the original type of fork used in the West by both the Old Californians and Texans and can be traced back many centuries to the very earliest saddles in Europe and the Middle East.

Around 1900, somebody got the idea of putting swells on the fork as an aid to staying on a bucking horse. Prior to that, a rolled slicker or artificial leather swells were used by some bronc riders to help keep them in the old A fork saddle. By the 1920's, saddles were being built with extreme swells sticking out and slightly back as much as 20 inches. The swells were deeply undercut where the fork joins the bars to give plenty of knee grip. This coupled with a high dished cantle gave rise to the name bear trap, implying that once a rider got into the saddle it would be as hard to get out of as a trap. These saddles did give the bronc rider an advantage. However, they were dangerous if a horse fell, because of the difficulty of getting out of them in a hurry. Not many of these extreme saddles are being made now but forks do still show considerable variation in the amount of swell. Ropers tend to select saddles with little or no swells because they stand up and lean ahead to rope and big swells tend to interfere with this. Horse breakers and cutting horse riders usually prefer a fairly good swell because of the extra security the swells give them. Cowboys chasing cattle or horses in rough country may want some swells for the same reason. Rodeo rules specify that saddles with 14 inch swells with a one inch undercut on each side must be used in the bronc riding. The rider might prefer a little more swell, the owner of the bucking horse less; however, this width has been agreed upon as being the most fair for both horse and rider. In general, if you want or need security you will want some swells on the fork.

From the standpoint of comfort for both horse and rider, the width of the fork where it joins the bars, or width of gullet is more important than the width of the swell. Some trees are made with extra wide gullets to fit down over low withered horses. This is fine for the horse with poor withers, but not so good for a sharp withered one. Unless considerable padding is used, the top of the gullet may rub the top of the horse's withers. It may not be so good for the comfort of the rider either, particularly short-legged ones. A saddle that is wide on the inside gullet is also wide on the outside where the rider's upper leg hangs. Extra wide saddles may prove quite uncomfortable on long hard rides where many hours are spent in the saddle.

A properly made saddle should fit almost any horse's withers, have as much swell as desired and yet be narrow enough in the outside gullet measurement to be comfortable. Saddles with as much as 14-inch swells can be cut back under the swells to 10–11 inches wide. If you are a horse breaker, you will want some swells, but if the saddle is made correctly, it can still be narrow enough under the swells to be comfortable. Riders who use gentle horses and ride for pleasure, and thus may be most interested in comfort and enjoyment, should consider an A fork. They are hard to beat for comfort.

SADDLE FORKS

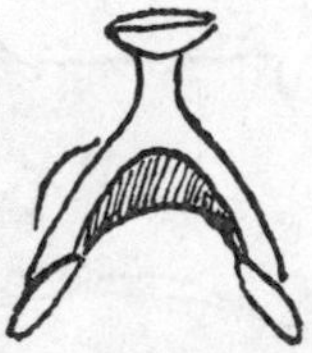

Illus. 49. Old time A Fork. A good fork if you want comfort.

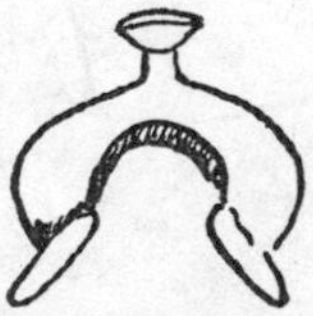

Illus. 50. Moderate swell. Popular today.

Illus. 51. Fifteen-inch swell.

TYPE OF CANTLE—ILLUS. 52–55.

Prior to 1900, cantles were almost always 5 inches high with no dish, that is, they were a straight piece of wood, rounded on the top and attached across the rear of the bars. The trend to lower cantles started with the early rodeo ropers who wanted to dismount in a hurry to tie a calf or steer. Saddles with the Cheyenne roll were the first to be used by the ropers and it's still a popular cantle today. After 1900, the bear trap trees were developed and the dished cantle became an essential feature of these saddles. The dish keeps the rider's seat from slipping sideways in the saddle.

Modern saddles can be ordered with cantles from one and one-half to five inches high, all with more or less dish and with a variety of rolls or turns of the top of the cantle. Ropers and steer wrestlers use the low, rolled cantles. Horse breakers, cutting horse riders and others riding performance horses or riding in rough country generally prefer 2–4-inch cantles. The higher cantles, like the bigger swells, give more security.

CANTLES

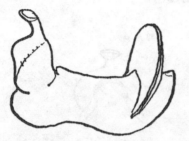 

Illus. 52. Old-time five-inch cantle with no dish.   Illus. 53. Modern roping cantle.

Illus. 54. High dished cantle with under-cut swells, bear trap style.   Illus. 55. Four-inch cantle with dish. A good one for breaking colts.

TYPE OF HORN

There is a wide variety of horns in size, shape and height. Ropers prefer the larger ones, with dally ropers wanting not only a big horn but also a big, high throat to aid in dallying. Horse trainers who like to keep their hand low may prefer a smaller, low-set horn which allows them to keep their hands close to the withers of the horse. Hands in this position are more conducive to a low head set.

Riggings

We have said the tree is the foundation of the saddle. Now we will talk about the rigging which holds the saddle on the horse and determines its position relative to the center of balance of the horse. Obviously, the strength of the rigging must match the strength of the tree if the saddle is going to stay on the horse under hard use. Also of considerable importance is the position the saddle is held on the horse. The common types of riggings are ring, plate and skirt and the common positions are full, 7/8 and 3/4.

TYPE OF RIGGINGS—ILLUS. 56–59.

The original type of rigging in the early California and Texas saddles was what is called a ring rigging. Heavy leather straps coming down from the fork and cantle were attached to a round metal ring about 4–5 inches in diameter. The latigo and billet were in turn fastened to this ring. Just prior to 1900, the Texans changed the ring slightly to a D shape and also some saddle makers began making a flat ring rather than a round one. All of these types of rings are still being put into saddles today although the round ring is not common. The D ring has been and still is particularly popular in roping saddles because it makes a very strong rigging. The first major change in types of riggings came around 1930 when plate rigged saddles began to appear. The plate was a double thickness of leather sewed together and extended in one solid piece from the fork down and around to the cantle on each side of the tree. If properly made, these were strong and also were not as bulky as the ring rigged saddles. The rider's legs were a little closer to the horse, making it easier for the horse to feel leg pressure and making it more comfortable for the rider. This type of rigging is most often found in saddles with 7/8 or 3/4 position.

The next major change in riggings came around 1950 when saddle makers discarded both the ring and the plates and started making the rigging and skirts all in one piece. The principal advantage of the skirt rigged saddles is less bulky leather between the rider's legs and the horse. Skirt riggings are now common in all types of saddles and if properly made are strong enough for roping.

For the horse trainer, the most important consideration about type of rigging is that it have as little bulk as possible and still have adequate strength. The closer the trainer is to the horse, the easier it is to transmit body and upper leg cues to the horse. It also makes the saddle more comfortable if the rigging is not bulky.

TYPES OF RIGGING

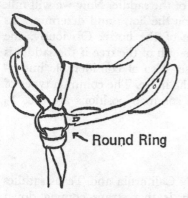

Illus. 56. The original type, a round ring.

Illus. 57. D ring, an early modification of the round ring. Still popular with ropers because of the strength.

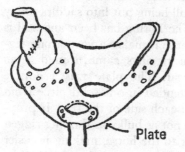

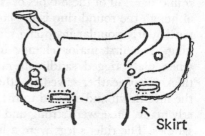

Illus. 58. Plate rigging. A good rigging, but not widely used today.

Illus. 59. Skirt rigged saddle, the newest type. Keeps the rider close to the horse.

POSITION OF RIGGINGS—ILLUS. 60–64.

We have just discussed type of riggings where strength and bulkiness were the major considerations. The position or point on the rigging where the latigos are attached in relation to the horn and seat of the saddle is also of considerable importance. There is some interesting history concerning position of riggings starting back in Old Mexico. Apparently

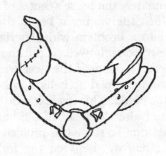

Illus. 60. Original Mexican saddle with a rim fire position (now called the full rigged).

Illus. 61. Original center fire rigging, seldom seen today.

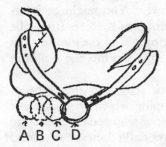

Illus. 62. Model showing positions full (A), ⅞ (B), ¾ (C), center fire (D).

Illus. 63. Modern full rigged saddle, same position as original Mexican saddle but with back cinch.

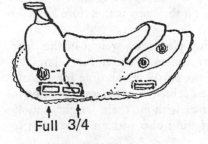

Full   3/4

Illus. 64. Modern saddle with changeable full and ¾ positions, also ⅞ if both slots used for latigo.

the earliest saddles used on Mexican ranches were the rim fire or now more commonly called full rigged saddles. In these old saddles, the rigging consisted of two strong leather straps hung over the fork and coming straight down to rings on either side. Latigos went from the rings to the cinch. The cinch went around the horse just back of the elbow or at approximately the horse's center of balance.

When the vaqueros began using ropes to catch and hold cattle, they ran into a problem with this rigging. The position appeared to suit the horse reasonably well. It put the pull or jerk of the rope directly over his center of balance if the steer was off to the side or to the rear. However, the saddle tipped up behind rather abruptly when the rope horse was facing the cattle. This made it a little difficult for the rider to stay in the saddle and also the front of the bars could hurt the horse when the saddle tipped up. To solve this problem, someone moved the cinch ring back to about halfway between the fork and the cantle and brought a strap around behind the cantle and down to the ring on each side. Thus the center fire rigging was born. It is not clear if this development occurred in Old Mexico and was brought to California with the first missions or if it was strictly a California idea. In any event, it was the predominate position of rigging used from the earliest mission days through the first third of this century in California. As we pointed out earlier, California equipment and techniques including the center fire rigging slowly spread to adjoining states and eventually to the Northwest. You might be interested in the origin of the terms center fire and rim fire. It comes from rifle cartridges, some of which are fired when the firing pin of the gun hits the center of the cartridge. Another type fires when the pin hits the explosive cap on the edge or rim of the cartridge.

Apparently the center fire proved very satisfactory for the type of horses ridden during that time and for dally roping which was practiced in California and the surrounding states. The rider who rode a center fire also used a long rawhide riata which was always dallied, never tied hard and fast to the horn. The cattle were slowed down and turned by slowing the horse gradually, letting the dallys run when necessary to prevent a jerk. The dally roper never jerked cattle for two reasons: a jerk might break his riata and his rigging was not in a position to protect the horse from a hard jerk. With a center fire rigged saddle, the horn is well forward of the center of balance and a jerk on the horn is therefore hard on the horse.

On the other hand, a center fire rigging places the weight of the rider over the center of balance and therefore makes it easier for a horse to carry the rider. Undoubtedly, this fact was partly responsible for the old Californian's reputation of having the best reined cow horses ever known. They could sit down and rein their horses without their weight unduly hampering the horse. This position of rigging also was an advantage to the bronc stomper because it kept him over the center of balance and made it easier for him to ride a bucking horse. Will James, Montana cowboy author, artist and noted authority on the range horse, who rode in the early 1900's pointed out in one of his books that he had used both positions or riggings available at that time, the center and rim fire. He said it was easier to sit a bucking horse with the center fire than the rim fire. This verifies what we discussed earlier about the rider being over the center of balance.

Interestingly enough, the last saddle perfected and used by the U. S. Cavalry was center fire rigged. This was the famous McClellan which appeared just before the Civil War. It was the standard equipment for the cavalry riders up to the time of the disbandment of the U. S. Cavalry in the 1940's.

Now let us return to the original Mexican rim fire saddle and how it influenced the Texans. When the first Americans rode into the area which was to become Texas, they found the Mexican residents using the rim fire rigged saddles that they had been using for some 300 years. The early Texans soon found that this position of rigging suited their style of riding and roping quite well. One improvement was necessary, they added a back cinch to prevent the saddle from tipping up when they roped. As a matter of fact, they liked this arrangement so well they are still using it. The full rigged saddle is by far the most popular in Texas today. Why did the Texans find the full rig satisfactory when the early Californians didn't? The explanation lies in the different style of roping. We have already explained that the Californians dally roped. The Texans on the other hand had developed a technique of roping in which the rope was tied hard and fast to the horn. They used short ropes made of plant material which did not break easily even though subjected to a hard jerk. The fact that the horses were jerked made the Old Mexican full rig ideal because it put the jerk or pull of the rope directly over the center of balance of the horse. Since the Texans still rope in this same manner, it is not surprising they still prefer the rim fire rigging.

So much for the history of the original two positions of riggings. Both played an essential part in the development of our western riding heritage. Interestingly enough, only one survives today. The rim fire is still widely used, the center fire rarely. Why did the center fire disappear? I have never heard a real good explanation; but apparently it was a change in use, in type of horse or, more likely, because another position evolved which worked better. The new position which evolved in the early 1900's was the ¾ rigging. This was a compromise between the rim or full rig and the center fire. The ¾ rig had the ring placed three quarters of the way from the cantle to fork. This position was halfway between the two original ones and has now replaced the center fire. The ¾ rig puts the rider over the center of balance almost as well as the center fire and yet can be used for roping. Today it is preferred by many horse breakers, cutting and reined horse riders. It is the only rigging position allowed for rodeo saddle bronc riders. Others who ride for pleasure or youths performing in equitation classes should certainly consider the merits of the ¾ rig. This position would make it easier for them to ride in balance with their horse.

Historically, the ¾ rig is supposed to have evolved in the northern states where riders have always been noted for their ability to ride bucking horses. One authority (Wellman, 1939) states the ¾ rig was also used around 1900 in the Southwest. In the early 1900s, there were hundreds of thousands of wild horses running in Montana, Wyoming and the Dakotas and the men who broke and rode these horses had to be some of the best riders the world has ever known. Originally many of these men had used the full rig because of the Texas influence in these states. Eventually they realized that they needed all the advantage they could get to ride the big, wild horses of the North. The center fire was not suited to hard and fast roping which they preferred. So the ¾ rig evolved which could be used for roping and was particularly well suited for breaking horses.

Riders found another compromise in the ⅞ rigging which is halfway between the ¾ and full rigs. Also a ⅝ position is available which is most like the old center fire. Many dally ropers use the ⅞. One of the recent innovations in saddles is to make the rigging easily convertible from full to ⅞ to ¾ by moving the latigos from one position to another. For some riders who may want to rope and break horses in the same saddle, this may be very useful. Also, because of the differences in the conformation of horses, one position may fit a horse better than another.

DOUBLE RIGGINGS

No doubt, some of you are wondering why I haven't mentioned anything about double riggings. There is a common misunderstanding about what double means. It simply means that the saddle is rigged with two cinches. The position or type of rigging may be any of the ones we discussed, except the center fire, which, as far as I know, was never double rigged.

The idea of using a back cinch apparently originated in Texas. We pointed out earlier that the early Texans and Californians used a single cinch coming straight down from the fork. The Texans had the same problems as the Californians with their saddles tipping up behind when roping but they solved their problem in a different way. Instead of moving the rigging back to make a center fire, they left it where it was and added a back cinch with a separate and lighter rigging pulling straight down from the cantle. We would now call this a full double rigged sad-

RIGGING POSITION AND PERFORMANCE

Illus. 65. Roping horses handle cattle easier when the pull of the rope is over their center of balance.

Illus. 66. Performance horses, such as this one cutting cattle, carry the weight of the rider easier if he is over the center of balance. It is also easier for the rider to stay in balance with the horse.

dle. The full indicates that the front cinch pulls directly down from the fork and double indicates two cinches. A full rigged saddle is seldom made without a double cinch because it would tip up too easily while roping without the back cinch. Most ⅞ riggings are also double and ¾ riggings may be.

There seems to be a current fad that all saddles should be double rigged. This is very questionable unless you are going to be roping or riding bucking horses. The extra cinch is just extra weight and bother and has little real value for most riding including breaking horses.

In summary on rigging positions (Illus. 60–64), if you're a hard and fast roper, you will probably prefer the full double rigged saddle because it's easier on the horse when the pull comes over his center of balance. If you're riding a performing horse or breaking horses, you may prefer the ¾. It puts your weight over the center of balance, making it easier for you to ride the horse and easier for the horse to carry your weight. If you ride simply for pleasure, you may find it more comfortable to be over the center of balance where a ¾ rigging puts you.

Stirrups

STIRRUP TYPES—ILLUS. 67–70.

The principal difference in stirrups is their width at the bottom which may vary from ¾ to four inches. The bronc riders and many barrel racers and cutting horse riders use the narrow ¾ inch one called an oxbow which fits into the instep of their boot and is not as easily lost as a wider one. Ropers and steer wrestlers prefer the wider, heavier ones which allow them to get a foot out quickly for rapid dismounts.

You may find the wider stirrups more comfortable because you ride with your weight on the ball of your foot rather than the instep. Also you may be a little less apt to get your foot hung up in a wide stirrup and thus they may be a little safer.

POSITION OF STIRRUPS—ILLUS. 67–70.

Historically since early Mexican days, the stirrup straps on western saddles have been hung over the bars. This is still true on most saddles today. Some early rodeo riders hung their stirrup leather straight down from the fork to make it easier for them to keep their feet ahead on a bucking horse. A few saddle makers have gone back to this idea in recent years to provide greater comfort for riders because it keeps them forward over the center of balance.

On a ¾ rigged saddle, the stirrups hang over the cinch and thus about over the center of balance. This also puts the rider's weight over the center of balance. On a full rigged saddle, the stirrups hang behind the cinch and thus behind the center of balance. This makes it difficult, if not impossible, for the rider's weight to be over the center of balance.

Saddles used at rodeos for riding bucking horses must have the stirrup

TYPE AND POSITION OF STIRRUPS

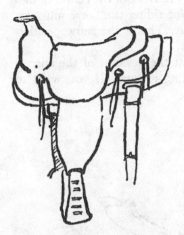

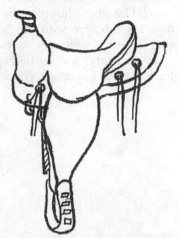

Illus. 67. Full rigged roping saddle, four-inch-wide stirrups hung slightly behind the D ring. Rider's weight will be slightly behind the center of balance.

Illus. 68. Three-quarter rigged saddle, three-inch-wide stirrups hung over the cinch. Rider's weight will be over the center of balance.

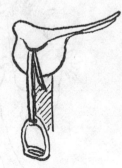

Illus. 69. Rodeo bronc saddle with ¾-inch-wide stirrups tied forward of the ¾ rigging. Keeps the rider well over the center of balance.

Illus. 70. Jockey saddle with stirrups hung in the same forward position as the bronc saddle.

leathers hung over the bars. This means they are over the cinch and thus about over the center of balance of the horse because these are ¾ rigged saddles. However, bronc riders tie the stirrup leathers ahead to the fork which in effect puts the stirrup leather slightly in front of the center of balance. This gives the rider the best position for riding the horse and also does not interfere with the horse in any way. This is the same position that the stirrups on a jockey saddle are hung.

In summary, it must be kept in mind that the position of the stirrup leather is an important consideration in riding a horse. If you want to

Illus. 71. Bucking horse rider. The ¾ rig, forward hung ¾-inch stirrups and 14-inch swell makes an even match for the top rider and the tough bucking horse.

keep your weight over the center of balance of the horse, your stirrups must be hung in the correct position. Thus the position of the stirrup, as well as the position of the rigging, is involved in keeping your weight over the center of balance. If you ride standing up all of the time, stirrup position would be most important, while if you ride without stirrups, rigging position would be most important. In actual practice, you'll be putting some weight on your stirrups and some on the seat of the saddle and, therefore, both are about of equal importance.

One more thought about stirrup position. If you do considerable riding in rough mountainous country where you spend half your time riding downhill, you may want your stirrups hung more to the front of the tree. This allows you to keep your feet out in front of you to absorb more of the jar when coming downhill.

HEADGEAR

A wide variety of headgear has been and is being used to train horses. In the 5,000 years that the horse has been domesticated, there have been more different types of headgear tried and discarded than any other piece of horse equipment. Even today there are still supposedly new devices being promoted which will solve all the horse trainers' problems. There is a lot of truth in an old saying that it is not what you use on a horse, but how you use it, that gets results. With this in mind, we will stay with the old, proven headgear and not be concerned with all the various gimmicks that are available.

We will discuss what is considered standard or basic training equipment. This will include the bar or snaffle bit which has been in almost continuous use since the horse was domesticated, the curb bit which has been used for at least 2,000 years, and the doubled reined bridles, pelham and weymouth which have been used for several hundred years.

Bits

Bar and Snaffle—Illus. 72, 73

The oldest form of headgear still in use for training today is the bar bit. Although not commonly used on saddle horses today, it is still used on harness and draft horses. This type of bit apparently was the first one ever put in a horse's mouth. It was originally made of bone or wood and eventually metal. From the bar bit evolved the snaffle which works on the same principle but is jointed in the middle and therefore is a little more severe and gives the rider more control.

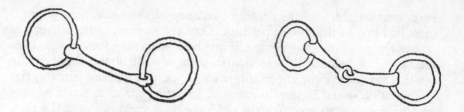

Illus. 72. Bar and snaffle bit. Left: The first bit ever used was probably a straight piece of wood or bone; later it was made of metal. Right: Eventually a bar bit was jointed to make the snaffle, a bit commonly used today for starting young horses.

Note: Horses were probably first ridden with a rope in their mouths. This practice was widespread among American Indians. However, they did use metal bits when they could get them. In this discussion, we are not considering the rope bridle to be a bit, although it could be.

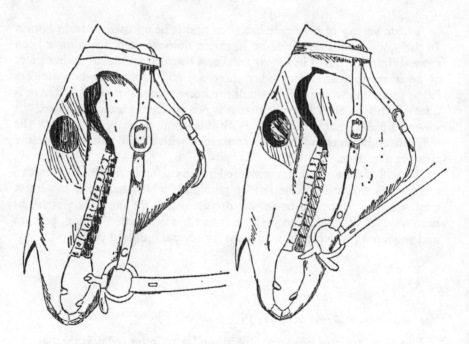

Illus. 73. Snaffle bit in relation to the teeth. Left: Correct position, about halfway between the bridle teeth (single tooth above and below) and the molars (back teeth). This position is obtained when the bit touches the upper corner of the mouth. Right: An incorrect position with the snaffle pulling on the molars. Hands are too high or the horse's nose is up and out.

Note: The tongue is not pictured but would be below the bit.

The bar and snaffle bit works by pressure or pulling on the tongue, bars and lips of the mouth. Notice in Illus. 73 that the snaffle should be adjusted to hang between the molars and the bridle teeth. If the horse is responding properly and if the rider's hands are low enough, the bit will pull about halfway between the bridle teeth and the molars. If the horse has his nose extended out or the rider has his hands too high, the bit will pull against the molars making it uncomfortable for the horse and probably will result in head throwing or at least a higher head.

The snaffle is the most commonly used headgear for breaking horses in this country and probably the world. When properly used, most horses can be taught to respond to gentle pulls and slacks and some horses to only slight tremors of the fingers. In expert hands, most horses can also be taught to flex at the pole with a snaffle. Eventually, however, many western horses tend to get hard in a snaffle and the horse must be transferred to a curb bit. Thus, the snaffle is considered a breaking bit and a western horse is not finished until he is responding properly to a curb bit.

As we mentioned earlier, the snaffle works by pressure on the mouth. The fact that it is not a leverage bit, as is the curb, may create considerable problems when changing from the snaffle to the curb. The most intelligent horse cannot be expected to automatically respond to the leverage action of the curb, regardless of how well it is responding to the pressure of the snaffle. It is a totally different action.

Expert horsemen can and do make the change from snaffle to curb with little or no problems. If you're not an expert, then you should consider using an intermediate step between the snaffle and the curb. This intermediate step involves the use of headgear which has both the snaffle and curb action and two pair of reins. We will discuss this after the section on curbs.

Curb Bits—Illus. 74–80.

A curb bit has a leverage action. The curb strap attached to the shank above the mouthpiece and the reins attached to the shanks below the mouthpiece provide this action. When the reins are pulled, the tongue and bars of the mouth are caught in a vice-like leverage action between the mouthpiece and the jaw bone of the horse. Obviously, this is a totally different action on the horse's mouth than the pressure applied by a pull on a snaffle bit.

Any bit, regardless of the mouthpiece would have this leverage action if the curb and reins are attached as described above. The mouthpieces of curb bits can vary from a simple straight bar with no port or curve to the very high port of the spade bits. A common training bit called a long shanked snaffle has a snaffle mouthpiece but this is still a curb if arranged as described above. Bits with a low curve or port in the bar are supposed

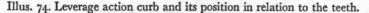

Illus. 74. Leverage action curb and its position in relation to the teeth.

to be less apt to cut the tongue than a straight bar. The tongue can fit up into the curve of the port and not be caught against the bars. However, this will not prevent cutting the tongue if the horse is really jerked hard or falls on the bit.

The type of mouthpiece on a curb which horsemen will use depends mostly on personal preference and some on the horse. Some horses get along better with a low port, some with a higher one. Some horses seem to carry a light bit better than a heavier one. As a horse trainer, you should have two or three different bits on hand to try on a horse. You might want a long shanked snaffle, a medium port in a light bit and about the same port on a heavier one.

SPADE BITS—ILLUS. 79–80.

One of the most misunderstood curb bits is the spade. Horsemen who do not understand its proper use look at a spade and wonder who in the world would ever use such a cruel bit on a horse. They often remark that

CURB BITS

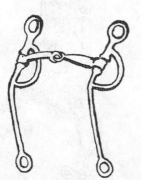

Illus. 75. Long shanked snaffle, a mild form of the curb.

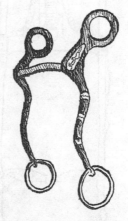

Illus. 76. Curb with straight bar mouthpiece.

Illus. 77. Curb with slight port, also grazing type shank.

Illus. 78. Curb with halfbreed mouthpiece (this means about half as much port as a full spade).

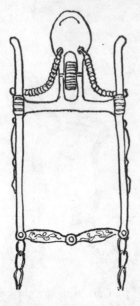 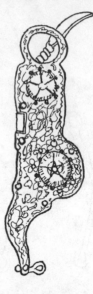

Illus. 79. Spade with spoon mouthpiece.   Illus. 80. Side view of spade showing correct position of spoon.

it must be for rank, hard-to-handle horses that can't be ridden with the ordinary curb. Actually, a good spade bit, properly fitted to the horse and properly handled, is just the opposite of being cruel. It is really designed to keep horses very light and soft mouthed. The horsemen who perfected its use wanted a horse to respond to the very lightest pulls or tremors on the reins. Over a long period of time, after using many different bits, they decided the spade was the bit to do the job. Exactly where or when the spade originated is not known for certain. It was introduced to Old California by the Spanish and had probably been used in Spain for several hundred years prior to that. The Californians found that it worked especially well on their horses. They wanted their horses to work with light contact on the bit and to be prepared to respond to the rider instantly. This is essentially the same way cavalry horses were trained in Spain when men were fighting on horseback with swords. The period prior to the development of gun powder in the early 1500's saw this type of horsemanship reach its greatest perfection.

The high port of the spade is designed to provide maximum contact of the bit and mouth thus enabling the horse to feel only the very slightest movements of the bit. The properly trained spade bit horse will respond to very light movements of the bit. The high port will not cut the tongue of the horse because it moves away from the tongue when the reins are used. Neither can it cut or hurt the roof of the mouth if the curb strap is adjusted properly. The proper adjustment is just snug enough to allow two fingers to be placed between the strap and the jaw bones.

Illus. 81. Two fingers laid between jaw and curb strap is about correct adjustment.

In addition to providing maximum contact of the bit and mouth by using a high port, the Spanish also used copper on some part of the bit. Copper stimulates the salivary glands to produce saliva, thus insuring a moist mouth which many horsemen feel is conducive to a light mouth. Also all good spades are made with a roller or cricket which gives the horse something to roll with his tongue when he is standing. This serves to quiet the horse and may also stimulate the salivary glands. Many spade bits nowadays are what is called loose jawed, that is, the side pieces are not fastened rigidly to the mouthpiece. This allows the horse to feel the shanks move before the mouthpiece does and serves as a preliminary cue. This is another way in which the spade keeps a horse light mouthed. From all this, it would appear that the Spanish were certainly not being cruel but were trying in every way to help their horses not only respond easily to the bit but actually enjoy it.

The spade bit is still very popular west of the Rockies today. However, the halfbreed bit, which is a modification of the full spade, is more widely used at the present time than a full spade. The halfbreed does not require quite as much skill or time to teach a horse to carry and more horses will learn to carry it well.

My discussion of the merits of the spade is not meant to imply that everyone should be using one. A good spade is expensive and you shouldn't have one if it is not a good one. In addition, it takes considerably more time and patience to train a spade bit horse. You really need to work with someone to learn how to do it properly. We have discussed it here because I think a student of horsemanship should understand that such a bit was developed for very good reasons. If the bit is properly used, excellent results can be obtained.

DOUBLE REINED BRIDLES—ILLUS. 82-84.

From the very earliest days of the range riders east of the Rocky Mountains, there was a very strong tradition that said no cowboy used a double reined outfit. There were just too many reins to handle and still be able to swing a rope. Besides, it was strictly an eastern dude outfit suited to the high tailed and tallyho riders. Later on we'll see there was a different tradition in California but in the area influenced by the Texans, which now includes all of the eastern as well as the Great Plains states, this was the tradition.

For well over 100 years, cowboys in this big area broke horses in snaffles and went directly to the curb bit. Their horses were not noted for their soft mouths or correct head set but for their ability to work cows. The cow can be a much better teacher than a rider when it comes to teaching a horse how to turn and stop and work a rope. In recent years, however, there has been a change in all this because of fencing and smaller ranches. There is not nearly as much cow work for horses to do and besides, the vast majority of the horse owners are not cowboys. Without the cow to teach horses how to work, it is undoubtedly more difficult to change a horse from a snaffle to a curb. The mouths of many young horses are now being ruined in the process of this change.

In the last 25 years, the use of the pelham has been introduced in the West. It is gradually being recognized as an acceptable type of headgear for changing horses from a snaffle to a curb. It is not uncommon for professional trainers nowadays to use pelhams, although not many of the older cowboys will go that far. In my opinion, it is an excellent method for young or inexperienced riders to change a horse to a curb because it can be done gradually over a period of time. You don't take the snaffle off one day and put the curb on the next.

The pelham, as Illus. 81 shows, has a snaffle and curb action and is commonly used on jumping horses and polo ponies. When the bit is first

DOUBLE REINED BRIDLES

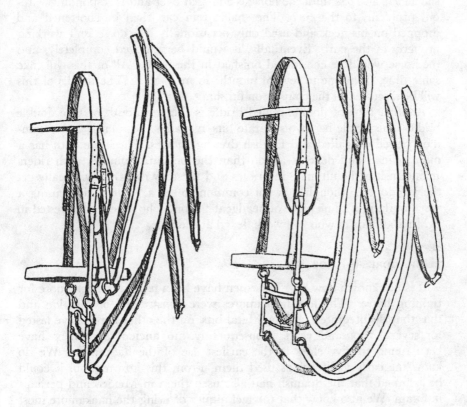

Illus. 82. English pelham with snaffle and curb reins.

Illus. 83. Weymouth or true double bridle with separate snaffle and curb bits.

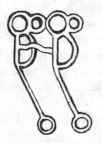

Cowboy Pelham

Illus. 84. Popular western pelham.

put on the green horse, the snaffle is used until the horse has learned to carry the new bit. Gradually, the curb is used more and more and the snaffle less and less until the horse is changed over and is responding without problems to the curb. The snaffle rein can then be shortened and dropped on his neck and used only occasionally if a horse isn't working properly in the curb. Eventually, it would be removed completely, and the horse would be considered finished in the bridle. All of this will take some time, from one to several months in most cases. The details of this will be discussed in the chapter on finishing.

Another type of double reined bridle is the weymouth or true double bridle. This bridle has two separate bits, a snaffle and a curb and is commonly used on gaited and English dressage horses. The weymouth has a more refined and delicate action than the pelham. Some English riders maintain it is the ultimate in bridles and the only one that will really get the job done. Although it is not common to see a western rider using a weymouth, it is a fine piece of headgear for one who is really interested in light reined horses who will work flexed at the pole.

HACKAMORES—ILLUS. 85.

It is not known how long horsemen have been using the hackamore for training horses. The first hackamores were constructed of rawhide and thus they disintegrated rapidly. Metal bits, on the other hand, have lasted for several thousand years. Consequently, no ancient specimens have been found to give clues to the earliest use of the hackamore. We do know the early Californians used them. From this information, it could be assumed that the Spanish had also used them in Mexico and perhaps in Spain. We also know that the techniques of using the hackamore most likely reached their peak of perfection in Old California where the vaqueros put a great deal of emphasis on light reined cow horses.

The hackamore, when properly used, may be the best headgear ever developed for use on a young horse when he must be worked on cattle while still green and when the ultimate goal is a light, soft mouth. All of his cow training can be done with the hackamore and his mouth would never be touched during this time. When he is doing all he would ever need to do in working cattle, he can gradually be changed from the hackamore to the bit. This change is necessary because almost all horses will tend to get hard and lose their responsiveness in a hackamore if kept in one too long. In other words, the hackamore is a breaking and training device just like the snaffle. A hackamore horse is not considered finished until he is working in a curb bit. The curb bit to the Old Californians was the full spade, however, to the modern Californians it is most apt to be the halfbreed.

The Old Californians might ride a young horse in nothing but a hackamore for 6 months or a year. Then they would take another 6 months or a year to transfer him from the hackamore to the bit. If they started with a four-year-old horse, the horse would be at least five and possibly six years old before he would be finished. Today, the time required for this process is about the same, maybe longer if the horse is not ridden regularly or if there is not enough cattle to work.

The method of transferring the horse from the hackamore to the bit is most interesting because it involves double reins, one set of hackamore reins, one set of bridle reins. We said earlier that no early day cowboy east of the Rockies would ever consider using double reins because it was considered an eastern dude outfit. Now we find that cowboys to the west of the Rockies did use double reins long before there were any cowboys to the east. So double reins can't be considered an eastern trick since California is about as far west as you can go in this country.

For two hundred years cowboys, who followed the Old California tradition, have been using double reins as an essential step in finishing

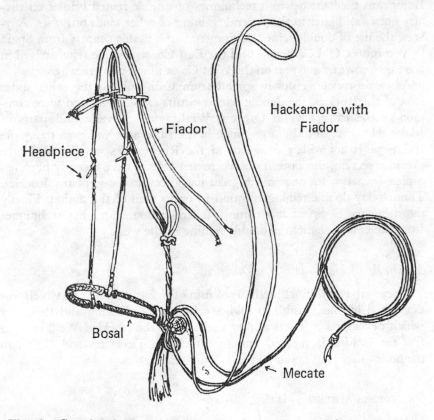

Headpiece

← Fiador

Hackamore with
Fiador

Bosal

← Mecate

Illus. 85. Complete hackamore with 22-foot hair mecate tied for reins and lead rope. A strong fiador and tie rope can be used as a halter when breaking colts.

their horses. When the horse is doing all that can be expected in the hackamore, the bridle is put on over a light bosal. For the first few weeks the horse learns to carry the bit. Because the spade bit is heavy and is a mouthful, it takes some time for the colt to learn to hold it in his mouth and keep it from bouncing. When he learns to hold and carry the bit, the bridle reins are gradually used more and more and the hackamore reins less and less. Eventually, the hackamore is taken off and the horse is considered finished.

One more interesting thought about double reins. The Californians were obviously greatly influenced by Spain. Historical records indicate that some of the young horsemen in Old California went to Spain to study horsemanship. They applied the Spanish techniques, one of which was double reining, to produce the reined cow horse. Earlier, Spanish techniques had also influenced the rest of Europe and England. Spain had been world famous for its horses and horsemanship from 1200 to 1600 A.D. and thus had a great influence on neighboring countries. The Europeans used the Spanish techniques of double reined bridles on cavalry horses and later in the general training of other kinds of horses. Anyway, the use of double reined equipment came to this country from Spain by two routes, Old California and the East Coast. Double reins arrived in the east 300 years ago and on the West Coast about 200 years ago.

As cattle ranching slowly spread from California to the other states west of the Rockies, the double reined outfits came along and were common in the early days in Oregon, Washington, Nevada and parts of Idaho. However, it did not go much beyond this area and even today the technique is not widely used east of the Rockies. As we discussed in a previous section, the eastern double reined bridles have recently been accepted by a few trainers in the great cattle country east of the Rockies. Thus, today double reining is found in every area of the nation. Finally the influence of Spain has come full circle, double reining techniques from the east have met the double reining of the west.

Methods of Using the Hackamore

There are two distinct methods of using the hackamore, one which was developed by the Spanish in Old Mexico and California and the other which developed in Texas and spread east of the Rockies. We'll call the first the California method and the other the Texas method. The two methods differ considerably in technique and results.

CALIFORNIA METHOD—ILLUS. 86–87.

As we have said before, the Spanish in Old California were interested in producing a light reined cow horse. The hackamore was an essential tool for accomplishing this goal. They learned to adjust it on the horse in such a way that the horse would respond to very light touches throughout a training period of six months to a year or more. They adjusted the bosal so that the side pieces just above the heel knot would touch the jawbones of the horse a couple of inches back of the lower lip when the reins were being pulled. If the reins were not being pulled, the bosal would fall clear of the jaw bone. To get this type of action, the nose button must be

CALIFORNIA HACKAMORE

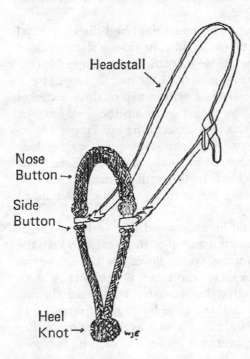

Headstall

Nose
Button →

Side
Button →

Heel
Knot →

Illus. 86. Bosal and head piece. Most California hackamore users prefer a bosal about ¾ inches in diameter with a rawhide core for starting young horses. In general it is advisable to use as soft and light a bosal as will provide results as training proceeds. Note: Headstall has no buckle. Slip knot allows for easier adjustment.

Illus. 87. Proper adjustment of bosal on the nose. Note absence of brow band and fiador which are not needed once a colt is started. Heavy fiadors tend to interfere with the free action of the bosal. Working part of bosal moves one to two inches to contact lower jaw. If the bosal moves too far, raise the nose button by shortening the headstall. Adjust the size of bosal by increasing or decreasing number of mecate wraps at heel knot.

fairly high on the horse's nose and the bosal shaped to move easily past the upper jaw. The lower part of the bosal is fit tight enough so that it moves only one to two inches when the reins are pulled, but is free of the jaws on a slack rein. The bosal will bring light pressure on the lower jaw only when the mecate reins are pulled. This is why a fiador is generally not used because it may interfere with the heel knot falling away from the jaw. Note in Illus. 86 how the heel knot is tied.

This method of adjustment, which allows the bosal to fall away from the sensitive jaw bones, is the real secret of keeping the horse working in the bosal for an extended period of time. It is also the basic difference between the California and Texas method.

When the rider wants the horse to do something, he brings the bosal up to touch the jaw lightly. The rest of the time, he rides a slack rein and keeps the bosal away from the jaw. As we pointed out in Chapter I, continuous pressure on any area of the horse such as the mouth, lower jaw or ribs soon deadens the area. The lower jaw, within two or three inches of the lips, appears to be more sensitive than further up the jaw. For best results, the bosal should work on this area close to the lip. Proper adjustment and use of the hackamore can keep the lower jaw sensitive long enough to teach the horse all he needs to know about reining. Even when handled this way, most horses will eventually get hard in a hackamore. Therefore, it is considered a training device and a horse is not finished until he is working in a bit.

In the Spanish method, it should be understood that with one exception, the only purpose of the nose button on top of the bosal is to keep the bosal in the proper position for working on the lower jaw bone. The one exception is that some hackamore men, who never use the snaffle at all for breaking, will drop the nose button down low on the nose for the first few rides on a green colt. This gives them more leverage for doubling in the event that the colt tries to run or buck. As soon as they're certain they have him under control, the nose button is moved into the higher position.

A bosal will handle a little differently on each horse. Also a bosal may work differently when you first get on a horse and later on when the same horse is warmed up. The good hackamore man watches the position of the bosal very carefully and may raise or lower it slightly one or more times on a ride. Usually the bosal will fit a little tighter at the start of a ride. Therefore, it may be necessary to drop the nose button slightly to allow the heel knot to move properly. As the horse warms up, the rawhide warms also and may change in size and shape enough to require moving the nose button higher on the nose.

It is difficult to explain properly, in writing, the correct adjustment of the bosal. It is much easier to actually demonstrate it. Therefore, unless you're acquainted with a hackamore man who uses the Spanish method,

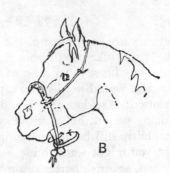

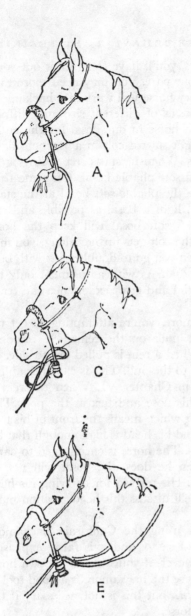

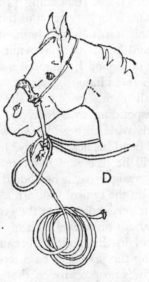

Illus. 88. Tying mecate heel knot, California style.

A. Place round knot of 22-foot mecate through bosal.

B. Wrap mecate snugly above heel knot until within about 1½ inches of the jaws.

C. Pull rein loop from front to back above last wrap. Put loop over the neck and adjust length. You may want rein about six inches longer than normal hand position.

D. Now take one more wrap above the reins and pull the end of the mecate through this wrap to form a half hitch around the bosal.

E. Tighten the knot. To make major changes in the fit of the bosal loosen knot and take off or add wraps below the reins. Make minor adjustments with the headstall.

and they are scarce east of the Rockies, you'll have to figure it out your-self. It will take careful thought on your part. You may need more than one young horse to try it on as not every horse will work in a hackamore. You also would need at least three bosals of different size and stiffness because it is seldom you would keep a horse in one bosal for the entire training period. For example, you might start a colt in a ¾ inch diam-eter, fairly stiff bosal for the first rides. When he starts responding prop-erly, you might want to use a ¾ inch soft pliable bosal. On some thin-skinned, sensitive horses you might use the pliable soft bosal at the start. In general, you would use as soft and light a bosal as possible and still have the horse responding properly. A soft bosal will keep the horse lighter for a longer period of time. As the colt gets further along, you may need only a soft ⅝ inch bosal and when you go to double reins with both a bit and bosal you may want a ⅜ bosal. As with adjustment only the advice of a good hackamore man or trial and error experience can teach you when to change bosals.

In all of this work with the hackamore, you're attempting to get the colt responding to lighter and lighter pulls on the reins. He responds properly with his head in two ways. When a rein is pulled out to side, he should bend his neck and give his nose to the pull. This is called doubling and will be discussed in more detail in Chapter VI. When the rein is pulled straight back, he should tuck his nose and flex at the poll. This gives him the typical California headset which means the front of his face is about perpendicular to the ground and his head is high enough that his eye is about on a level with his withers. The horse is encouraged to carry his head in this position because when he does, the bosal will not be touching the jawbones on a loose rein. His reward for carrying his head properly is no pressure on the jaw. We'll discuss this head position more in the last chapter on finishing horses.

Not everyone will be interested in using the California hackamore method. It takes a lot of time, a lot of savvy and it is fairly expensive because several bosals are needed. However, if you want to break a horse and finish him as a soft, light reined horse the hackamore is a good tool to use. It would help to have cows to work but this is not necessary if the horse will not be used as a reined cow horse.

Summary of the California Hackamore Method

1. It takes considerable time.
2. You will need several bosals.
3. You must ride on a slack rein except when actually making the horse execute a move.
4. You must use a pull and slack, never a steady pull.
5. Your pulls must be as easy and light as possible and still get the

desired response. The more finished the horse, the lighter pulls should be if he is progressing properly.

6. You must adjust the bosal so that it falls clear of the lower jaw except when the reins are pulled.

7. The heel knot should move about one to two inches from its resting position, which is free of the jaws, to its working position against the jaws.

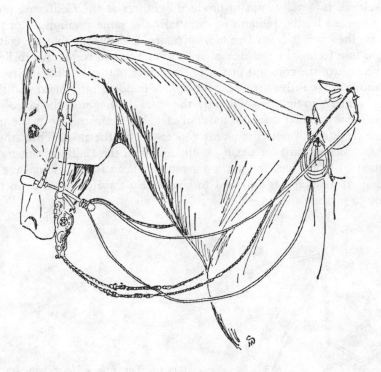

Illus. 89. Complete double rein outfit for gradual change from hackamore to curb bit. Bridle is placed over a ⅜-inch bosal.

TEXAS METHOD—ILLUS. 90.

The Texas method is a modification or alteration of the original Spanish method. It may have been introduced into Texas from California in the early days or came directly across the border from Mexico with the rim fire saddle. About the only similarity between the Texas and California method is that a hackamore is used, because the way it is used and the end results are considerably different. The most obvious difference is the position of the bosal. In the Texas method, the nose button is the principal working part of the bosal and is usually kept lower on the nose. The bosal is fit quite loose and the heel knot pulls up high on the jaw, several inches back of the lower lip. This puts the pull of the reins mostly on the nose button rather than the lower part of the side pieces and heel knot.

It was pointed out earlier that the advantage of dropping the nose button was more leverage on a green colt. The Californians do this but only for a few rides. In the Texas method, the bosal remains in this position. Although some horses will learn to respond to light pulls with the bosal in this position, it is not as apt to produce lightness as the California position. The nose button remains in essentially the same position all of the time and the horse is never free of its pressure. This means that the colt is likely to lose feeling in the area or will never become responsive to light pulls because of the constant pressure. The lower part of the bosal hits the jaws above the sensitive area near the lips. A fiador is often used and this is not conducive to lightness if it keeps the bosal tight against the jaws.

The Texas method does not naturally teach a horse to flex at the poll because flexing will not eliminate the pressure on the nose. Thus, there is not as much reward for flexing as there is with the California method. The method works well for starting green colts and for occasional use in finishing. It generally is not used to completely finish a horse as in the California method.

Illus. 90. Texas hackamore. Nose button is adjusted low on the nose, heel knot is loose and works high on the jaw.

HEAD STALLS—ILLUS. 91–93.

In general, I believe it is best to put as little on a horse's head as is necessary to hold the mouthpiece or hackamore in place. The less on his head, the less he has to irritate him and make him sweat and rub. In other words, I prefer split ear head stalls on bits without a nose band or throat latch and a simple, strap head stall on hackamores, with no fiador. These kinds of head stalls would be for colts after they have been ridden for a month or so and are well under control.

For the first month or so of riding a colt, a snaffle bit head stall should have a throat latch. Once in awhile if a colt really bucks hard, he can flip a head stall off if it doesn't have a throat latch. I've had them throw the saddles as well as bridles off over their heads. You may also want a chin strap on the snaffle, especially if the bit has small rings. The chin strap prevents the bit from pulling through the colt's mouth if it is necessary to double him hard.

It is a good idea to have a fiador on a hackamore for the first rides, too. The fiador prevents the colt flipping the head stall off his ears and also makes a halter out of the hackamore. A hackamore without a fiador will pull off a colt's nose if he backs away from you. However, many hackamore trainers take the fiador off as soon as possible. It tends to interfere with the action of the bosal and is not really needed once the colt gets started reasonably well.

HEADSTALLS

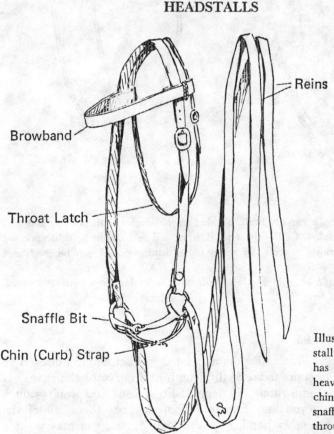

Browband

Reins

Throat Latch

Snaffle Bit

Chin (Curb) Strap

Illus. 91. Good head-stall for riding colts, has throat latch, heavy reins and a chin strap to prevent snaffle from pulling through the mouth.

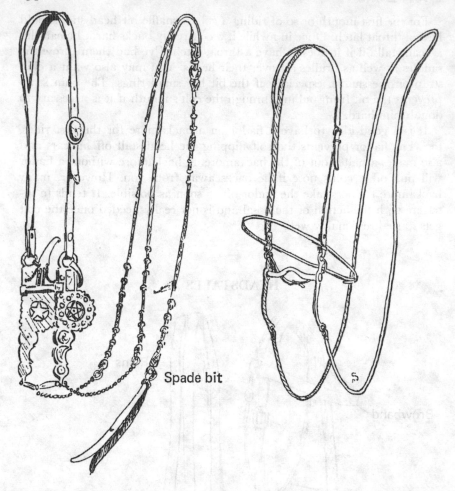

Spade bit

Illus. 92. (Left). Split ear headstall, braided rawhide reins with buttons and rein chains, romel, spade bit, California style. Buttons and rein chains help balance bit. Chains also keep rawhide reins dry when horse drinks. Romel can be used as a quirt.

Illus. 93. (Right). Light, split ear headstall, nose band, low port curb and closed reins, calf roping style.

SPURS—ILLUS. 94, 95

We have already discussed spurs as related to disciplining horses. The main difference in spurs today is the length and curve of the shank. If you're short legged and riding big deep bodied horses, you won't want a long shank because you may find it difficult to keep them out of the horse's ribs. On the other hand, if you're long legged, you may want a

SPURS AND SPUR STRAPS

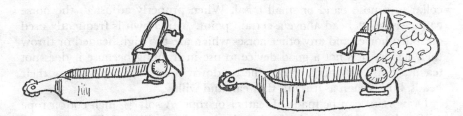

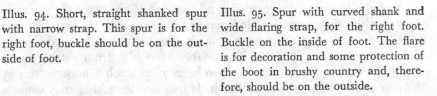

Illus. 94. Short, straight shanked spur with narrow strap. This spur is for the right foot, buckle should be on the outside of foot.

Illus. 95. Spur with curved shank and wide flaring strap, for the right foot. Buckle on the inside of foot. The flare is for decoration and some protection of the boot in brushy country and, therefore, should be on the outside.

longer upward curved shank to make it easier to touch the horse. The rowel of most modern spurs is small and, regardless of size, should be dull. There are two types of straps, a narrow one which buckles on the outside of the foot and a flaring one which buckles on the inside.

Martingales and Draw Reins—Illus. 96–98.

There are three types of martingales, two of which can be used as training aids and will help teach the horse to carry its head correctly. The two useful ones are the running and German martingale. In the running martingale, the reins are passed through rings which are attached to a split strap which, in turn, is fastened to the cinch or breast collar. The reins slide freely through the rings and tend to lower the head and flex the poll when properly adjusted and used. The martingale can be removed when the horse gets the idea he can carry his head correctly. It can be used with a snaffle or curb bit.

The German martingale also has a split strap running up from the cinch to the reins. However, the ends of the split straps are run through the rings of the snaffle and then snapped to small rings on the reins. This martingale, when adjusted properly, does not tighten or touch the horse's mouth unless the horse gets its head too high or its nose too far out. It also allows a rein to be pulled out to the side in a leading or lateral action which is essential in training horses. Although not as commonly used in the West as the running martingale, the German martingale can be useful in helping to solve some problems of head position.

The third type of martingale is the standing one or generally simply called a tie down. It is a single strap running from the cinch or breast collar to a nose band or small bosal. When properly adjusted, the horse cannot raise its head above a certain point. A tie down is frequently used on rodeo horses and any other horses which are too high headed or throw their heads. It is not a good device to use in training because it does not teach a horse anything. When the tie down is on they can't throw their heads, but as soon as it is off, they can and will.

Draw reins can be made of leather or rope. A soft ⅜ inch cotton rope 16 feet long with snaps braided on both ends works well. The snaps are run through the rings of the snaffle and snapped to the cinch rings. Draw reins give the rider considerable leverage on a colt and are useful in two ways. If a colt is apt to stampede or buck, draw reins can be used to turn him in a tight circle which will probably keep him from getting away with his bad acts. Draw reins can also be used to teach a horse to flex at the poll and give their head to the bit. If used too long, they may cause a horse to over flex and bring his jaw back against his chest which would be very undesirable. They are useful on certain horses for a short period of time.

MARTINGALES AND DRAW REINS

Illus. 96. German martingale has a split strap running up and through the rings of the snaffle with each end snapping to a small ring on the reins. Provides lateral control as well as improving flexation at poll.

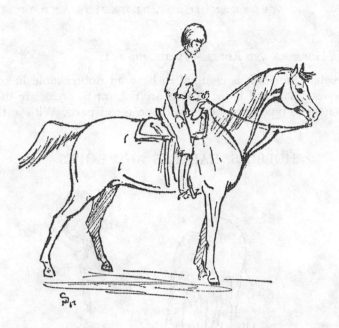

Illus. 97. Running martingale is useful for improving flexation at the poll. Cannot be used effectively for lateral control.

Illus. 98. Draw reins provide extra leverage for horses that are difficult to control or that refuse to flex at the poll.

HALTERS, HOBBLES AND ROPES—ILLUS. 99–101.

For breaking horses it is essential to have an unbreakable halter and rope. The only halters I know of that are not apt to break are the ones made from some type of polyester with no metal parts. With a 10 foot

HOBBLES, HALTERS AND ROPES

Illus. 99. Grazing hobbles, used to limit the distance a grazing horse can travel. Leather straps connected by chain with a swivel buckle around pastern.

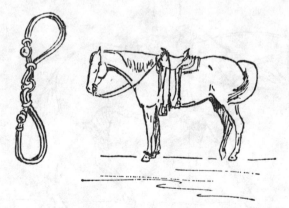

Illus. 100. Rawhide hobbles used to immobilize a horse for short periods of time. Not suitable for grazing because they may injure the skin around the pastern. All hobbles should be placed around the pastern rather than above the fetlock, where they might injure the tendons running down the leg.

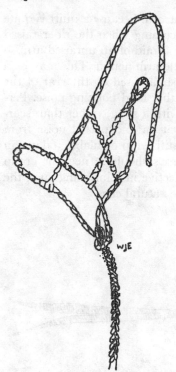

Illus. 101. Unbreakable polyester halter with nylon tip rope.

nylon rope attached to a solid snubbing post, everything should hold together regardless of how hard the horse fights. The nylon rope should be at least ⅝ of an inch in diameter. Smaller ropes may be strong enough but are difficult to hold and pull on.

If a rope is to be used for tieing up feet, it should be soft cotton, ¾ to one inch in diameter and 35 feet long. The cotton rope is used to reduce the chances of rope burning the horse. A hobble made out of cotton rope is also desirable if you plan to break your horse to hobbles. As illustrated in Illus. 99, 100, hobbles may be for turning horses loose to graze at night or for making them stand in one place.

WHIPS—ILLUS. 102–104.

The use of whips was discussed in an earlier chapter as it related to reward and punishment. Some horses definitely need to be whipped occasionally, while others should never be. Old timers whipped with a quirt which had to be used with a big swing of the arm because a quirt is quite flexible. Their horses knew something was coming when the rider raised his arm. Nowadays, it's best if a horse is not afraid of an upraised arm so most trainers use a whip which requires little arm action. This may be a stiff double leather, popper type which is usually used on the rear of the horse. In addition to stinging, it makes a rather loud popping noise. Personally, I prefer to discipline a horse only with a sting, rather than scaring him with noise, because he may jump at an unexpected noise from some source other than a whip. The light, stiff whip available today can be used with mostly wrist action on a horse's shoulder, neck or croup without his ever seeing it coming. To be effective in reinforcing cues, the sting must be preceded by one or more of the natural cues.

QUIRTS

Illus. 102. Old style flexible quirt, not commonly used today.

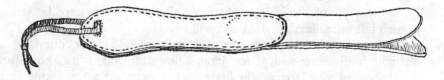

Illus. 103. Double leather popper, stings and makes a popping noise.

Illus. 104. Light stiff whip, usually made of plastic. Disciplines the horse with mostly wrist action and no noise.

PARTS AND TYPES OF SADDLES

ROPING SADDLE

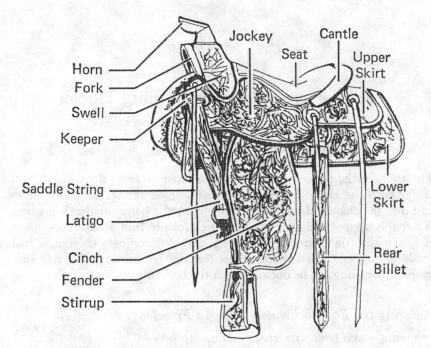

Horn

Fork

Swell

Keeper

Saddle String

Latigo

Cinch

Fender

Stirrup

Jockey

Seat

Cantle

Upper Skirt

Lower Skirt

Rear Billet

CUTTING HORSE SADDLE

RODEO CONTEST SADDLE

Illus. 105–107.

CHAPTER IV

Leading and Handling Young Horses

BREAKING HORSES TO LEAD

The younger the age at which a horse is broke to lead, the easier it will be for both the horse and the trainer. The older horses will fight more and thus the chance of hurting themselves or the horse breaker is greater. If a foal is normal and healthy, it can be broke to lead at about 4–5 days of age, with little chance of its getting hurt. Interestingly enough, a foal broke at this age will not forget his lessons. He may need a refresher course at weaning but he doesn't forget the basic idea.

Breaking the Foal to Lead at Four to Five Days

STEP ONE—CATCHING THE FOAL—ILLUS. 108.

If the foal has been born in a barn and handled each day, he will be no problem to catch. If he was born outside and not handled, he will be a little spooky. In this case, the mare and foal should be put in a box stall or small corral and the foal carefully cornered and caught and held. The girl in this picture has one hand under the foal's neck and the other around its rump. By being quiet and careful, she can hold the foal until it is over the initial scare. The handler should not catch and hold the foal with both hands around its neck. Not only is it difficult to hold the foal in this manner, but it generally scares it more. The mare should be allowed to stay with the foal as they will both become very agitated if separated. It is best to have two people working, one holding the mare while the other catches the foal.

STEP TWO—HALTERING THE FOAL

Usually it works best to back the foal into a corner after it is caught and with the help of an assistant carefully put on the halter. The foal may be especially sensitive to a touch on its nose or around its eyes and ears.

STEP THREE—MOVING THE HALTERED FOAL—ILLUS. 109.

This step is the one that can be dangerous for the foal. They frequently

Illus. 108. Catching and holding the foal. Note a hand is under the neck and under the rump. Although not pictured, the mare should be nearby.

Illus. 109. Using the rump rope. The mare is moved a few steps and the rump rope is used to move the foal. Great care must be used to prevent the foal from falling.

rear up when the rope is tightened and are very apt to throw themselves. When this happens, they can seriously injure their head if it hits the ground or a wall or fence. Thus, several precautions need to be taken. If possible, use a corral with soft ground or a stall with plenty of bedding. Keep the mare with the foal and use a rump rope. This is a rope long enough to go around the foal's rump in a loop and back to the trainer as he stands in front of the foal. The loop may be a running one as in a lariat rope or a tied one.

Use the halter only to keep the foal straight. Don't try to pull the foal with the halter, this will almost always make him rear. Use the rump rope to move the foal ahead. It usually is best to have the mare alongside the foal and to move her a few steps and then the foal a few. In a matter of minutes, the foal should be following the mare.

As soon as the colt takes a few free steps without much pulling on the rump rope, the lesson should be ended for that day. Most foals can be caught, haltered and led a short distance in about 10 minutes. If they have fought any, they will be plenty tired in this time and no young one should be worked if he is very tired.

STEP FOUR—SECOND DAY

On the second day, follow about the same procedure as on the first. It shouldn't be as much trouble to catch and halter the foal. If he follows his mother easily, then at the end of the lesson make him move away from her a short distance and then return. If he has done all this reasonably well in 10 minutes or less, a few minutes could be spent rubbing and handling his legs. It usually works best to have the foal backed into a corner with the mare close by while doing this.

STEP FIVE—THIRD DAY

Most foals, by the end of the third lesson, will be leading quite well even away from the mare for short distances. The rump rope will still be needed but won't be used much. If the foal's feet were handled the second day, they should be picked up and held on the third day. Some foals may need another day or two of leading and handling.

It would help to catch the colt and handle it several times before weaning, however, this is not necessary and would depend upon the availability of the foal. Mares and foals will be more satisfied if they can run in fairly large pastures and not be handled too much.

Breaking the Weanling to Lead

At weaning time, most foals are big and strong enough so that they can definitely hurt a trainer by striking or kicking and even biting. They can also hurt themselves. Thus, one must be careful when handling them. In most cases, at least with ranch or range raised foals, they would be more difficult to catch than a newborn foal. Therefore, their handling is considerably different than that of the little ones.

STEP ONE—CATCHING THE WEANLING

If the weanling has not been handled, he will likely be a problem to catch and halter. The best method of catching is some type of chute or swinging gate which can be used to hold the colt in close confinement while a halter is slipped on. Some careful planning and thought will be needed to have the proper setup. If a box stall is available, a good, strong, high panel can be used in one corner. In any event, be quiet and easy while putting on the halter. Make certain the halter and lead rope are strong enough to hold regardless of how much the colt fights. Most leather halters will break if really tested. Rope or nylon halters are best when the colt is tied.

STEP TWO—TYING THE WEANLING—ILLUS. 110 AND 111.

After the halter is on, the handler may wish to tie the colt solid to a good plank or pole fence post and let him pull back until he learns to stand tied. This usually makes leading a little easier because their head is sore from pulling. Some trainers prefer to break them to lead, as in step three, before breaking to stand tied. Either way, all well-broke horses should be taught to stand tied; although it's surprising how many horses never are taught this.

Illus. 110. Tying up the weanling. Note, dally around the post and the trainer standing by in case of trouble. You may prefer breaking the colt to lead before tying solid.

When tying the weanling solid, it is essential that a good, strong rope and halter be used and that, of course, the post be solid. A strong metal ring bolted into the wall of the barn or box stall works very well also. If you want to spoil a horse so that he will always try to pull back and get away, just let him break loose a time or two by using a breakable rope or halter. Tie the colt high enough and short enough so that if he lunges ahead he won't get a foot over the rope (Illus. 110). Usually about two feet of rope between the halter and the post is about right. Always tie with a knot that can be jerked loose if the colt gets into trouble as in Illus. 111. It is also best to take a dally or complete turn around the post before tying. This prevents the knot from pulling as tight.

The first two or three times that any age horse is tied solid, you should not leave the area. Regardless of how carefully you tie them, there is a very good chance that they will get tangled up in the rope and go down, and unless you are there to turn them loose, serious consequences may result. You will remember that in breaking the foal to lead, nothing was said about tying them solid. In my experience, it is very risky to tie a baby

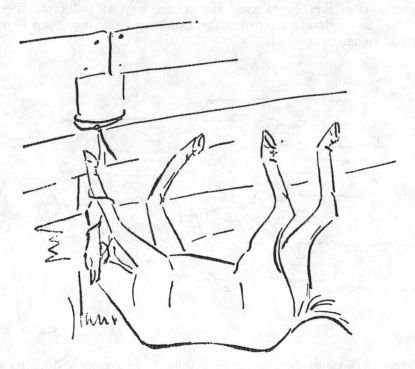

Illus. 111. A weanling in trouble. This is why young horses should never be left unattended when first tied.

foal solid. One more thought, don't leave them tied too long at a time. A weanling will learn about all he is going to for one day, in 15 to 20 minutes of being tied.

STEP THREE—LEADING THE WEANLING

Most weanlings will pull back several times the first day they are tied and maybe once or twice the second day. Anyway, when they stop pulling back, it's time to start leading them. If they have pulled back, their head will be a little sore from the halter and this will make them easier to lead. A rump rope can be used successfully on most weanlings. A few spooky ones, however, really go sky high when a rump rope touches them. On these kind, it is best to use the method in Illus. 112.

It would take great strength to pull a weanling straight ahead. They can brace their feet and be almost impossible to move. To avoid this problem, step to the side, speak to the colt by saying, "come here," or some such phrase. Then pull hard enough to make him take a step sideways to keep from falling, then give him slack. Step to the other side and do the same. Usually in a few minutes he will step to the side fairly easily and eventually he will take a step ahead. When he does this, reward him by talking and also walk up and pat him on the neck.

If he will take two or three steps, it's probably time to quit for that day. In any event, don't work him too long, maybe 15–20 minutes, and be sure to stop immediately after the weanling has done something good.

Breaking Yearlings and Older Horses to Lead

Needless to say as the horse gets older, he will definitely be more dangerous to handle while breaking to lead. Ropes, halters and posts must be stronger and greater care must be taken by the handler.

STEP ONE—CATCHING YEARLINGS AND OLDER HORSES

Some type of well-constructed chute is the best way to catch these horses. It takes a little planning and work but will pay off in the long run. Old timers would rope such horses either by the neck or the front feet. If the horse was roped around the neck, a snubbing post was used to hold the horse until he choked down enough to get a halter on. If he was front footed, he was jerked down and the halter put on while he was on the ground. Either method was tough on the horse and took a top hand with a rope. Such methods were used at that time because of the wild horses, but nowadays there are more suitable ways.

STEP TWO—TYING YEARLINGS AND OLDER HORSES

As already stated, a good rope and halter are essential. The best rope is nylon of the length and diameter as discussed in Chapter III. Halters are more of a problem. It's difficult to find a good one. With these older

Illus. 112. Leading the weanling. Step to one side and give a good pull. Then reward the colt with a pat when he takes a step. Move to the other side and repeat.

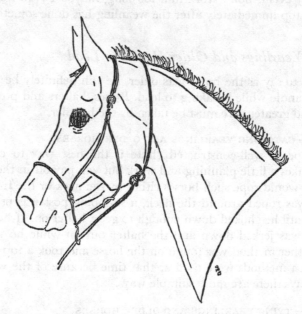

Illus. 113. Using a neck rope. A nylon lead rope run through the halter and tied with a bowline should be unbreakable. How to tie a bowline is described in the next chapter.

horses, it is best not to rely on a halter alone but to run the lead rope through the halter ring and around the colt's neck as in Illus. 113. The knot used under the throat must be a bowline.

Occasionally, a horse will fight a rope hard enough to pull neck muscles loose from their attachments. This produces what is called a "kinked neck." If a horse is real spooky and of a breed which can be expected to put up a fight, such as a Thoroughbred, it is wise to tie them as in Illus. 114. The best rope to use is a nylon lariat. The loop is put around the heart girth, then the end is run between the front legs, through the halter ring and then to the post. Remember to take a dally around the post and tie with a slip knot. The rope around the heart girth is also good medicine for spoiled horses that pull back. It's amusing how surprised they look when they fall back and the rope tightens around their middle instead of on their head.

Illus. 114. Tying around the heart girth. Good for breaking older horses to stand tied or for halter pullers.

STEP THREE—LEADING YEARLINGS AND OLDER HORSES

Leading these horses involves about the same process as followed with the weanling. It will take more time and harder pulls. Using the rump rope is a possibility, but may not be advisable with a spooky horse.

LEADING HORSES

Illus. 115. Well-broke horse should lead up at about the handler's shoulder. It should move when the handler moves, without being pulled.

Illus. 116. This horse is being pulled, not led.

SUMMARY OF BREAKING TO LEAD

The younger the horse when it is broke to lead, the easier it will be on both the horse and the horse breaker. From weaning time on, the horse is big and strong enough to seriously hurt a person, so be careful. When you tie one up solid, be certain that everything is strong enough to hold. Remember too, that a horse, well broke to lead, does not have to be pulled wherever you go; he moves when you move, stops when you stop. The horse should move alongside the handler as in Illus. 115–116.

GENTLING AND HANDLING YOUNG COLTS

If the foal is broke to lead shortly after birth, it can be gentled at that time. Its feet should be handled and it should be brushed all over its body. Horse owners who keep their mares and foals around the barn in small pastures usually gentle their foals at this early age. If the mare and foal are not kept close, then the gentling would probably be done at weaning time. The following discussion concerns handling weanlings and yearlings. As used here, the term yearling will include the weanling or short yearling, and on up to 18 months of age or a long yearling.

A limited amount of training can be done after the weanling settles down and is on feed. The training should definitely be limited because at this age they are just too young to do very much. Their bones are still growing rapidly and extra strain on the bones or joints can lead to unsoundness. Also, they do not have much strength or endurance and if forced too hard, it may in effect break their spirit and they will lose interest and desire to learn and perform. With this in mind, the training of the yearling should be limited to gentling, handling feet, showing at the halter, and possibly some work on a longe line. Keep each training session short, perhaps 10 minutes or less, and don't spend all year on them. Try to train them to do what you want and then leave them alone to grow.

Gentling

After the young one is broke to lead, he should be gentled by handling a little each day. He should be brushed gently and carefully, first, mostly on the shoulders and back, then in a day or two on the croup and quarters and eventually down the legs. The colt should be made to stand quietly while this is done. On many young ones it works best to do this while they are eating their grain. Talk to them as you work around them and make them understand that the word "whoa" means to stand. If they won't stand, some discipline may be necessary. A jerk on the halter or a good slap on the belly is usually enough. This is the time to let them know who is boss. If they start any bad habits such as biting or kicking, discipline them immediately and severely enough so they know they have done something wrong.

Handling Feet

If the yearling has not had its feet handled previously, they should be done as soon as it has gentled down. A system perfected and used by the U. S. Army when they used horses is shown in the following pictures. There are other methods but this one is especially safe for the handler. Regardless of the method used, the colt should not be tied when you are first handling the front feet. If it pulls back while you are picking up a front foot, it might come down on you. Back the colt into a corner and have an assistant hold it while you handle its feet. When handling the back feet, it is best to also have an assistant hold the colt, but it is not dangerous to have them tied.

To pick up the near front foot (Illus. 117), face the rear of the horse and place the left hand on the shoulder or withers. You can take some mane in your hand if you wish. Run the right hand down the colt's leg and grasp the back of the fetlock. Pull the foot ahead to get it off the ground. It may be necessary to push some with the left hand to get the

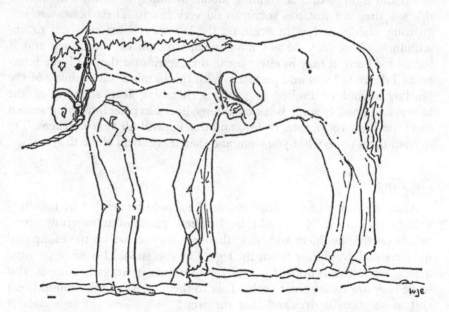

Illus. 117. Picking up front foot. Note, left hand is on shoulder of horse, right hand at back of fetlock.

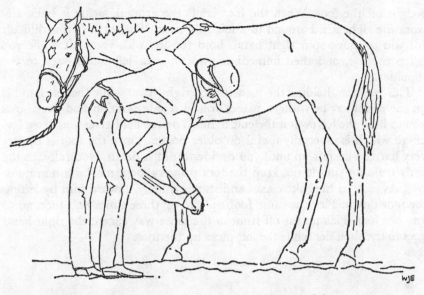

Illus. 118. Toe hold on a front foot gives good control if colt fights.

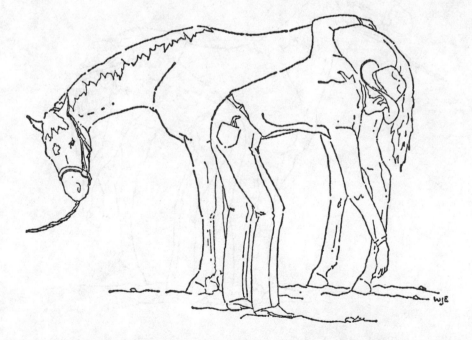

Illus. 119. Picking up hind foot. Note, left hand on hip, right hand behind fetlock.

weight off the foot. When the foot is off the ground, swing it back and work the right hand around to a toe hold as in Illus. 118. If it is difficult for you to move your right hand, hold the leg with your left while you grasp the toe, and then immediately move your left hand back to the shoulder.

This position, holding the toe with the right hand while the left hand is on the shoulders or withers, places you in a safe position and yet allows you to hold the leg even if the colt fights. The toe hold gives you extra leverage which is especially useful on older horses. Once the foot is up, try very hard to keep it up until you decide to put it down. Naturally, in the early training you do not keep the foot up very long, maybe a minute or two. As soon as the colt relaxes and stands quietly, reward him by letting the foot down. Pick the same foot up two or three times and then go to another foot. Pick up the off front in the same way except the right hand goes to the shoulder while the left picks up the foot.

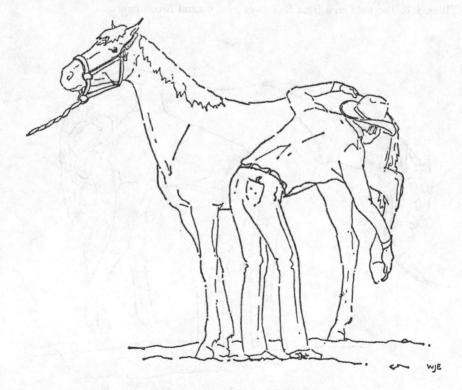

Illus. 120. Toe hold on hind foot. A safe way to hold a colt that wants to kick. Handler in this drawing should have his body farther away from horse.

The rear foot is picked up in essentially the same manner. For the near hind, place the left hand on the hip and carefully run the right hand down the leg to the back to the fetlock (Illus. 119). Pull the foot ahead and up and get a toe hold. With the left hand on the hip you are in a safe, strong position (Illus. 120).

After several days of picking up the feet on a young horse, the handler may wish to trim the feet. Illus. 121 shows the proper position for holding a front foot for trimming. Sometimes, putting a front leg between your knees will unduly frighten the colt. As an alternative, the leg can be merely held against your legs (Illus. 122) and cleaned and rasped in this position. If there is not much trimming to do, this method works well.

Illus. 123 shows how to place a hind leg for trimming. The leg is held on both knees and the left hand is brought down and just to the rear and below the hock as in Illus. 124. Both hands are then free for working on the foot.

Illus. 121. Holding front foot between knees while trimming.

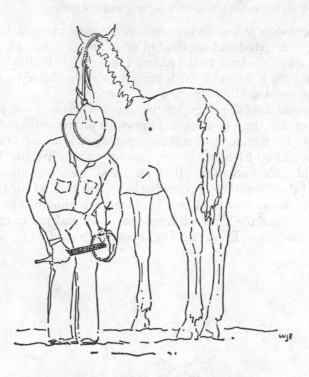

Illus. 122. Alternate method of holding front foot. Hold against your leg just above your knee. May be less scary for foals and weanlings.

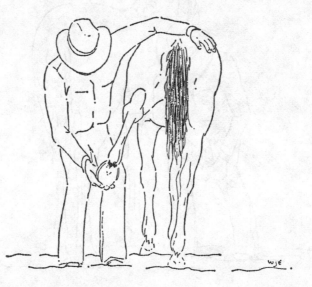

Illus. 123. Getting under a hind leg.

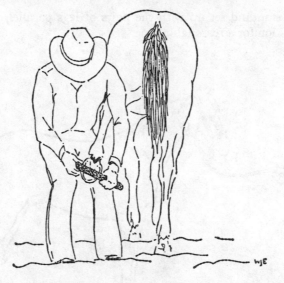

Illus. 124. Holding a hind leg. It is best to rest foot on your knees and not allow horse to lay on your hip with upper leg.

SHOWING AT THE HALTER

If the yearling is to be shown at the halter, there will need to be some training done at home to prepare for the show. The colt must be taught to position its feet properly while standing, to walk and trot easily, and to turn properly.

Foot Position

If is often rather difficult to teach a horse to stand on its legs in such a way that the judge can see the best qualities of the horse. A desirable show ring position is seldom the way a horse would stand naturally. Show ring position varies among breeds so we will use a western horse as an example. They are taught to stand with their legs perpendicular under them and with the front feet parallel to each other and hind feet also parallel to each other. As in Illus. 125, notice the showman is standing in a position where he can observe all four legs of the colt. This is slightly to the near side which gives him good vision and also is a relatively safe position if the colt should jump ahead. The principal problem is to get the horse to stop and set up with the pairs of legs parallel, and then to hold this position for a reasonable time.

Illus. 125. Correct position of colt and showman. Note the showman is in position to observe all four feet and the head and body of the colt.

STEP ONE—MOVING ONE FOOT AHEAD—ILLUS. 126.

The first thing to teach the horse is to move forward or backward a step at a time. Stand alongside the colt facing its head with the left hand on the lead rope about 12 inches from the halter and the right hand held close to the point of the shoulder. Now try moving the horse forward. Because of your position he will not understand at first that you want him to move. It may be necessary for you to move sideways to cue the horse to take a step. Stay in position to touch him with the right hand when you want him to stop. Work on this for several days until you can make him move any foot ahead.

STEP TWO—MOVING ONE FOOT BACK

If you have not yet taught the colt to back freely, this must be done next. Stand as described above, say "back," pull back on the lead rope and push back with your right hand in the area of the chest and lower neck. Sometimes it may help to use your thumb to push with because the colt may feel this more. As soon as he takes one step back, pat him on the neck and tell him he has done well. If he will back two or three steps the first day, that will be enough. Within several days he should be backing 5 or 6 feet straight and free. Not only will this training be useful in showing at the halter, but also when you start riding the colt.

Once he is backing freely, it does not usually take long to teach him to back a step at a time. Stay in the same position, that is, left hand on the lead rope about 12 inches from the halter and your right hand on the point of the shoulder. Then touch him on the chest as you say "back." The lead rope is used to stop him from backing too much. When the colt will move forward and backward a step at a time, he is ready to be set up square.

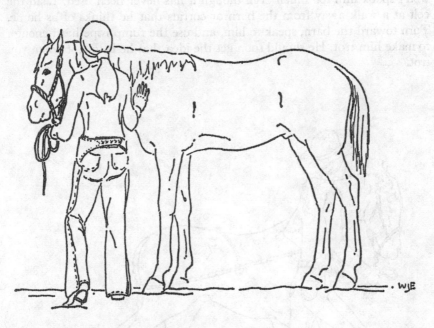

Illus. 126. Controlling foot position. The handler must teach the colt to move any foot ahead or back. Left hand leads the colt forward. Right hand on shoulder helps push the colt backward.

STEP THREE—SETTING UP THE COLT

Teaching the colt to set up straight and square each time he stops will take some time, probably 12 to 20 ten minute sessions. The colt could be worked twice a day on this if necessary to get ready for a show. Remember to keep each training session under 10 minutes. Once this has been learned, as with all other things a horse learns, don't work him too often, just once or twice a week to keep him tuned up.

Leading at Walk and Trot

Leading at the walk should be no trouble if the yearling has been properly broke to lead. Remember, you must walk alongside the head and neck of the colt. He must move when you move and stop when you stop. If it's necessary to get out in front and pull the colt, he is not broke to lead.

Leading at the trot may be a little more of a problem. One of the best ways to train a colt for this is with the rump rope. If he was broke to lead this way, he will know what it means. If not, you can teach him in a short time. The colt should be gentle enough by now that the rump rope won't spook him too much even though it has never been used. Lead the colt at a walk away from the barn or corrals that he thinks of as home. Turn toward the barn, speak to him, and use the rump rope hard enough to make him trot. He should soon get the idea that he is to trot when you trot.

Illus. 127. Leading at the trot using a rump rope.

Another method is to use a 5 or 6 foot buggy whip held in your left hand and pointed behind you. Walk the colt along a fence, speak, pull on the halter, and just touch him lightly on the rear quarters with the whip. The fence will keep him from jumping sideways so he should move ahead. (Illus. 128).

Illus. 128. Leading at the trot using a whip. Encourage colt to trot by touching it lightly on the rear quarters with a long whip. There should be a fence on the off-side.

Needless to say, the use of the two artificial aids, the rump rope and whip, must be discontinued as soon as possible or the colt may learn to cue on them rather than on you. Also as soon as the colt will trot reasonably well toward the barn (this should be in 2 or 3 days) be sure to make him go away from the barn too. Walking and trotting your colt can be done every day if you and he need the exercise.

Turning the Colt

It is common for show ring judges to want to see the action of a horse as it goes straight away and straight back to them. When the horse turns to come back to the judge, it must come back on the same straight line as it went away on. If not, the judge will be forced to change his position to see the action properly. Thus, the good showman and the properly trained horse will stop at the end of the line away from the judge, pivot 180 degrees to the right on the hind legs and return on the same straight line. Anything but a 180° pivot will not put the horse back in line. A pivot on the hind legs means that the horse keeps its hind legs planted in one area while it moves the front end around.

Pivoting 180 Degrees—Illus. 129.

Have your horse standing facing away from the barn. Have your left hand on the lead rope about 12 inches from the halter and your right hand touching him on the point of the shoulder. Speak to him, a clucking noise is commonly used as a turn signal, push his head and shoulders away from you with the lead rope and your right hand until he takes two or three steps with the front feet only. Reward him with your voice and a pat on the neck and then ask for a few more steps. Remember this is to be a pivot on the hind legs, so don't let him walk ahead, back up or move the rear end sideways. This will require the proper use of your hands. When he gets the idea of what you want, be sure and turn away from the

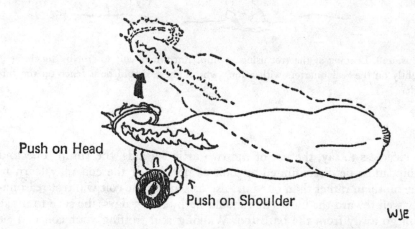

Push on Head

Push on Shoulder

WJE

Illus. 129. Pivoting on the rear hand. Teach the young one to pivot both directions.

barn part of the time. It will probably take 4 or 5 sessions to get a colt to go the 180° reasonably well. Teach a western horse to pivot to the left as well as to the right because when you start riding him, you will want to pivot both ways. This early training on the ground will not be forgotten and will be beneficial when you start riding the colt.

LONGE LINING THE YEARLING

Working the yearling on a single line or longe line (French meaning long line) can be used as a method for exercise and also to teach a few simple moves and voice commands. Remember though, don't overwork them. A few minutes a day is plenty.

Starting on the Single Line

If a good sized box stall is available, it would work very well for starting a colt. If there is no stall, a small corral or pen 20 to 30 feet square would be very useful. Have a halter on, with a lead rope long enough to reach about two-thirds of the way across the stall or corral. There are some special-made headpieces and lines for longeing, but they are expensive and not necessary on a yearling. The idea is to get the colt to move around you as you stand in the middle. This is an entirely new experience for the colt so don't expect him to do it immediately. Have the colt standing against the wall or fence, step toward his rear and at the same time give him slack on the rope and speak to him to move. It might be necessary to slap your hand on your leg to make a little noise. A spooky colt will generally move. When he moves, he will probably want to come to you. To keep him away, shake the lead rope at him, at the same time staying toward the rear. If he doesn't want to move and is gentle enough so that you are sure he won't kick, you can get hold of his tail and pull it gently. (Illus. 130). Keep the lead rope short enough so he will turn in a small circle around you. This works well in a box stall but not too satisfactorily in a bigger area.

If the colt is too quiet and gentle and won't move, it might be necessary to use a light touch with a whip on the rear quarters. It's best to use a buggy whip so you will be at least 6 feet away from the colt and keep your lead rope at just the right length so he can move ahead but not turn his tail to you and try to kick. Sometimes using a whip will make him want to kick. An especially nervous colt may try to kick, even though you don't use a whip. Always keep your lead rope just right so you can pull his head to you if he starts a bad move.

If you have trouble with the colt wanting to come to you, obtain a light pole 6 to 8 feet long (a stout fishing pole works well), tape a snap on one end and snap it into the halter. This will make him stay away the length of the pole. If nothing seems to work and you can't get the colt moving around you, have an assistant lead him while you stay in the middle. Once you get him going one way reasonably well he shouldn't be as much trouble going the other way.

Remember, *this is a new experience for the colt. Be patient and use your head to figure out which system would best suit the nature of the young one.*

Illus. 130. Starting on a longe line. One method is to pull a gentle colt's tail to start him moving. Be very careful he doesn't kick you. A touch of a long whip can also be used, or a slap of your hand on your leg may start a spooky one.

Working on the Single Line

Yearlings can be worked at the walk and trot on a line but it may not be wise to work them at the lope. Loping in a small circle puts considerable strain on the hocks and this can lead to unsoundness in the young ones. If a colt is well developed and getting along toward 18 months of age, he can be loped some on a line without danger of hurting himself.

An important aspect of working a young horse on a line other than exercising is the teaching of voice commands. The yearling should be taught to respond to the words—walk, trot, whoa and some sound such as clucking for turning and a smacking noise with the lips for increasing speed. You will be surprised how quick a horse will learn to respond to words. Speak the same way each time. It is not necessary to speak loudly; the horse has excellent hearing. In two or three weeks, he should be responding rather well to these words.

After a colt is walking around you both ways, it usually is not difficult to get him to trot. If he is feeling real good, it may be more difficult to make him walk than trot. If he doesn't want to trot in a box stall, move to a bigger area. It will be easier for him.

A good method for teaching the colt to stop is to say "whoa," raise your hand that is on the longe line and step toward the front of the colt. Stepping in front will usually surprise one enough to make him stop. To start him again, step toward the rear and say "walk" or "trot." As the colt progresses, it will not be necessary to get in front to stop him. Eventually, all you should have to do is say "whoa."

Illus. 131. Working on a longe line teaches the young colt to respond to simple cues.

To turn the colt the opposite direction, stop him, then pull him away from the fence or wall so that he faces the middle. Don't let him come toward you, only face you. Walk around to the other side of him, throw some slack at him with the line and ask him to walk or trot. When you have finished working, always make him stop on the fence and you walk to him. Some trainers prefer to use a whip to cue the horse for stopping, starting and turning. This works well but teaches the horse to watch the whip more than the trainer.

SUMMARY

This section has discussed the training of a weanling or a yearling. Remember, this age of horse can be compared to pre-school children and, therefore, they should not be expected to learn very much nor to work very hard. Be patient, work slowly and don't expect too much. Make certain that no bad habits are started, be ready to discipline them when needed but also reward them when they have been good. One of the best rewards is to stop working them for that day.

The training which has been described would take 4 to 6 weeks, working 5 or 6 times a week. If at all possible, when you have finished training or showing yearlings, turn them out in good pasture and leave them alone. Like young children, they need time to grow and play. Ideally, they should be turned out for 6 or 8 months as yearlings.

CHAPTER V

Breaking Horses to Ride

Training horses can be divided into two major categories, breaking and finishing. In the previous chapter we discussed breaking horses to lead and to be gentle. In this chapter we will deal with the basic principles of breaking horses to ride. All horses, regardless of the breed and their specific use, should be gentle, reliable, trustworthy and obedient. We will discuss how these four attributes can be developed by using methods which are easy on the horse and safe to the handler. These methods are based on an understanding of the natural behavior and learning processes of the horse, as discussed in Chapters I and II. In the next chapter we will discuss finishing horses to do certain specific jobs.

The colts should be at least coming two-year-olds before they are started. Some horse breakers prefer three- and four-year-olds. In the old days in the West, horses were not broken until they were four or five years old. They wanted the horse old enough to stand hard use while he was being broken. These older horses were mighty tough to handle and it took a top hand to get the job done. For those who have not had much experience in breaking horses, it would be much better to start with a two-year-old. They are usually considerably easier to handle than the three- and four-year-olds, because they are not as strong nor do they have as much fight. Special care must be taken not to get two-year-olds too tired nor try to teach them too much. However, if one is careful, any normal, healthy two-year-old can be broken to ride with excellent results. Any age horse should be in strong condition and feeling good. It is wise to feed grain while you are breaking them, especially to the younger ones. Be certain the colts are free of internal parasites.

Getting back to the old days, there was no preliminary gentling of the horses. They were run into a corral, roped by the front feet, jerked down, and hog tied. The horse was saddled on the ground and when he was untied, the rider got on as he got up. The horse naturally enough thought he was going to be eaten alive by this thing on his back and his instinct was to buck it off or run out from under it. The horse was ridden until he played out and after several days of this treatment, was called a green-broke horse. Such methods of breaking horses were suitable to the wild horses of the range country but produced, in general, a type of horse which only a cowboy could ride.

Nowadays, not only are the majority of the horses raised under different conditions, but the majority of people who ride them are not cowboys. The horse of today, to fit the rider of today, must be gentle, reliable, and trustworthy. Thus, today, most horse trainers use methods which will produce a horse that anybody can ride. Usually every effort is made to keep the horse from bucking and to make them as gentle as possible.

As with all phases of horsemanship, there are many different methods which can be used to obtain the same general end results. Keep in mind that what follows here is not the only way to break horses. However, it is one which has worked well for many years for my students and their horses.

The following techniques of this method will be discussed: Ground work, mounting, preliminary riding, and reining.

GROUND WORK

It's a good idea to do as much as possible of the initial training of a horse on the ground before riding him. It is usually easier for the horse and much safer for the horse breaker to teach the following on the ground: understanding "whoa," sacking, preliminary reining, head set, and backing.

By far the most important word a horse learns is "whoa." If "whoa" is properly taught and learned by the horse when it is first being handled, it will not only save many problems later but will make the horse much safer. The basic idea is to impress very strongly on the horse that he is to stop all movement and stand completely quiet when "whoa" is said. The basic problem is to have some method of punishing the horse if he does not respond and to reward him when he does. Discipline on a well-trained horse may involve only speaking sharply to the horse and a slight pull on the halter. For greener horses, it may require a sharp jerk with a halter or hackamore (never with a bridle). Reward is a pat on the neck and a soft word or two. Several methods of teaching "whoa" will be discussed.

Halter or Hackamore Method of Teaching "Whoa"

"Whoa" is commonly taught to barn-raised horses in their first handling as foals. This method usually involves disciplining the foal with a slight jerk of the halter and speaking sharply the word "whoa." To illustrate this method, we can use a two-year-old horse which is halter broke but does not understand "whoa." The horse might be barn, range or ranch raised. It could also be a horse that has been handled a good deal but is somewhat spoiled. Remember the basic idea is to discipline the horse when he does not respond to "whoa." The discipline is in the form of a downward flip or jerk on a heavy halter or rawhide hackamore. If a hackamore is used, it should be five-eighths to three-fourths inches in diameter and fairly stiff. When the horse responds to "whoa," the reward is a soft-spoken word or two and a pat on the neck.

If you plan to ride the colt in a hackamore, you may want to use some other method of teaching "whoa." It is a little confusing to the colt to use the same device for teaching "whoa" and for reining.

STEP I—TEACHING "WHOA"

Get the colt moving around you at the walk as described in the section on longeing yearlings. This could be in a corral or large box stall.

STEP II—TEACHING "WHOA"—ILLUS. 132.

When the colt is moving reasonably well, say "whoa" in a sharp clear voice, step slightly to the front of him and flip down lightly several times on the lead rope. This is done in such a way as to make him feel the

Illus. 132. Teaching "whoa" with a hackamore. The colt is first taught to move around the handler as in longeing. The handler then says "whoa" and gives a light flip down on the lead rope. This flip bounces the bosal on the colt's nose and is done by throwing a little slack toward the colt in a downward motion. Most colts will soon learn to respond to "whoa."

halter or hackamore on the top of his nose. It may take several easy flips or downward jerks to get him to stop. Do not use the rope any harder than is necessary to make him respond. As soon as he stops, reward him by ending the flips and walk to him for a pat on the neck. Let him move again and repeat. Work him both ways. Most colts will learn to stop at the word "whoa" in a few minutes. Once they stop, keep them stopped until you tell them to move. If they take even as much as a step, say "whoa" and give them a flip or two to make them stop. Walk up and pat them on the neck and talk to them but don't let them move and never allow them to come to you. If they try to come to you, keep them away with the lead rope by throwing some slack at them.

STEP III—TEACHING "WHOA"

The second day, work him at a trot and make him stop dead when you say "whoa." Make him stand while you walk around him and pat him on all parts of his body.

STEP IV—TEACHING "WHOA"

By the third day, or as soon as the colt definitely understands "whoa," you could start to sack him. For sacking,* you or an assistant, must keep a hand on the lead rope. If the colt moves, say "whoa" and give a light flip or two until he stands. In three or four days, you should be able to sack him all over as he stands with the lead rope down. From here on, the process of bridling, driving, etc., is about the same as described in the following section on tying up a foot.

This method of teaching "whoa," or variation of it, is very commonly used in teaching horses "whoa." It's a good method that will work on many horses and is widely used on foals and weanlings. With these young ones all that is needed is a leather halter. Light flips of the lead rope to make them feel the halter on their nose is usually very effective in teaching them "whoa." Once properly learned they should never forget the lesson.

A few expert trainers can accomplish a great deal in a short time with this method and a hackamore. It is possible to take a colt that has not been handled except to halter break and be riding him in an hour. The trainer, in about 30 minutes, teaches the horse to stop dead anytime he says "whoa." Then he sacks the colt, saddles it and works it some more and then puts a rider on. This system works if the colt has been taught to fear the jar of a hackamore more than anything else that may be done to him.

* See later section in this chapter on sacking.

Foot Rope Method of Teaching "Whoa"

After many years of working with all kinds of experienced and inexperienced student horse breakers and unbroke horses, I have come to the conclusion that the best way to teach "whoa" to a horse under these conditions is by tying up a hind leg. This method has proven to be safe for the horse breaker and very effective for the horse. Most of our horses have been ranch or range raised. In many areas of the country where horses are raised in close association with people and have no fear of them, it would not be necessary to tie up their foot. If this is your situation, then you may never use the following methods. However, if you have a spoiled one who won't let you pick up its feet, mount safely, or is spooky about slickers or ropes, then a foot rope might be good medicine.

In addition to teaching a horse "whoa," tying up a foot produces some other important results. The most important is its psychological effect on the horse. The horse learns that he can be completely helpless yet stay alive. As we discussed in Chapter I, a horse has a mortal fear of being caught or held because as a wild horse this would mean he was going to die. You teach him that when you tie him up nothing bad will happen to him and that when he quits fighting he will be rewarded by getting free. The wilder the horse, the more profound is this psychological change.

A horse that accepts the fact that he will not be eaten alive because he is helpless will associate you with this phenomena. He learns that what you do to him is not really going to hurt or destroy him. He learns to trust you and also that you are the boss. If you want to pick up his feet, shoe him, sack him, mount him and all the other things you need to do, he knows you can do it and it isn't going to hurt him any. If he ever gets tangled up in a rope or even in wire, he will likely remember not to fight, he will remember you will be along to turn him loose. I have seen horses get tangled in barbed wire in such a way that they would cut a foot off but they did not fight because their feet had been tied up.

As I said at the start of this section, tying up a hind foot is a good method. Other methods will get about the same results but this one has worked especially well for my students.

STEP I. TYING UP A FOOT—ILLUS. 133.

Tie the colt to a corral post. The post must be solid and the halter and rope unbreakable. Remember to take a dally around the post and tie with a slip knot. Hold one end of the foot rope (a 35 foot, one inch, soft cotton rope) and throw the coils of the rope away from you and the horse. Do this quietly so as not to spook the horse. Be sure there are no twists or knots in the rope as it lies on the ground stretched out its full length. The reason it is stretched out on the ground is to prevent you from getting tangled in it in any way. It is very dangerous to get caught in a rope while working around horses.

Make the horse stand against or near the fence with his right side. This will give you plenty of room to walk up to the horse on his left (or near side) with the end of the foot rope. Do not go up to the horse until he is standing correctly as it could be dangerous to get trapped between the fence and the horse. Put the end of the foot rope around his neck and tie with a bowline.† The loop around his neck should be large enough to come back against his shoulders and fit like a collar on a work horse.

Next, take hold of the foot rope and stand a safe distance behind the horse, with the rope on the ground in the area of his hind feet. Move to the right or off side and encourage him to step towards and over the rope, then pull it up between his hind legs. Many horses will kick at the rope when it touches them, so be certain you are standing well back. Keep the rope above his hocks and work it back and forth, touching both legs and his tail, until he is over the initial scare.

Illus. 133. STEP I. Preparing to tie up a foot. Halter rope should be dallied completely around post and then tied with a slip knot. A bowline should be used on neck rope. Keep the rope high between his legs until he quits spooking.

STEP II. TYING UP A FOOT—ILLUS. 134.

When the horse has quit spooking at the rope between his legs, bring the rope round and pass it through the loop around the neck. The rope is passed around the neck loop from the outside to the inside. This gives you

† See end of this chapter for tying *this knot*.

Illus. 134. STEP II. Tying up foot. Bring rope around and through neck rope. Keep the rope above the hock while passing the end through the neck loop.

a complete turn around the neck rope when you are standing at his shoulder. Keep it snug and do not let it fall below the hock, because if he starts kicking he may skin the back of the cannon bone. After you pass the rope through the neck loop, be sure to throw it away from you and the horse so there will be no coils to step in.

STEP III. TYING UP A FOOT—ILLUS. 135.

Get enough slack in the rope coming around the leg to let it drop from the hock to the pastern. Drop the rope in one easy motion. As soon as the rope is below the fetlock, start shortening the rope and picking up the foot. If you do this quietly and easily, some horses will let you get the foot up and tied before they fight. However, some will start to fight as soon as the rope drops below the pastern. If they do this, get away from them fast but hang on tight to the long part of the rope and take up any slack that you can as he kicks. If it's a big stout horse, you may need help on the rope to get his foot up. You will have better leverage with the rope if you can stay toward the front of him (at a safe distance, of course) while he is kicking, Illus. 136.

Illus. 135. STEP III. Dropping rope and picking up foot. Drop rope below fetlock in one easy motion. Avoid scaring horse if possible. Tighten rope slowly and pick up foot.

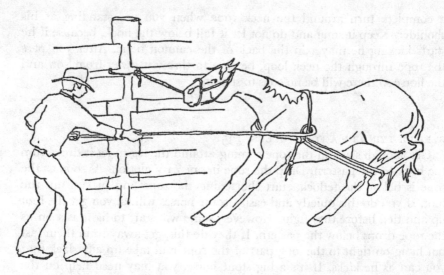

Illus. 136. Picking up foot. If colt fights, take up slack as you can. Note turn around neck loop prevents horse from kicking slack into rope if you stay to front and hold strongly.

STEP IV. TYING UP A FOOT—ILLUS. 137.

When he has stopped kicking, or hopefully before he starts, bring the loose part of the rope down to the foot and completely around it (a dally), then back to the neck rope. Now tie the rope with several half hitches. There will be four ropes running to the foot. The dally or complete turn around the pastern helps to prevent the horse from kicking out of the ropes. Some horse breakers use a half hitch here. Others wrap the loose end of the rope before they tie it several times around the ropes running from the foot to the neck rope. This is to prevent the horse from kicking out of the ropes. The height the foot is tied up from the ground will depend upon the horse. In general, it is best to have the foot high enough so that he cannot use it for any support. However, on some horses who have trouble standing on three legs, it may be necessary to let the foot just touch the ground the first couple of times they are tied up.

STEP V. TYING UP A FOOT—ILLUS. 138–139.

As soon as the foot is tied up, untie the horse from the post. If he starts to fight the foot rope, which most of them do, he will be more apt to throw himself if he is still tied to the post. It might be necessary to have him take one step so that he realizes he is on three legs. When he starts to

Illus. 137. STEP IV. Taking final turn on foot. Be careful here as you lean down to take dally around fetlock. Tie off end of rope with half hitches. If the horse kicks out of the rope, take several turns around the ropes coming up from the foot (Illus. 138) when you put it on again.

fight the rope, say "whoa" sharply and repeat it until he stops. This is his first lesson in associating the word "whoa" with standing still. When he stops fighting and has stood quietly for a few minutes, reward him by untying his foot. He soon associates being good with this reward. From the time you started tying him up to when you let him down should not be more than about 10 minutes. Standing on three legs is very exhausting to a horse. Walk him around a few minutes and tie up the same leg again. This time he shouldn't fight as much.

Horses will often fall down as they fight and when they do, it is usually best to get them up immediately. Use the halter rope to help pull them up and with a few good slaps on the croup, they will usually stand up. If the horse refuses to get up, try letting him lie for awhile, maybe five minutes or more, then try him again. As a last resort, you may have to untie the foot. If so, put the rope right back on when he gets up but tie him long and let his foot touch the ground to lend some support.

Occasionally you find a horse that refuses to stand on three legs even when he is tied long. Usually this type of horse has been handled quite a lot and is inclined to be sullen. The wilder ones will fight harder to stay on their feet because they are afraid to be down. If a horse refuses to stand with a foot tied up, then some other method will have to be used to teach him "whoa."

Remember, *when they fight the rope, it is because of their basic fear of being caught and held. You are teaching them that they need not fear such confinement.*

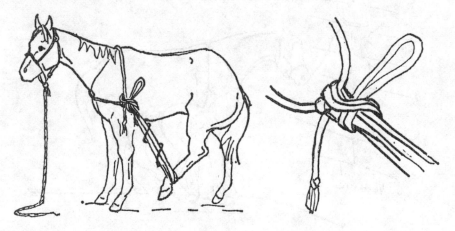

Illus. 138. STEP V. Standing on three legs. As soon as the foot is tied up, untie the lead rope. He will be less apt to fall down. It is best to hold the lead rope to steady colt if he fights.

Illus. 139. Note how first half hitch is tied on neck loop. Should use one more half hitch.

STEP VI. TYING UP A FOOT—ILLUS. 140.

The second time the horse's foot is tied up and he quiets down, you should begin working around him. Start at his neck on the near side and pat or rub him easily with your right hand along the shoulder, back and croup. Keep your left hand on him as you move along. If he should try to move and in the process fall toward you, your left hand would push you away from him.

As you move by the leg that is tied, keep your body away from it. A horse can cow kick out to the side a short distance with his foot tied up. Move on around the back of the horse and keep your left hand on him while patting with your right. If he spooks and trys to move, say "whoa" sharply. When you have been around him a couple of times, it will probably be time to let his foot down and quit for the day.

Notice in Illus. 140, the foot is tied with a rope around the neck and to the foot, but the rope is not around the foot. Instead a regular western saddle cinch is dallied around the foot. This is a substitute method if you do not have a soft cotton rope. The rope around the neck and to the cinch can be any kind of rope, provided it is strong enough. The soft cinch will prevent any soring of the fetlock area. Inasmuch as the cinch

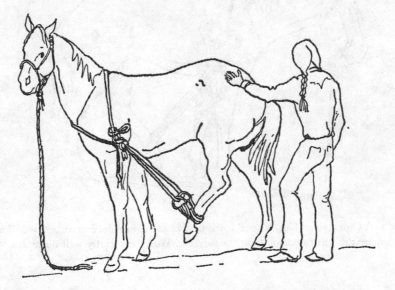

Illus. 140. STEP VI. Handling colt with foot tied up. For safety reasons keep one hand on colt as you move around him. If he falls toward you he will push you away. Say "whoa" if he moves. Note in this drawing a cinch is used around the fetlock.

must be put on by hand, so to speak, it could be used only on horses that will let you pick up a back foot.

We have discussed a method of tying up a foot called sidelining. That is, the foot is picked up on the same side of the horse as the final half hitches are tied. Another method involves cross tying, that is, tying up the opposite foot from the half hitches on the neck, Illus. 141. It is more difficult for a horse to stand if he is cross tied because of the way the ropes pull. Also the foot must be tied high and short or he will kick himself on the opposite hock. Cross tying would be used if a horse is very bad about kicking as you worked around him with a foot tied up. Remember we pointed out a sidelined horse can kick out to the side, the cross tied horse cannot. Cross tying is by far the best way to tie a mule, since they are especially handy at kicking, even while standing on three legs. In general, the sidelining method is the best to use because it is easier to put on, and is easier on the horse.

Remember, *we said at the start of this section many gentle horses will not need their legs tied up. We have described it here in some detail because you might need to use it sometime.*

Illus. 141. Cross tying. The off hind leg is tied to the near side. Prevents cow kicking but is more difficult to put on than the sideline. Works especially well on mules.

Hobble Method of Teaching "Whoa"

Using hobbles to make a horse stand and learn the meaning of "whoa" is successfully used by some horsemen. A ranch or barn-raised colt whose feet have been handled should be easy to hobble. On the other hand, a wild range colt would be difficult as well as dangerous to hobble. To hobble the wild ones, the handler would need to tie up a hind foot or use a chute. Two methods could be used to hobble the colt, one involves hobbling the front feet only, the other hobbling all four feet.

HOBBLING FRONT FEET—ILLUS. 142.

The hobbles should be soft and pliable to reduce the chance of skinning or bruising the colt if he fights. The colt should be held by the halter rope as the hobbles are put on quietly and rapidly. When the hobbles are in place, the halter rope should be dropped and the handler should say "whoa" and back away quietly toward the rear and side of the horse. Walking directly away from the colt may cause him to try to follow and fall down.

When the colt does try the hobbles, the handler should say "whoa" sharply. After the colt has stood quietly without fighting for a few minutes, reward him by removing the hobbles.

If the colt fights the hobbles hard the first day, he will probably try them again the next day and then give up. Some colts will learn to run with the hobbles. If they do this, a short soft rope should be run from the hobbles to a hind foot or tied into the tail of the horse. This will prevent him from putting his front feet out to run.

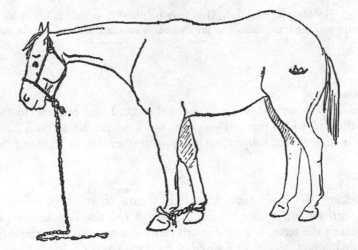

Illus. 142. Hobbling front feet. Remember horse can kick or rear while hobbled in front. Note hobbles are placed below fetlock to avoid injuring tendons above fetlock.

HOBBLING ALL FOUR FEET—ILLUS. 143.

Some horse breakers hobble both the front and back feet and the two hobbles are tied together under the horse. This really immobilizes the horse but it is slow and dangerous to put on, particularly the rear hobbles. If the horse is spooky, it would be necessary to tie up a hind foot to put on the hobbles. Once in place and the horse tries them and quits fighting, he can be worked around safely because he could not strike or kick.

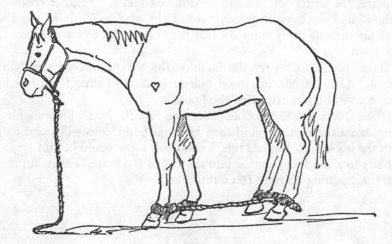

Illus. 143. Hobbling all four feet. They may be difficult to put on, but horse is completely immobilized. Remember to say "whoa" anytime the horse tries to move.

SUMMARY

It is very important that a horse understand and respond to "whoa." Regardless of which method you use, work on the horse until he is well confirmed. The next subject, sacking, is another step in teaching "whoa."

Sacking

"Sacking" is an old-time term that means to rub and gently slap a horse with something like a sack. Although old timers may have used a sack, hence the term, it is now much more common to use something like a saddle blanket, slicker, or a piece of light canvas 2×6 feet.

Sacking is actually a continuation of the process of teaching a horse "whoa." You will learn, as we discuss sacking, that it takes the spook out of even the wildest ones, and if a horse has been properly sacked out he will be a long way toward being a reliable horse. He would certainly know the meaning of "whoa."

A properly sacked horse will allow a rider to swing a rope all around and under and between its legs. He would also allow a mounted rider to take off or put on a coat or slicker. In other words, the horse should not be spooked by anything moved around or under him.

SACKING GENTLE HORSES

If the colt has been barn raised or otherwise gentled, sacking should be no problem. However, regardless of how gentle he may seem to be, it is a good idea to sack him thoroughly on the ground and mounted.

The steps for sacking a gentle horse are essentially the same as the following detailed description with the hind leg tied up. Of course, if a leg is not tied, the horse must be well confirmed on what "whoa" means. When he moves away from or spooks at the sack, the handler must be able to quiet him by saying "whoa" or by disciplining him as described in the section about teaching "whoa."

It may be best to take the edge off the colt by riding, driving, or longeing before sacking him the first couple of times. If he is a little tired, he will take the sacking quieter. Without a foot tied, the handler must be very careful not to get in a position where he could be kicked as he sacks the horse. The horse is rewarded for standing quietly by ending the session and a pat on the neck.

Sacking With a Foot Tied Up

Any colt that is not confirmed on "whoa" would be much easier and safer to sack if a foot is tied up or if he is immobilized with double hobbles. A horse hobbled in front would be handled similarly but precaution must be taken to avoid being kicked.

STEP I. SACKING—ILLUS. 144.

Sacking could be started the first day a colt has its foot tied up. However, since he has a lot to think about the first day, maybe it's best to wait until the second day. Tie up the near hind, or the same foot that was tied the first day, by the methods already discussed. Untie the colt from the post, move him one step and say "whoa." From now on if he moves, say "whoa" to him sharply and make him stand. Walk up to his head and let him smell your sack (we will use this term even though you are probably using something else), then rub him on the neck and shoulders. Do not bother him around the eyes or ears. Move on around him, keeping your left hand on his body as you rub with the sack in your right hand. When you have rubbed around him once or twice, start slapping him gently with the sack. It's usually best to start at the near shoulder and move around. Remember to keep the left hand on the horse. If he spooks, say "whoa" but keep on sacking gently. Watch your time and don't keep him tied up for more than 10 minutes. Let him rest for awhile and then tie up the off hind foot. He will probably fight this a little, but not nearly as much as when the near foot was first tied. Sack him again for a few minutes and then reward him by stopping for the day.

Illus. 144. Sacking with a foot tied up. Gentle horses can be sacked with little or no restraint. Note the girl keeps a hand on the colt to push herself away should the colt move toward her. Be quiet and easy the first session. It is usually best to untie them from the post.

STEP II. SACKING—ILLUS. 145.

In the next three or four days, gradually increase the vigor of the sacking until you can stand out at the end of your sack, say five or six feet away from the horse, and slap him all over his body and legs. Remember, you are not trying to hurt the horse, only getting him accustomed to the noise and action of the sacking. Remember not to hit him around the eyes or ears; this might make him head shy. Also, alternate the legs tied so that the horse will stand quietly with either one up.

Illus. 145. STEP II. Sacking vigorously. Within three or four days the colt should allow you to sack him rather vigorously from a distance of several feet. Do not sack him around the head. Remember you are not trying to scare him, just showing him there is nothng to be afraid of by the noise and movement of the sack. Next step is to sack without a foot tied up.

STEP III. SACKING

After four or five days of sacking with a foot tied up, the horse should be ready to be sacked without a foot tied. The ultimate in sacking a horse on the ground is to have him stand in the middle of the corral with the halter rope dropped while you sack him all around. If you have done the initial training properly, he should stand without moving.

STEP IV. SACKING WHILE MOUNTED

The final step in the sacking of the horse is to be mounted and have him stand without moving while you sack him over the body and legs. Since we are getting ahead of ourselves, we will discuss this after we finish the groundwork.

FIRST BRIDLING AND SADDLING

As soon as the horse responds to "whoa" properly and has been sacked, he can be bridled and saddled. On some colts, this might be as early as the second day or on others, several days might be needed. If the colt is going to be ridden in a snaffle bit, he could be saddled a day or two earlier than if he is to be started in a hackamore. The reason for this is that with the bit in his mouth for the first time he will be busy trying to spit it out and will not pay as much attention to the saddle. The hackamore colt will have only the saddle to think about. He might decide to get rid of it if he is saddled too soon, that is, before he is confirmed on the meaning of

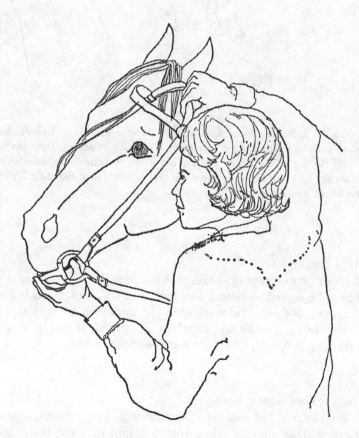

Illus. 146. First bridling. Be very careful about the eyes and ears. Note how fingers hold the bit and the thumb opens the colt's mouth.

"whoa." A discussion of the merits of the snaffle and hackamore for breaking horses was given in Chapter III.

In the following discussion, the colt is bridled and saddled with hobbles on or with a foot tied up, whichever method was used in teaching "whoa" and preliminary sacking. Gentle colts who are well confirmed on "whoa" would not need to be restrained in this manner.

STEP I. BRIDLING—ILLUS. 146.

Have the colt hobbled or a foot tied up if necessary and untied from the post. Quietly and carefully slip on the bridle, being especially careful around their eyes and ears. Most colts will open their mouth for the bit if it is rubbed against their incisor teeth. Sometimes it may be necessary to open their mouth with your thumb. If this doesn't work, try pressing their lip against a tooth until it hurts enough to open their mouth. It will be the second or third time you will have the most trouble getting them to take the bit.

STEP II. FIRST SADDLING—ILLUS. 147.

Lay the saddle up carefully and quietly and do not allow the cinch or the off stirrup to flop over and hit him. When he gets gentler, you can throw the saddle on but not now. Even then do not allow the cinch or

Illus. 147. First saddling. Place it on quietly and easily.

stirrup to hurt him. Walk to the offside and adjust the cinch, stirrups and strings properly. Back on the near side, pat him on the belly with your right hand as you reach under for the cinch. Keep your left hand on his shoulder in the event he should jump. Some colts are very ticklish the first few times they are cinched. Pull the cinch up snug enough so the saddle will stay in place if he makes a jump, but do not cinch tight. It is very important not to cinch young horses any tighter than necessary. If cinched too tight they will soon learn to protect themselves by taking and holding a deep breath just prior to cinching and maybe become what is called cinch bound. After he is cinched, move the stirrups back and forth gently so he knows they are there. Sometimes a colt will spook at a stirrup if it should move unexpectedly.

STEP III. SADDLED AND BRIDLED FOR THE FIRST TIME—ILLUS. 148.

When the colt is saddled and bridled, take the foot rope or the hobbles off. Run the reins to the cinch or D ring on each side and tie them there or if they are long enough, run them through the ring to the horn and tie. Leave them loose enough so they will not touch the colt's mouth even when he raises his head. Tie up the halter rope to the horn. If the colt is one that might try to buck, tie the halter rope short enough to keep his head up. Of course, if he starts anything, shout "whoa" and hope for the best. You definitely do not want him to buck. If he has been confirmed on "whoa" and sacked out properly, there is little chance that he will buck with the empty saddle. Let him work around the corral carrying the

Illus. 148. First saddling and bridling. Reins are tied loosely to cinch rings. Halter rope should be tied shorter if there is any chance colt might try to buck.

saddle and worrying with the bit. You could let him work for thirty minutes to an hour if you wanted to. Usually, he will learn all he is going to in that time.

BITTING AND HEAD SET

While the horse is learning to carry the bit, you can also teach him to respond to pressure on the bit and to flex at the poll.

The following discussion will describe how this can be done with an ordinary western saddle. Some professional trainers have a special piece of equipment called a bitting rig. This is used in place of a saddle and has a couple of advantages. First it is light and easy to put on. Second, the rig is usually equipped with several places to tie the reins depending upon how the horse is carrying its head.

The disadvantages of a bitting rig are: First, you may not have one. Second, they do not teach a colt anything about carrying the weight of a saddle nor accustom him to the flapping of the stirrups. Actually, a western saddle has three different heights at which to tie the reins: the cinch ring, the D ring (or part of the rigging where the latigo fastens) and the horn. It is usually best to start at the cinch ring. You can move the reins higher at larger sessions if the colt carries his head too low.

STEP I. BITTING AND HEAD SET

The second day the colt is saddled, you can start making him give to the bit and develop a proper head set. Saddle and bridle the colt again with a foot tied or hobbles on. This time when you free him, have the reins short enough so there will be some slight pressure on his mouth. Remember to run the reins to the cinch or D ring, not directly to the horn. Most colts will resist this pressure at first and try to throw their heads up. Usually a colt won't throw his head more than two or three times. As soon as he shows signs of giving to the bit, reward him by ending the training session. Usually a colt's head should not be tied down more than 10–15 minutes. What you are trying to teach him is to respond to pressure on the mouth by giving to it, rather than throwing his head up. This is a very important preliminary step in bitting a colt.

If elastic rope or a small piece of inner tube is available, a 12 inch piece can be snapped in between the bit and rein. This allows for some give when the colt does throw his head.

STEP II. HEAD SET—ILLUS. 149.

The third day the colt is saddled, the reins can be shortened a little more. By the 4th or 5th saddling, the reins should be short enough to make the colt carry his head perpendicular to the ground as in Illus. 149. During this process of bitting, do not make them go more than about ten to fifteen minutes with their heads tied down. It is uncomfortable to the horse because this is not a natural head position. Nevertheless, it is important the colt learn to carry his head perpendicular and be flexed at the poll if you want him to become a horse that is easy to handle and responsive to the bit. This head set is not found on all western horses.

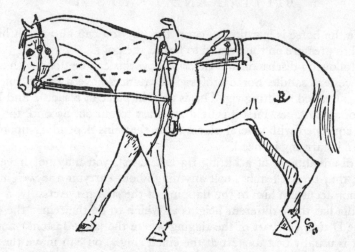

Illus. 149. Developing head set. The horse is taught to flex at the poll by gradually shortening the reins over a period of several days. Note forehead of the horse is about perpendicular to ground. Reins could be tied to the D ring or horn if colt carries his head too low.

You can see now why the reins are run to the cinch or D ring. This makes him tuck his nose down and back and flex at the poll. If the reins were run directly to the horn, it would only push his head up. Don't worry if he seems to carry his head and neck a little low in these early stages; it's usually easier to bring it up than down. However, if the colt is carrying his head too low, you can run the reins to the D ring on the saddle rather than the cinch ring. In a rare case, it might be necessary to go to the horn. This would be a colt who was really dragging his head on the ground.

Some trainers tie one rein around to the cinch ring to teach the colt to turn and give to the bit. We have not elaborated on this method because if the colt is to be driven in double reins, it may not be necessary. We will discuss driving in a later section.

STARTING ONE IN A HACKAMORE

The preceding section has discussed starting young horses in a snaffle bit. A different technique is used if the colt is to be ridden from the start in a hackamore. In Chapter III, the merits of the hackamore were discussed. Remember, we pointed out that if you think the horse may buck or try to run with you, it would be best to start him in a snaffle. The hackamore is used with a pull and slack and thus the reins should never be tied solid as was illustrated in Illus. 148 and 149. If the hackamore reins were tied like this, it would very likely skin the jaws of the horse which would be a poor way to start a colt. There is a way which they can be tied which will teach the colt something without hurting him.

STARTING IN A HACKAMORE—ILLUS. 150.

If you are starting the colt in the hackamore from the beginning, you may wish to wait a day longer to saddle him for the first time than if you were using a snaffle. Let's say you saddle him on the third day rather than the second. Tie up a foot or hobble him if necessary and sack him out good and then saddle him. Take the halter off and put the hackamore with a fiador on and adjust it properly as described in Chapter III. Tie the reins to one stirrup short enough to pull his head around and turn him loose.

This should make the colt turn around in a circle. A saddle with heavy stirrups is best to use because it puts more pull on the reins. The stirrup will give and take as he moves his head and thus simulate what you will be doing with your hand when you start riding him. If the colt will turn

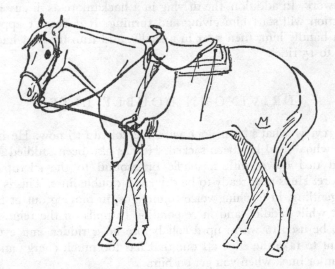

Illus. 150. Starting in a hackamore. The mecate is tied short enough to the stirrup to pull the colt's head around. To work properly the stirrup must be heavy and the colt willing to move. At this stage it is best to have a fiador on the hackamore.

and move around some, then in about 5 minutes, change the reins to other stirrup and let him turn for another 5 minutes. Reward him by ending the training session.

Some colts will not want to move with their head tied in this manner. It may help to pull them around in a circle a few times but if they won't work by themselves, you just as well untie them. With this type of a colt, about all you can do is pull them from the side as you would in halter breaking a colt. That is, step off to the side and give a good pull, not a jerk, and make them come to you. Do this from both sides several times. This helps to loosen the colt up and give him the idea of bending his neck when the hackamore is pulled. Usually in 2 or 3 sessions the colt will learn all he is going to on the ground about responding to the pull on the hackamore.

Old timers had several other methods of starting colts in a hackamore. One common method was to put him on a picket line tied to a log. The colt would fight the rope hard, skin his head as well as his legs but in the process certainly would become responsive to a hackamore and careful of a rope. Needless to say, this method was a little tough on the horse. Another method was to put a hackamore on with a long lead rope and then spook the colt to run alongside of a corral fence. When he got to the end of the rope, he was turned back hard, then run the other way and turned back. With most of our colts today, it probably is not a good idea to make them run away from you, a necessary part of this latter method.

If the colt is gentle enough to start in a hackamore, then tying his head to a stirrup or pulling him some both ways will usually be sufficient ground work. In addition, the driving in a hackamore as discussed in the next section will start him giving and turning. If it doesn't appear that you can handle him, then start in a snaffle and transfer to a hackamore after 10 to 15 rides.

DRIVING IN DOUBLE LINES

Let's review what's been done with the colt up to now. He has been taught "whoa" and has been sacked. He has also been saddled and had his head tied down with a snaffle or around to the stirrup with a hackamore. He is now ready to be driven in double lines. This is another step in gentling, in teaching voice commands, in moving out at the walk and trot while saddled and in responding to pulls on the reins. Driving can also be used to warm up a colt before he is ridden and even more important to take the edge off one that has too much energy and might try to run or buck when you get on him.

From a safety standpoint, there are two items that must be watched when driving. First, never get close enough behind to be in any danger of being kicked. If you will stay about a horse's length behind, you should be safe. Never trust any colt regardless of how gentle it might appear to be. A sudden surprise may cause even the gentlest colt to revert to the wild type and kick at anything behind him. The second item is to be very careful not to get your hands or feet tangled in the driving lines.

A square corral 35 to 40 feet to the side works best for driving. Ideally, a driving corral should be boarded or planked solid to prevent the colt from looking out and thus not watching you. However, this type of corral may not be available so a simple one with one or two planks around could be used.

STEP I. STARTING IN DOUBLE LINES—ILLUS. 151.

You can start the average colt in double lines about the second or third day he has been saddled. He needs to be over any fear of the foot rope or hobbles and to stand quietly while you sack him thoroughly on the hind legs and quarters. He should be well confirmed on "whoa." He may still have some things to learn about sacking, and giving to a snaffle or hackamore, but as discussed in Chapter II it's all right to be teaching him more than one thing at a time.

On the day the colt is to be driven, go through the regular steps of sacking, saddling and let him work a few minutes with the snaffle or hackamore. If the colt has been worked on a longe line, he will be no trouble to start on double lines. If he has not, it would be best to have an assistant to help you because your principal problem may be to get the colt to move. Another problem would result if the colt had not been sacked out enough. The lines touching him on the hind legs could make him kick or try to run. You must use your judgment as to when he has been sacked enough.

The end of your driving lines with the snap should be run through the stirrup on each side and snapped into the ring on the halter, not to the snaffle bit. You may have to make some hard pulls the first few times you drive and you do not want to hurt the colt's mouth. If you are using a hackamore, it will be necessary to devise a method of fastening the lines to the bosal. Take a piece of heavy string like bailing twine or a leather thong about 16 inches long and tie the ends together. Run one end of the loop through the bosal from rear to front just above the mecate, then drop this end down and around the end of the bosal. Snap the lines into the loop left behind the bosal, as in Illus. 153.

When the lines are attached, have your assistant lead the colt around the breaking corral and you follow directly behind but at a safe distance from the colt. Work the lines gently against his rear legs to let him know they are there. After about three times around the corral, have your assistant quietly and gradually get away from the colt. The colt will probably stop and you will need to encourage him to move with your voice and gentle slaps with the lines. Be patient because this is entirely new to the colt. He has never had you behind him before, holding lines and trying to get him to move forward. If he doesn't want to move, you may have to slap harder with the lines and maybe even have your assistant lead him again. When he does move by himself, he may want to come to you. Avoid this by pulling hard on the outside line and at the same time move yourself rapidly to keep directly behind the colt. When you get him around the corral three or four times without too much trouble, reward him by quitting for the day.

Illus. 151. First driving. An assistant leads the horse around corral as driver gently works lines on rear legs. Although not pictured, stirrups should be tied together under the belly of horse with a light rope. This prevents the stirrups flipping up if lines are pulled out or up.

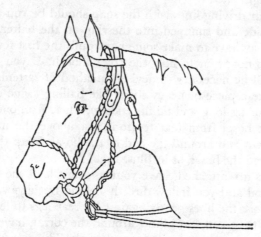

Illus. 152. With snaffle bit training, driving line attached to halter.

STEP II. TURNING IN DOUBLE LINES

The second day you drive him you can start him on some turns. With double lines the colt turns away from you and toward the fence using the corners to make the turns. When turning, make your pulls on the lines as easy as possible and don't, under any circumstances, jerk on them. The first few times you turn, the colt will probably fight the pull on the line. This is the reason you should have the line fastened to the halter or hackamore rather than the snaffle. You won't hurt his mouth if he fights the pull. When the colt starts to respond well to the pull, probably in 3 to 5 days, then you can drive with the snaffle. Driving in a hackamore is especially effective since the pulls are very similar to the way you will pull the reins when you ride. Don't work him too long, stop before he gets tired. As soon as he makes a few good turns, reward him by stopping for the day.

STEP III. TROTTING ON THE DOUBLE LINES

After two or three days driving, the colt should be walking around reasonably well with you following. The next step in his training will be to get him to trot. First, however, unless you need the exercise and figure

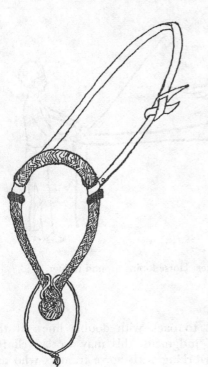

Illus. 153. Driving lines can be snapped to loop around bosal heel knot.

that you can trot as fast as the horse, you may wish to teach the horse to work around you while you stand in the middle. This should be started at the walk and is usually not difficult to do. Have the colt walking with you following and then you gradually make a smaller and smaller circle while you keep the colt on the original circle. Eventually you will be standing in the middle with the colt going around you. If the colt is feeling good, it is usually not difficult to get him to trot. You may need to slap him with the lines some and, of course, speak to him. In time, you can teach the horse to trot when you say trot.

STEP IV. LOPING IN DOUBLE LINES—ILLUS. 153–154.

It is difficult for horses to lope in a circle in a small area. A square corral with at least 35 feet to the side is about the minimum size that can be used. You will need to have your colt trotting freely and really eager to go before you can expect him to lope. Usually you would need to have driven the colt 8 to 10 times before trying to do this. Be certain that the colt takes the correct lead, both front and hind, at the lope. If he doesn't, slow him to a trot and start again. If they ever get the idea of going cross leaded it's difficult to get them over the habit. Don't lope a two-year-old too much, it's hard work for them.

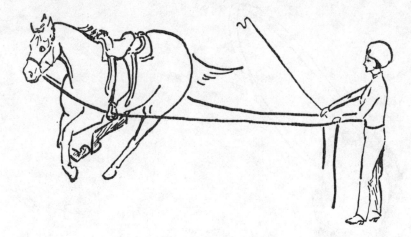

Illus. 154. Advanced driving in double lines. Horse loping around trainer.

STEP V. BACKING IN DOUBLE LINES

Some trainers teach their horses to back with double lines. If the handler has good hands and good judgment, this may work well for them. However, in my experience working with horse trainers who are still learning, they are very apt to hurt the colt's mouth or nose by trying to back with double lines. We will discuss another method of teaching a horse to back in a later section.

What Can Be Accomplished By Driving

Driving a colt for a week to 10 days will teach the colt a number of important lessons. First, he learns to move with you behind him, which is more similar to your being on top of the colt than leading would be. Second, he gains experience in carrying the weight and feel of the saddle, the movement of the stirrup and touch of the lines on his legs. Third, he learns to turn in response to pulls on the snaffle or hackamore. Since the lines are run through the stirrup, the pull will be low, thus encouraging the colt to flex at the pole. When you start riding the colt, you must remember to keep your hands low to simulate the same pull on the reins as in driving. Fourth, he learns, or at least begins to learn, three more voice commands, walk, trot and lope. In addition, you have given the colt more experience in responding to "whoa" and to stopping correctly from a walk, trot or lope.

If you wish to continue on with the driving and in effect put a finish on your horse, this could be done with a three-year-old or older horse. You can, in about a month or six weeks, have him working rather well. You can teach a sliding stop, roll backs over the hocks and correct leads. The horse will get real sharp at responding to voice commands. This type of work will also improve the head set of the horse. As stated earlier, the pull on the lines on a hackamore horse is similar to the pull you make while riding. With snaffle bit horses, it might be necessary to tie bridle reins down to the cinch or D rings to get the horse going flexed at the poll while you drive him with the long lines. If the horse carries his head too low, the lines should be taken out of the stirrups. They could then be run through loops dropped down from each side of the horn. The loops of rope or leather could be adjusted to give the proper height to the lines. Finishing a horse in double lines will get results but is time consuming. A few trainers have had very good results by driving their horses to a two wheel cart.

Review–Let's review what we have accomplished up to this time with the colt. If all has gone well you should have modified his self-protective behavior considerably. He should no longer fear ropes, sacking, bridling or saddling. He should be well on the way to becoming a gentle reliable horse. In addition, he has learned to listen and watch for cues from you. You have taught him a language of words and signs. All of this will be very useful when you start riding him.

MOUNTING

Up to this point, we have been discussing the ground training of horses. Although there is some chance of a handler being hurt while working a horse on the ground such as by kicking, striking or biting, the dangers increase considerably when the riding starts. The danger really starts when the horsebreaker puts his foot in the stirrup to mount. Mounting and dismounting can be the most dangerous part of breaking horses, or for that matter of riding even gentle horses. Thus, we'll discuss the first mounting in some detail.

If the colt is barn-raised, gentle, and well confirmed on "whoa," you would be tying up a foot or hobbling him to mount. However, everything else discussed in the following section should be carefully studied and used wherever appropriate.

The following material outlines in detail the procedure of first mounting with a foot tied up. This method is discussed in detail because it has been my experience that it is the safest way to mount a ranch or range-raised colt for the first time. Of course, the horse must have had its foot tied up on at least three different days to be certain he understands first, that he can stand on three legs and second, that he must stand without moving while being saddled and sacked. Although it is possible a horse prepared in this manner would spook and fall down when first mounted, this has been very rare in my 30 years experience in using this method. I don't mean a horse might not be scared and make a move or two on three legs, but for one to spook enough to fall down, which could be dangerous to the rider, has been very rare. Now, obviously, to tie up a foot for the first time on any horse and get on him right at that time would be very foolish. You couldn't blame the horse if he threw himself and caught the rider. But, as pointed out above, if the horse has been tied up at least three times, he should be safe to mount.

Horsebreakers who use hobbles to teach "whoa" may also have the colt hobbled when they first mount. Naturally the colt must be completely confirmed on standing while hobbled regardless of what is happening to him. Mounting a hobbled horse is more dangerous than one with a foot tied up. If a hobbled horse should make a jump, he would be much more apt to fall down and roll over on the rider than would a horse with a foot up.

One other big advantage to mounting a horse for the first time with a foot tied up or hobbled is that he learns right from the start to stand while being mounted. Mounting is potentially a very dangerous act for the rider particularly if the horse won't stand.

First Mounting

STEP I. FIRST MOUNTING WITH FOOT TIED UP—ILLUS. 155.

After the colt has decided he can stand on three legs without moving and you have had him saddled two or three times, you can get on him for the first time. Do this with a leg tied up. It may look a little risky to get on with him standing on three legs, but it may be much safer than if he were on all four. Of course, by now he is, or should be, confirmed on standing on three legs, he has been saddled, turned loose carrying the saddle, sacked a number of times and probably driven in double lines.

If you are breaking a rather small horse and you are on the heavy side, it would be best to tie his foot low enough so he can bear some weight on it. On the other hand, if there is reason to believe he might try to make a

Illus. 155. Mounting with a foot tied up. Note position of left and right hands. For safety reasons, only the toe is placed in the stirrup. The right leg *does not* go over the horse the first time up. The rider can step down and away from the horse easily if there should be trouble. Pat horse on neck then dismount. Step up again and, if all is well, swing your right leg over easily without touching his rump. Repeat several times.

jump, pull his foot up high. Use your own judgment on this. Anyway, tie up his foot, saddle and bridle him and have him untied from the post. Mount first slowly and carefully by standing up in the stirrup, Illus. 155, with your right hip against the saddle and without throwing your right leg over the horse. Be sure only your toe is in the stirrup, that your left hand has a mane hold and that your right hand is on the horn. In this position you can step down and away from the horse if he should make a bad move. If he is properly confirmed on "whoa," he shouldn't do much, but you want to be prepared.

As you stand in the stirrup, reach up and pat him carefully with your right hand on the neck and shoulder, then step down. The next time you go up, if he has behaved all right, swing your leg across and sit in the saddle. Talk to him quietly and pat him on the neck. Shift your weight very easily in the saddle so he can feel it move. Carefully and quietly move your legs one at a time forward and backward so he will feel the touch of the stirrup and fender on his shoulder and ribs. Step off easily and quietly pat him on the neck if he stands, then remount.

Dismount and mount on the offside of the horse too. If your horse is to be well broke, you should be able to mount and dismount on either side. When you have mounted 3 or 4 times, quit this for the day and go on to something else. Each time you mount, pat him on the neck as a reward.

STEP II. SACKING WITH FOOT TIED UP—ILLUS. 156.

The second day you mount the colt with a foot tied up, use the sack on him while you are mounted. Do this gently the first day. By the third or fourth day you mount with his foot up, you should be able to sack him rather vigorously all over his body and legs. Remember to pat him each time you mount. Also reward him with a pat on the neck after he has stood quietly for sacking. After several days of sacking with the horse restrained, sack him without the foot rope or hobbles. When he is properly confirmed on sacking, you can swing a rope, put on or take off a slicker, wave at a friend and he should not be spooked by any of these actions.

STEP III. MOUNTING WITHOUT FOOT TIED UP

When the colt will stand without moving while you mount and dismount on both sides and sack him vigorously, you can discontinue tying up his foot to mount. This will usually be within 3 or 4 days of the first mounting. Continue making him stand without moving while you mount and dismount. Don't ever give him the idea he can move until you tell him to. When you are mounted securely and all set, pat him on the neck as a reward for standing and give him a voice and leg to move.

One of the most dangerous things that can happen to a rider is to get a boot hung in a stirrup as he mounts or dismounts. If a horse will stand without moving while you mount or dismount, there is much less chance of this happening. So, be certain you break your horse to stand. Also, as

Illus. 156. Sacking while mounted. On the second day of mounting with a foot tied up, sack the colt gently. Repeat each day, gradually increasing the vigor of the sacking. Bring the sack over and under and around his legs. In 3–4 days you should be able to sack him vigorously without a foot tied up. Do not sack around his head.

you continue to ride him, be careful not to get into a situation which is apt to make him move as you mount. For example, don't try to mount as another rider moves away from you. Ask the rider to stay right with you until you are mounted. Remember to return the courtesy too, when you are riding with someone.

How the Horsebreaker Should Mount

While we are on the subject of mounting, we should discuss the matter in more detail. There are a number of ways which a horse can be mounted but only one correct way for a horsebreaker. All old-time western horsemen mounted this correct way and all modern horsebreakers should. Basically it involves keeping full control of the horse while you mount in an easy, safe manner.

KEEPING CONTROL WHILE MOUNTING

To lose control of a young horse while mounting can be dangerous. Always have your left hand free to check the horse regardless of what stage of mounting you may be in. To maintain control, gather the reins in your left hand and lay the left hand on the neck of the horse. You must have contact with the horse's mouth as you mount, but do not have a tight rein or it will cause the horse to back up. With the reins run through the palm of your hand and held by the thumb and the palm resting on the horse's neck, you can check the horse by rotating your palm up on the little finger as in Illus. 157.

Remember, *we said earlier there are many ways to break horses. We are describing one system that does work but it is certainly not the only way to get the job done.*

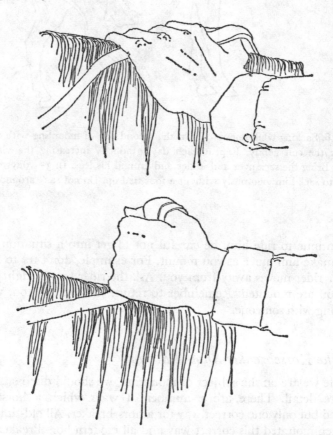

Illus. 157. Holding reins for mounting. Left hand is laid on the neck with reins run through the hand as indicated. A mane hold can be taken if desired. If the horse moves, the hand is tipped up and pulled back to check the horse.

Old timers had a couple of other tricks to keep control of the horse but in general they are not advisable under today's conditions. If a horse was a little hard to get on, that is, he wouldn't stand, they would hold the reins as described but slip their left elbow over the near rein to check the horse and turn him toward them by pulling the rein with their elbow. If a horse was real bad to get on, they would do what is called cheeking. The left hand holding the reins would also have ahold of the cheek piece of the bridle. As they swung up on the horse, his head would be pulled toward the rider. With either method, the elbow or cheeking, the horse was pulled in a tight circle to the left, which prevented him from starting a bad move until the rider was up. It is easy to get on a horse if he turns toward you, rather awkward and difficult if he turns away. However, since the horse is moving, it is more dangerous than if the horse will stand. For this reason it is much better to make a horse stand for mounting. Then most any kind of a rider can get on safely.

MOUNTING AS A HORSEBREAKER SHOULD

STEP I. STAND FACING TO THE REAR—ILLUS. 158.

As you adjust your reins properly in your left hand, you should be standing at the shoulder of the horse and facing directly to the rear. Standing at the shoulder keeps you as far away from the hind legs as possible, a position of safety which men riding the wild horses of the past were always very careful to maintain. Most horses today won't try to kick

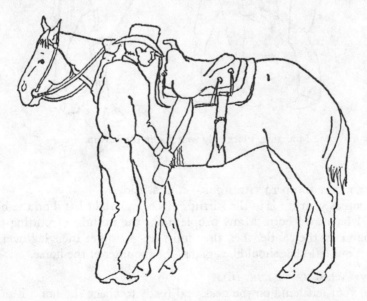

Illus. 158. STEP I. Mounting. Note left hand on neck. Reins should be even and snug.

you as you mount, particularly if you have tied up their feet and sacked them out. However, there is still a good reason for using this position. If the horse should, for any reason, start to move ahead as you swing up, you will be pulled into the saddle rather than land behind it. The latter position might prove embarrassing even on a gentle horse.

STEP II. PLACING FOOT IN STIRRUP—ILLUS. 159.

From this position, use your right hand to turn the stirrup and then place the toe of your left foot in the stirrup. Notice I have said place the toe, not the foot, in the stirrup.

If the horse should jump as you start to mount, your foot would be much more apt to come out of the stirrup if only your toe is there. Remember this point, it's the most important safety factor concerning mounting.

Illus. 159. STEP II. Mounting. Place only your toe in the stirrup.

STEP III. RIGHT HAND TO THE HORN—ILLUS. 160.

As soon as your toe is in the stirrup, place your right hand on the horn. Notice I have said horn. Many people make the mistake of putting their right hand on the cantle, then they must let go to get their leg over the cantle. Your left knee should be against the shoulder of the horse.

STEP IV. SWING UP—ILLUS. 161.

With your left hand on the neck and ready to check the horse if necessary, with your toe in the stirrup, your knee against the shoulder and your

Illus. 160. STEP III. Mounting. Note right hand is on horn, left knee against the horse.

Illus. 161. STEP IV. Mounting. Swing your leg over, keeping head and shoulders low and body close to the horse.

right hand on the horn, you are now ready to mount. Start off the ground by rising up quickly on your right toe and try to swing on smoothly by pivoting on your left knee, keeping your head and shoulders low and over the horn of the saddle. In effect, you roll on to the horse. Keep your body close to the horse and do not start to swing your right leg over until your head and shoulders are over the horse. This will take some practice on a gentle-broke horse, but it's the way a horsebreaker should get on. When you think you've mastered the technique, try getting on without the cinch fastened. You will need a reasonably good-withered, gentle horse, but if you are getting on correctly, it can be done.

STEP V. DISMOUNTING

To dismount, just do it all in reverse. Remember, the first thing you do is pull your left foot back in the stirrup until only your toe is touching it. Then shorten your reins and with your left hand on his neck and your right on the horn, pivot on your left knee and step down again facing the rear of the horse.

MOUNTING GENTLE HORSES ALTERNATE METHOD—ILLUS. 162–163.

While we are on the subject of mounting, we should mention another method which can be used on gentle horses. Your hands are used the same as for mounting green horses. The left hand holds the reins and is placed on the neck ready to check the horse if he moves. The right hand may be used, if necessary, to hold the stirrup, and is then placed on the horn. The difference from the horsebreakers' method is that the rider stands alongside of the saddle, facing slightly toward the front of the horse. He then puts his left foot in the stirrup and steps up keeping right hip against the horse and then throws his right leg over the saddle. This method of mounting is the easier for many riders because it does not require swinging on from the front of the horse. It still gives good control of the horse. For the horsebreaker though, it is not as good because if the horse should jump or move rapidly as the rider mounts, he might land behind the saddle.

INITIAL RIDING

We have just discussed how to mount and how to break a horse to stand properly for mounting. We made a point of stressing safety. The next phase of horse breaking, that of riding the horse for the first few times, also can be dangerous. Young horses, regardless of how gentle, may buck, shy or stampede suddenly and for no apparent reason. The real reason, of course, as was explained in Chapter I, is that these young

Illus. 162. Mounting gentle horse. Note position of hands is the same as in Illus. 160–161.

Illus. 163. The rider stands up in the stirrup before throwing his leg over.

horses may suddenly and unexpectedly return to the wild horse and think you're a mountain lion on their back. Ground work reduces the chances this will happen but cannot eliminate the possibilities entirely. The following section discusses the first few rides on a colt and how to minimize the chances of his getting out from under you.

Before the first ride, the colt should be well confirmed on "whoa," should stand quietly for mounting and should have been driven a number of times. The amount of driving will depend upon the colt. It is wise to drive a nervous, spooky one at least 4 to 6 times before he is ridden. The driving helps take the spook out as well as teach him to respond to the reins. It is better to spend an extra few days driving a colt than it is to hurry the first ride and have him get away from you.

First Ride

On the day you plan to make the first ride, start the training session by warming him up by driving. Drive him long enough, maybe 10 minutes or so, mostly at the trot, to definitely get the edge off him. If you have been using a foot rope, tie his foot up and mount and sack him. Then let his foot down and mount quietly, being certain to make him stand. Be ready for any unexpected move the colt might make. Get a snug tight hold on the reins as described in a later section of this chapter. Put your free hand on the horn and brace yourself with it by pushing your body slightly back. You may want your legs slightly ahead of normal. In this position, a sudden jump ahead and up should not dislodge you, we hope. Don't be bashful about hanging on to the horn—that is what it is there for.

It would be best to ride in a small corral the first time and, if possible, have a rider in the corral on a gentle horse which the colt knows. The gentle horse serves to quiet the colt and to give him something to follow. Urge the colt forward with your voice and slight leg pressure. Leg pressure will be new so be careful. Some colts will spook when just touched with the legs. If you have driven the colt enough, he should respond to your voice command to move, particularly if the rider on the gentle horse moves along at the same time. An extra gentle, quiet colt might not move unless you whip him a little. If he takes a step or two and stops, pat him on the neck and start him again. Ride around the corral a number of times both ways. When you turn, try to pull his head around so that he gets a bend in his neck. Sufficient driving on the ground would help him respond to the pull.

In essence, you are trying to teach the colt two things on this first ride, one, to move with you on his back and, second, to turn around in a small circle when you pull him. Don't ride him too much the first day, especially if it is a two-year-old. Just get him moving and turning a little.

If you think the colt might try to run or buck, an experienced rider could lead you for awhile. This is called snubbing or ponying, and it takes a very experienced rider to snub a colt without getting tangled in the rope or jerking the colt down. Unless this type of help is available, it is best not to do this.

Illus. 164. First ride. A colt will usually move easier if he has a gentle horse to follow. Note horsebreaker's right hand is on the horn to steady himself if the colt makes a bad move. Also note colt has an ear back, which means he is watching the rider. The rider should be relaxed but very alert. *Remember,* even gentle colts can suddenly revert to the wild type.

SECOND RIDE

The second day you ride, go through about the same process of mounting and moving around the corral and turning. If you think you can handle him without trouble, take him for a ride outside the corral. Go with a rider on a gentle horse and do some trotting as well as walking. If he doesn't want to move out, it may be necessary to tap him some with a whip, as shown in Illus. 165. If you do need to whip him to get him moving, first, use your voice cue for moving ahead, second, squeeze or kick with your legs and, third, tap him with the whip. In a few rides, he should move with your voice and leg cues and not need whipping. Every 100 yards or so turn him around in a tight circle. Be careful not to ride too long and get your colt too tired if he is a two-year-old.

Illus. 165. Some colts may be very reluctant to move for a rider. A light tap with a whip may be necessary. Remember to use your voice and leg cues before using the whip. The colt should soon learn to avoid the whip by responding to the other cues. Use a light, stiff whip at the base of the tail to discourage tail switching.

THIRD RIDE

On the third day of riding you may wish to try to gallop. Get him warmed up good by plenty of trotting and then try to urge him into a slow gallop. Following a gentle horse will certainly help. You must be careful because some young horses will try to buck the first time they gallop. If he doesn't want to move out, you may have to use a whip. It is a good idea to use your whip directly over the tail of the horse. This helps keep his tail down. Too much whipping on the hip can make a colt start switching his tail. When he breaks into a lope, go a short distance, then slow him to a trot and turn him around. Repeat several times. When you get back to the corral, he will be tired so it would be a good time to practice dismounting and mounting on the offside.

Doubling and Early Reining

DOUBLING

We should explain the importance of teaching the colt to turn in a small circle. This is particularly essential with a hackamore because the only real control you have is if you can pull his head to the side and turn around. You could not hold him by pulling straight back if he were to try to buck or run. It will usually take at least 3 rides to get a colt coming around good or doubling (as it is called by hackamore riders). Illus. 166 shows a rider starting to double a horse. In a few more rides, the colt's head will almost touch the rider's knee as he is doubled. Remember as discussed in Chapter III, the hackamore will work only if you use it on a pull-and-slack basis. As you double, pull and slack, pull and slack, never jerk. You won't have control until the colt gets the idea that you can double him any time you want. From then on, if he starts anything bad, double him around 2 or 3 times one way and 2 or 3 the other way. You will be surprised how this will take his mind off his problems. You would dou-

Illus. 166. Doubling. Colt should be taught to give his head to the pull of the mecate. Note how mecate is held in the left hand and the low outward position of the right hand with the thumb pointed toward the rider.

ble him if he were to try to buck, run, shy or anything else where he needs discipline. If he should get real anxious to go back to the barn or to follow another horse when you didn't want to, double him. Under no circumstances should you try to hold a horse by merely pulling straight back on the reins. This is the best way in the world to get a horse to rearing and to make him hard mouthed.

Doubling is not as essential in a snaffle as in a hackamore. If you are big and stout, you can probably hold a colt because you have something in his mouth to pull on. However, it is still advisable to teach the snaffle-bit horse to double.

Holding the Hackamore Reins

Before we go further, we should explain how to hold the reins on a colt. Inexperienced horsebreakers will find it difficult to hold the reins correctly to insure control of the colt all of the time. You will get into trouble in a hurry with young horses if you can't keep a hold of them.

Illus. 166 shows the correct way to hold the hackamore rein or mecate. Notice that the right hand is on the rein with the thumb pointed toward the rider. With your hand in this position you can give a good strong pull with your entire arm, which will probably be necessary to start a colt doubling. Remember, after you pull, then slack. Later on, as the colt becomes more responsive, you can just wiggle your fingers to make him feel the bosal. Always use as light a pull as you can to get the response and give slack after each pull. To avoid jerking you must take the slack out of the rein before you pull. In other words, you should feel a light contact with the rein before you pull. The correct hand position also makes it natural to keep your hand low and well out to the side as you turn, again something essential if you wish to have a colt get the proper hackamore head set as described in Chapter III.

Your colt will learn to watch when your hand goes out to the side, as in Illus. 166, and this will serve as a cue to turn. If you do this correctly, it will take less and less pull to make him turn. As the training progresses, you bring your hands closer and closer together, so eventually the horse will not use the sight of your hand as a cue to turn. It is necessary to bring your hands together so the horse can be ridden straight up, as the old timers said, in preparation for neck reining. However, there is no hurry about bringing your hands together. It will take several months of steady riding before a colt should be ridden straight up in a hackamore.

Reining with a Snaffle Bit

Reins on a snaffle bit will be held somewhat differently than a mecate. Illus. 167 shows a good way to hold the reins for the first few rides on a

HOLDING SNAFFLE REINS

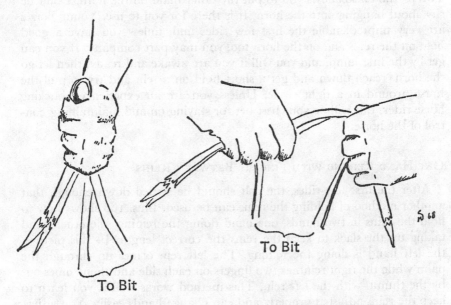

To Bit

To Bit

Illus. 167. Good method for first few rides, keep other hand on horn.

Illus. 168. One hand for reins, other hand for adjusting length of reins. In this drawing, left leading rein would be used for left turn. You must change hands to turn right.

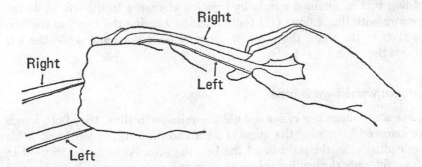

Right

Right

Left

Left

Illus. 169. Two hand reining. You can use a leading rein either direction without letting go of the reins. Also see Illus. 175–176.

colt. As indicated, the reins come up through the palm over the thumb and back through the palm of the hand. The advantage of this hold is that if a colt gives a sudden unexpected jump and tries to put his head down to buck, he will not be able to jerk the reins loose in your hand. This method also allows you to put the other hand on the horn. Don't be shy about hanging onto the horn. It is there for you to use. Young horses are very unpredictable the first few rides and, unless you have a good hold on the reins and on the horn too, you may part company. If you can get by the first jump, and you will if you are awake and ready, then let go the horn, reach down and get a short hold on a rein and try to pull the horse around in a tight circle. Unless you are an experienced bucking horse rider, this will be your best bet for staying on and maintaining control of the horse.

ONE HAND REINING WITH FINGERS BETWEEN REINS

After the first few rides, the colt should be settled down enough that another method of holding the reins can be used. Illus. 168 shows how to hold the reins in two hands, one hand doing the reining, the other hand taking up the slack to keep the reins the correct length. In this picture, the left hand is doing the reining. The left rein comes up through the palm while the right rein has two fingers on each side and then comes out by the thumb with the left rein. This method works well if you learn to keep the reins adjusted properly and can change hands easily. You adjust the length of the reins with the right hand. If you want the left rein shorter, pull it with the thumb and foref ger of the right hand. If you wish to shorten the right rein, grip it between the first two fingers of the right hand and pull. As pictured, you could turn the horse to the left by using the left or leading rein and also give some pressure with the right or bearing rein. The bearing rein should not be used until the colt has been ridden 5 or 6 times and should not be used alone until the colt is ready to be neck-reined. This will be discussed in a later section. The pull with the leading rein is obtained mostly by bending the wrist to the left while the pressure with the indirect rein is obtained by moving the hand to the left. To turn to the right, the right hand must hold the reins while the left adjusts the slack.

REINING WITH TWO HANDS

For some riders it is easier to hold the reins as in Illus. 169. Both hands are involved in turning the horse. To turn to the left, the left hand holds the leading rein, the right hand the bearing rein. As with the method in Illus. 168, only the leading rein is used in the early stages of breaking and the bearing rein is gradually used more as the training progresses.

To shorten the reins, the two outside fingers on each hand tighten on the end of the rein, the other two fingers relax and the hands are spread apart. One disadvantage with this method is that it is difficult to shorten the reins rapidly and pull a colt into a circle if he starts to make a bad move. It has the advantage of not requiring the rider to change hands on the reins each time the direction is changed. Remember, keep your hands low, pull and slack on the reins, never jerk and make the pull as easy as possible to get the desired result.

Summary of Initial Riding

By the time you have ridden the colt 6 to 10 times, he should be trotting easily and loping along fairly well. Most young horses will want to go fast or gallop rather than lope, but will want to go rather slow at the walk. Further training will be needed to slow down the lope and speed up the walk. In addition, at this stage, your colt should be standing still while you mount and dismount on both sides and sack him. If he won't, tie up his foot or hobble him again. He should be doubling easily without hard pulls. With these basics reasonably well learned, the colt is ready for further training.

FURTHER RIDING OF THE GREEN HORSE

If the colt is a two-year-old, another 8 to 10 rides may be enough. It is a real mistake to ride a two-year-old very much. They can easily be discouraged for life if they are expected to do more than they are physically and mentally mature enough to do. In 20 rides, the two-year-old should walk, trot and lope, stand quietly for mounting, dismounting, sacking and give his head easily for doubling. The colt should then be turned out until he is three. The remainder of this section will discuss cueing, teaching a horse to walk and lope correctly, to stop and back easily and to make simple turns. This further training of the green horse should be done only with three-year-old and older horses.

Now would be a good time to consider the condition and energy of your three-year or older colt. In the first rides on a colt, the emphasis is on getting him gentle and trustworthy and doing a few basic things. Extra energy could cause some problems in the early riding. I don't mean to imply that you want the colt weak so you can handle him, but it might be best if he is not just bursting with extra energy. Some early-day horse breakers did starve down wild horses to make them easier to break. This would most certainly not be recommended today.

For further riding, though, your colt will need plenty of energy because he must be feeling good to learn what you will be teaching him. The best energy producer is oats. The amount depends upon the condition of the horse and the other feed being used, but should probably be from 4 to 6 pounds per day. If the colt has not been wormed recently, it would be advisable to have this done.

Remember, *we are still using a snaffle or a hackamore because the colt is not far enough along to change to a curb or even a pelham. Some trainers do change back and forth with a snaffle and a hackamore at this stage. If the colt is not working well in one, they use the other for awhile.*

Cueing Horses

You might want to review Chapter II where we discussed the basic principles of cueing a horse. Some cueing begins during groundwork and in the initial riding. We have saved a detailed discussion until now because it becomes very important in the further riding of a green horse.

VOICE

We began a discussion of teaching cues to a horse in Chapter II and in the groundwork section of this chapter. The most important cue is the voice command "whoa." In addition, we also mentioned using a smacking noise with the lips as a cue for moving ahead and a clucking noise with the tongue against the roof of the mouth as a cue for turning. Voice cues used on the ground must be continued in exactly the same manner when you start riding the horse.

HANDS

The most frequently abused part of the horse is his mouth. The abuse often starts with the first ride and continues until the horse's mouth is ruined. The bad habits of head throwing, bit chewing and lipping the side piece of the bit often have their beginning in the early riding. Since the hands control the bit or hackamore, it is obvious that the hands are basically responsible for the mouth and head set on a horse. In this section, we will discuss the basic ideas involved in correct usage of the hands for starting young horses.

The two most important aspects, in my opinion, are the position of the hands and the method used in reining the horse. If you want a high head carriage, keep your hands high. If you want a moderate to low head carriage, keep your hands low. Most western riders want the latter but may not get it because they ride with their hands too high. By low, I mean keeping your hands down close to the fork of the saddle. In the first rides when you are doubling or turning, we stressed keeping your hands alongside or even below the swells of the saddle.

The method used to rein the colt in the first rides should be a pull and slack. You pull until he gives a little to the pull then give him slack, then pull again. In the first few rides, it may be necessary to pull fairly hard to make him give. Now I have said pull, not jerk. There are no circumstances that I know of when a rider should ever jerk a horse with a bit or hackamore.

The pull and slack of the reins will always be made with the leading rein when doubling or turning the green horse. The use of the bearing rein and the start of neck reining will come later. Remember you are riding the colt with a hackamore or snaffle bit at this stage, this is why you use the leading rein for turning.

For stopping or slowing the horse, you would use the direct rein. That is, you would pull straight back giving slack after each pull. Some trainers alternate the pull, first the right rein then the left, when backing. Pull just hard enough to get a response. As training progresses it should require lighter and lighter pulls.

LEGS

In the first rides on a colt, you would be using your start and stop voice cues. In addition, you would begin to use leg cues. Your legs would be used to reinforce your voice cue to move ahead. You should try squeezing the horse with the calves of your legs. If he responds, this would be very good. However, with most colts it will be necessary to kick with your lower leg. You would kick just hard enough to get the colt moving and then stop kicking as soon as he does move. Kicking will be used on most colts to get them to move, to urge them from a walk to a trot and from a trot to a lope. Kicking should be kept to a minimum and should be replaced as soon as possible with squeezing. Continued kicking tends to deaden the ribs of the horse and requires harder and harder kicks to get a response. On the other hand, by alternately squeezing and releasing the legs, the horse can be taught to respond to lighter and lighter squeezes. This will be discussed in more detail in the chapter on finishing horses. Anyway, in using your legs to move a colt ahead, start squeezing and releasing your legs as soon as possible.

WEIGHT

When you start turning the colt, you will want to start using your weight as a cue. I am not talking about doubling, which is a different proposition from turning. In doubling, you will not be using your weight because you are disciplining the horse. In turning, you would be teaching him to come around easily in a relaxed manner.

After the colt gets 6 to 8 rides on him, you will want to start doing some easy simple turns. At first you will be using mostly your hands to turn him with pulls and slacks on the leading rein. When he gets the idea of this, you can start using your weight as an aid to your hands. As you turn to the left, for example, you will be pulling his head easily to the left, with pulls and slacks, and at the same time stepping down slightly in the left stirrup. He will feel this slight shift of weight from the center of the saddle to left stirrup and will want to balance himself by moving under or with the weight. It won't be but a few rides until you can work him in a serpentine fashion, making little turns to the left and right, using only your weight and an occasionally reinforcing pull on a rein. Remember the withers on a horse are very sensitive to shifts in weight. Do not use much weight even at the start and keep using less and less. You will be surprised how a horse will learn to respond to a very slight shift in weight. The use of your weight in backing and stopping will be discussed later.

Teaching the Colt to Walk Properly

Since the walk is a natural gait, you wouldn't think there would be much of a problem to get a horse to walk. There isn't unless you want him to walk a certain way. Some riders, me for example, like to have a horse feel alive and really moving out at the walk. Other riders let their horses walk along at their own speed, which is usually a slow, flatfooted walk. A fast, flatfooted walk with the hind foot overstepping the front each stride will cover a lot of ground, but what I really prefer is what might be called a western running walk. In this gait, the horse steps a little shorter and feels as though he is up on his toes and really wanting to go somewhere. In a few horses this seems to be a natural gait, and others can be taught it. There are a certain number of horses which will not do it and a rider must settle for the flatfooted walk. We will discuss some ideas on how to get a horse to move out at the walk.

The horse should be well started before you begin pushing him at the walk. This will probably be 15 to 20 rides at least, maybe more. The most important aspect is that the horse must really be feeling good and really wanting to go somewhere. There is no use trying to push a tired, weak, uninterested horse into a fast walk. Of course, a horse can be feeling too good and will want to jog rather than walk. This problem can probably be solved by riding him far enough to get him tired and then pulling him down to a walk. It would be much better to have a horse with a little extra go than not enough. As we pointed out earlier, these young horses probably should be grained to give them extra energy.

Assuming the horse is feeling good and wanting to move out, urge him along with your voice and your legs. If he starts to break into a jog, check him back lightly with the pull and slack of your hands and push him again. At this stage, you should be squeezing not kicking. You squeeze with the calf of your leg and then relax, then squeeze, etc. At the same time, use your voice cue for increasing speed. Gradually use your legs less and less. Too much leg cue on a horse tends to irritate a horse and he may express his dislike by starting to switch his tail.

Don't expect him to walk out fast for too long. Just a few minutes the first ride, then let him relax to a slow, flatfooted walk. It will take several weeks of constant work on most horses to get the idea fixed that what you want is a fast walk. Eventually a mature horse can be expected to go fast all day at either the flatfooted or the running walk.

Most horses will want to hurry to get back to the barn after a ride and this is a good time to be certain they walk properly. However, a properly broke horse will go away from the barn just as easily.

Teaching the Colt to Trot

Trotting is a natural gait and it is the easiest gait to get a horse doing what you want because it is just a matter of speed. If you want a slow trot or jog, pull him down with pulls and slacks on the reins. If he wants to slow to a walk, squeeze slightly with your legs and use your voice. For more speed or an extended trot, use your legs and your voice. You will have the most trouble keeping a colt from trotting when you don't want him to. For example, he may want to jog instead of walk fast or he will want to trot fast rather than lope.

If you want to cover a lot of country at a good speed without exhausting your horse, use the trot alternately with the walk. Trotting is easy on the horse, hard on the rider, but eats up the miles. Since the domestication of the horse, horsemen have used the trot extensively to get the maximum amount of speed and endurance from their horses. In the next chapter, we will discuss how the trot is used to teach a horse collection, lightness of mouth and flexation of the pole.

Remember, *if you want to develop a light, responsive horse you must teach him to respond to lighter and lighter cues. When he does what you want, reward him with a pat on the neck, a soft word and rest or change.*

Teaching the Colt to Slow Lope

A well broke saddle horse should be able to do a collected slow lope. This is not a natural gait for a mature horse. Newborn foals will slow lope as soon as they get on their feet, but they stop doing this in a few months. Since it is not natural, it is difficult to teach many horses. The gallop is a natural gait, and when you slow them down, they drop to their next slowest natural gait, the trot. In the following section we will outline a method of getting a colt to slow lope. Teaching collection will be covered in more detail in the chapter on finishing horses.

STEP I.

One way to start teaching a colt to slow lope is to teach him to lope from a slower trot than he would naturally. The green colt will want to trot as fast as possible before he changes to the next fastest gait which is the gallop. You may need to use a light touch of a whip at the root of the tail as an aid to your hands and legs. Trot him along at a good rate but not extended. Give your voice and leg cue for increasing speed and then check him slightly with a pull and slack on the reins.

When he starts to slow, tap him lightly with the whip. Give him slack and lift your body in the saddle and lean slightly ahead. He should take a lope at least after a few tries. Practice this until he will lope from a medium speed trot. As soon as he breaks into a lope he will most likely extend this to a gallop which is all right at this stage.

STEP II.

When your colt will lope from a less than extended trot, then you need to teach him to maintain the slower lope. If he wants to increase speed, which most of them will, pull and slack with the reins to slow him down. If he tries to drop to a trot, use your voice, legs and whip to make him maintain the gait. It is often difficult to use leg aids correctly when a colt is between a trot and a lope because you are probably standing up in the stirrups. There is a tendency to kick too hard and therefore produce too much speed. It might be best to use your voice and reinforce your voice with a touch of the whip to make him maintain the slow lope. On some colts, it might be necessary to reverse step one and two. That is teach him first to slow from a gallop to a lope and then to lope from a medium speed trot.

Depending upon the riding area, you may want to work your colt in big circles when you are teaching a slow lope. This is especially useful on nervous horses which want to go too fast. Circling them tends to quiet them because they are not going any place.

Remember, *a slow lope is not natural for a horse and therefore, it will take some time and careful work to teach it. Remember too, pull and slack as lightly and softly as possible when slowing the colt down.*

Teaching Backing

Backing, like the slow lope, is also an unnatural move for horses. About the only time a wild horse would back is if he wanted to rub his tail on a tree or get into a better position to kick at another horse. In either case, it would only be a step or two not ten or fifteen feet, as we would want a broke horse to do. Since it is unnatural, it is difficult for some horses to do. They seem to freeze and absolutely cannot move a foot back. It is usually much easier and safer to teach a horse to back from the ground before he is backed mounted. To teach backing first on the horse, it may require too much pulling on the reins which may ruin his mouth or it may cause him to rear, which would be very dangerous. In the section on driving with double lines, we mentioned that some trainers teach their colts to back in double lines. Another way to teach backing which may work for you is described in the following steps.

STEP I. BACKING ON THE GROUND

If the colt had been backed as a yearling as described in Chapter V, then skip to step two. Stand facing the near side of the horse's head with your left hand on the snaffle bit or hackamore reins. Pull and slack the reins easily, say "back." Push on the colt just inside his shoulder joint, where his neck and chest join, with the thumb of your right hand. He probably won't back, so push harder with your right hand, but do not pull harder with your left. If he does take one step, immediately stop and reward him with a pat on the neck.

If it doesn't appear that he will back with thumb pressure, you may need to use a light stiff whip on his chest. Do everything the same, except tap him across the chest with the whip held in your right hand. Be careful because some colts will come ahead instead of back. Reward him as soon as he takes the slightest step back. If he will back a step or two on two or three different tries, that is enough for the first day.

Illus. 170. Backing. STEP I. Some colts may need a light tap on the chest to encourage them to back.

Repeat the lesson until he will back several steps easily. This may take 4 to 8 sessions. Remember, don't try to back him away from the barn or other horses. You would be fighting a very basic instinct, that of leaving the security of the barn or horses. It may help to back him out of or away from some place he doesn't like or even out of the corner of a fence. Remember too, reward him with a pat on the neck, a soft word and by ending the session as soon as he does what you want.

STEP II. BACKING MOUNTED

When the colt will back easily on the ground with only the voice and rein cues, try him mounted. Be sure to have him facing away from where he might want to go. Repeat the cues exactly the same way. If you have used a whip on the ground, you can use it on him. Hold it in your left hand and lean forward enough to tap him on the chest. If he doesn't want to back, have a helper stand at his head and do exactly as you had done previously. Expect to take 8 to 10 days to get him backing easily.

A horse seems to have more trouble moving his hind feet back than the front ones. It makes it easier for a horse to move his hind feet if you stand

Illus. 171. Backing. STEP II. Reins are held low, use voice cue to aid hands, keep your weight off the saddle.

in the stirrup and lean slightly ahead. This keeps your weight over or slightly forward of his center of gravity and lightens the rear legs. Remember your cues for backing will be voice, hands and lifting your weight off the rearhand.

Remember, *in this section we are describing the further riding of the three-year-old or older horses. We said two-year-olds should be turned out after about 20 rides until they are three.*

Turning

At this stage, the colt should be taught to turn easily in rounding-type turns. The teaching of more difficult turns such as pivots and roll backs will be discussed in the next chapter on finishing horses.

A rounding turn should be one of the easier moves taught to a green horse. If the horse has been driven a reasonable amount and has been doubled properly, he will have the basics of responding to your voice and the pull and slack on the reins. The next step will be to teach him to turn with weight and leg cues. The first two steps will be at the walk and trot.

STEP I. TURNING BY PULL AND SLACK AT THE WALK AND SLOW TROT

Turning by pulls and slacks of the leading rein has already been discussed in the sections on doubling and cueing. As the training progresses, the pulls should become smaller and smaller and the hands will be brought in closer to the withers of the horse. The hands will be supplemented and eventually almost replaced by voice, legs and weight.

STEP II. TURNING WITH WEIGHT AND LEG CUES

After 8 or 10 rides on the colt and he is handling well, you can begin to teach him to turn with leg and weight cues. If you have not been using a voice cue such as clucking to turn, you should start this now. As discussed in the section on cueing in this chapter, a horse learns to respond to slight shifts of weight in the direction to which he is turning. As you shift your weight, squeeze with the leg on the opposite side to which you are turning. The reason for using the outside leg will be discussed in the next chapter. The sequence for a left turn is as follows:

1. Pull his head easily with the left leading rein.
2. Cluck softly.
3. Shift your weight slightly to the left stirrup.
4. Squeeze with the calf of your right leg.

As he learns to respond, use your hands less and less. Eventually, you will also want to use your weight and legs less and less so that he will respond to only the slightest shift of weight and leg pressure. As soon as the horse responds reasonably well to the cues at the walk, he can be trotted into the turns using the same cues. You should spend much time turning at the walk and trot to get the horse confirmed on these cues.

NOTE: Teaching a horse to turn can be done in other ways than described here. This method has worked well for my students and may work for you. If it doesn't, try to develop a technique that will.

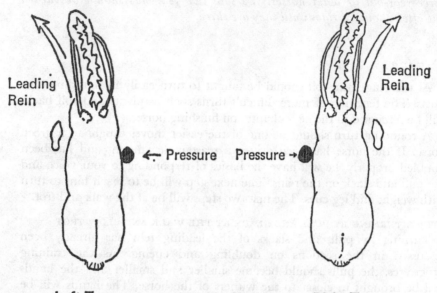

Leading
Rein   Leading
Rein

← Pressure   Pressure →

Left Turn   Right Turn

Illus. 172. Cues for turning. Use your voice as a preparatory cue, your hand to lead, shift weight slightly to be felt in the withers and use leg pressure to move and turn the horse.

STEP III. TURNING AT THE LOPE

A colt should be turning easily at the trot and slow loping reasonably well before he is turned at the lope. The colt should not be rushed into turning at the lope because there are some real problems with this move. First, remember we are not teaching roll backs or pivots, just a rounding turn; so don't try to turn too short. Second, you must remember at this stage to always turn in the direction of the lead the horse has. Third, do not change directions at the lope unless you drop to a trot. If you don't watch these last two items very carefully, you will be making him go cross leaded, which is very undesirable. If a young horse is allowed to go cross leaded, he soon thinks this is the thing to do and it is much more difficult to get him to go correctly.

When your colt is loping, you must know which lead he is in before you start to turn. If he is in the left lead, turn only to left. If you try to turn to the right, he will be very likely to cross up his leads. Now, say your colt is loping in a left lead and you want to turn right; drop to a trot and turn to the right at the trot and cue for a lope. When he takes the right lead, then make a rounding turn to the right at the lope.

You can make half circles at the lope, that is, you will be headed south and you make a rounding turn and head north. You can also make a full turn and go on in the same direction. It is best to lope out of each turn and go straight for a ways before dropping to a trot or stopping. This type of easy, big turns will be a prelude to making figure eights as discussed in the next chapter. Remember, don't make too tight of a turn and be sure to use the same cues in the same way as you did for turning at the walk and trot. Remember too, if the ground is slick, you must be very careful turning at a lope because a horse is much more likely to fall turning at a lope than at a trot or walk.

Stopping

A horse that is broke to ride but not finished should be able to stop straight and easy in 3 or 4 strides from the lope. At this stage, he should not be expected to do a sliding stop as would a finished horse. Great care must be used to avoid stopping the horse with the bit only. If only the bit is used, it almost invariably causes the horse to throw his head and become hard mouthed. It is very important to use a set of cues which combines voice, legs, weight, and finally hands for stopping. The hand should be used last and as little as possible, especially after the horse is in a curb bit. With a snaffle or hackamore, the horse can be pulled fairly hard, providing the hands are low and each pull is followed immediately by a slack.

Obviously, the voice cue to use for stopping is "whoa." If the horse has been properly taught the meaning of "whoa" in the early breaking, he should respond at least at the walk and trot. It will be necessary to reinforce the voice cue with other cues on the young horse.

Your legs can be a very useful cue for stopping. Some trainers squeeze with both calves of their legs as a signal for the horse to get his hind feet under him and prepare for a sliding stop. In stopping the young horse, you will not be expecting him to put his hind legs well under, that will come later. You may squeeze slightly with the knees and upper legs to steady yourself in the saddle, and the horse will learn to respond to this squeeze by stopping. Eventually he should learn to get his hind legs under him for a sliding stop. Some riders in place of squeezing, move their feet ahead 2 or 3 inches from their normal position. This may be a useful cue if the feet are not moved too far ahead and if the body weight is not put back on the cantle.

Weight, like the hands, can produce undesirable effects in stopping, if improperly used. Most of the problem with weight comes when it is shifted toward the rear of the horse as he is trying to stop. For example, some riders push their feet ahead as far as they can and lean back in the saddle as far as they can. The shift of weight toward the rear causes the horse to shorten the stride of the hind legs to keep his balance. If he strides short behind, his stop will be mostly on the front feet because he can't get his hind feet under him. Stopping on the front feet will be rough and bouncy and, therefore, uncomfortable to both horse and rider.

If you ride by standing up in your stirrups, the best way to use your weight as a cue to stop may be to sit down flat in the saddle, but do not

STOPPING

Illus. 173. If you tend to ride standing up or with most of your weight on the stirrups, the most natural weight cue for stopping would be sitting down flat in the saddle. Use your voice, sit down, squeeze with knees and upper leg and use light pulls and slacks on the rein.

lean back. If you ride mostly sitting down in the saddle, you may use your weight as a cue by taking it off the saddle and, in effect, rolling ahead slightly on your knees as the horse begins to stop and then sit down once the horse gets his hind legs well under him. Calf ropers use a shift of weight as a cue to stop. As they start to get off, all their weight is shifted to stirrup. The horse feels this through the withers and learns to start his stop as he feels this shift. Obviously the roper puts no weight on the loin of the horse and thus the horse can get his back legs well under for an excellent sliding stop.

Illus. 174. If you tend to ride sitting down in the saddle a shift of your weight up and then down as the horse stops may work best. Use other cues in the same sequence as above. In this drawing the rider is a little late sitting down.

Remember, *if you want a good stop on a light rein, you must use your hands very carefully. Ideally, what you really need to do is teach the horse to stop with your voice, legs and weight and not with your hands. This is the goal you should work toward at the walk and trot.*

One more cue that some riders use for stopping is to touch the horse on the neck just ahead of the fork of the saddle. As you will recall from Chapter II, this is a sensitive area on the horse and he will learn to respond to touches here. Such a cue should not be used in the show ring, so if you plan to show the horse, you may not want to use it. Naturally, he must be taught what you want him to do when you touch him. The advantage of this cue is that he feels it very easily and you are not hurting him with the bit or throwing him off balance with your weight. Calf ropers use this as one of their cues for stopping. As they start to dismount, their left hand goes to the neck of the horse and this touch signals the horse to stop.

STEP I. STOPPING AT THE WALK

As we pointed out in Chapter II, it is essential to teach each new move to a horse at as slow a gait as possible. This is very important in something like the stop. Here is a sequence which you might follow as the horse is walking along:

1. Say "whoa."
2. Sit down—you will probably already be sitting down but by taking the weight off your feet, it will put all the weight in the seat of the saddle. Do not lean back.
3. Squeeze with knees and upper leg.
4. Say "whoa" again.
5. If he stops, reward him. If he doesn't, and most colts won't in the beginning, pull and slack easily on the reins, keeping your hands low until he does stop.

Work on stopping at the walk until the colt will stop without using the reins. Do not stop too often maybe 4 to 6 times per session. As soon as he makes a good stop, reward him by ending the stopping lesson for the day.

If you ride at all gaits by sitting down tight in the saddle, you may wish to try the other method of cueing with your weight, that is rolling up on your knees as you stop. In this method, the sequence would be as follows:

1. Say "whoa."
2. Squeeze with knees and calves.
3. Roll up on your knees slightly.
4. Pull on the reins as necessary.
5. Sit down as he stops.

STEP II. STOPPING AT THE TROT

When the colt will stop satisfactorily at the walk, he can be taught to stop at a slow trot, then medium trot, and finally a fast trot. Obviously, you would need to use exactly the same cues in exactly the same sequence as you did at the walk. The dropping of your weight into the saddle may be more obvious at this gait. Also you may need to use your hands stronger which is all right, as long as you are still using a snaffle or hackamore.

Correct timing of the pull on the reins with the motion of the horse is important. Your timing can be practiced by coordinating the pull on the reins with posting. When posting properly, your hands must move back as you raise in the saddle and go forward as you sit down. This hand movement is necessary to keep contact with the horse's mouth. For stopping at the trot, this order would be changed and as you sit down, your hands would not go forward but instead would give a light pull on the reins, then a slack in time with your former posting motion.

STEP III. STOPPING AT THE LOPE

It is at the lope where timing of the pulls on the reins is most important and most difficult. You can try the same method at the lope as you did at the trot—that is pull as you sit down, then give slack and pull again in rhythm with the motion of the lope. It may sound easy but is difficult to do correctly.

Before stopping at a lope, you need to have your colt slow loping reasonably well and, of course, stopping easily at the trot. Most horses do not mind stopping at the walk and trot and will learn this easily. On the other hand, most horses do not like to stop from a lope or run. Since they do not like it, you should keep it to a minimum. Only do enough each day to make progress in his learning, never enough to make him dislike stopping. You should never try to stop your horse short on hard ground. It is very difficult for a horse to stop properly on hard ground and if done often can produce lameness and unsoundness.

If you have trouble with the colt throwing his head, you are pulling too hard or are out of time with the horse. Try to use your hands as little as possible and only when he doesn't respond to the other cues. Remember that, at this stage, all you should expect is a stop in 3 or 5 strides, not a sliding stop. The sliding stop will be discussed in the next chapter on finishing horses. When he makes the best stop he can, then do not stop any more for that session.

Stopping by Turning

In the early riding, you would be stopping or slowing your horse by doubling or turning. As the colt progresses and you start stopping him straight, you still should use a turn to slow and even stop him part of the time. As pointed out earlier, the horses do not like to stop straight from a lope or run. So, a good way to slow down or stop is to turn the colt into smaller and smaller circles. Be sure you turn him in the direction of the lead he is in.

Neck-Reining

We have not yet said anything about teaching a horse to neck-rein. All western horses should neck-rein, which is essentially riding the horse with one hand. The other hand then is free for roping, hanging on to the horn, rolling a one-handed cigarette, etc. However, there is no hurry about teaching a horse to neck-rein. In fact, some trainers never really teach a horse to neck-rein, it just develops as the training progresses. This is particularly true of the old Spanish hackamore method in which the hands are gradually brought closer and closer together. Eventually, the horse responds well enough to all cues so that he can be ridden straight up, that is, both hackamore reins in one hand. It is a common mistake of western riders to neck-rein a young horse too soon. Horses which throw their heads each time they are turned or turn their noses up and away from the direction in which they are turning have probably been neck-reined too soon.

When the horse is responding very well to all cues for turning, as described earlier, he can be taught slowly and carefully to neck-rein. This will usually be done much earlier in a snaffle than in a hackamore. There must be a very gradual change from using only the leading rein to using both the leading and bearing rein and eventually to using only the bearing rein. The bearing rein is the rein which touches the horse on the neck and causes the horse to turn away from the touch, in other words, results in neck-reining. It is usually not difficult to teach a horse to move away from pressure on any part of his body. Where the difficulty lies is in the action of the bearing rein on the bit. He has been taught to turn his head in the direction of the pull of the bit or hackamore and to go in that direction. Now, all at once, he is expected to go in the opposite direction from the pull. Obviously, it is very easy to confuse a horse at this point. If you want to end up with a light-mouthed, easy-reining horse, you must depend primarily upon voice, legs and weight to turn, rather than upon neck-reining alone. Until the horse is very well broke you must always have your hands in a position to use the leading rein, in case he fails to respond to the bearing rein properly.

STEP I. NECK-REINING AT THE WALK

After 8 to 10 rides on a snaffle bit horse, the preliminary steps of neck-reining can be started. This involves holding the reins as described earlier in this chapter. Holding the reins in one hand or in two can be used. In either case the leading rein must be used to turn the horse's head in the direction of turn, the bearing rein must be touching the neck lightly. The real secret here is to keep the reins adjusted at the correct length. If the bearing rein is too short, it will pull his head the wrong way, if it is too long, he won't feel it on his neck. You must learn to adjust the reins rapidly and smoothly each time direction and/or speed is changed. If you are using the one hand method, the reins must be changed to the other hand each time you change direction. When you are turning to the right, the reins must be in the right hand to properly use the leading and bearing rein, and changed to the left hand for turning left.

STEP II. NECK-REINING AT THE TROT

You may begin to work on neck-reining at the trot before the colt is completely confirmed on this at the walk. Some colts will respond more readily to weight and leg cues at the trot than at the walk. As you gradually change from using only the leading rein to turn, to using more

NECK-REINING

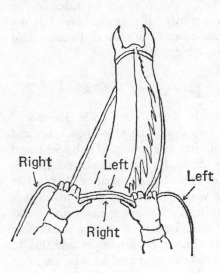

Illus. 175. Using two hands on the reins. The left hand leads the horse. The right one applies light rein pressure on the neck.

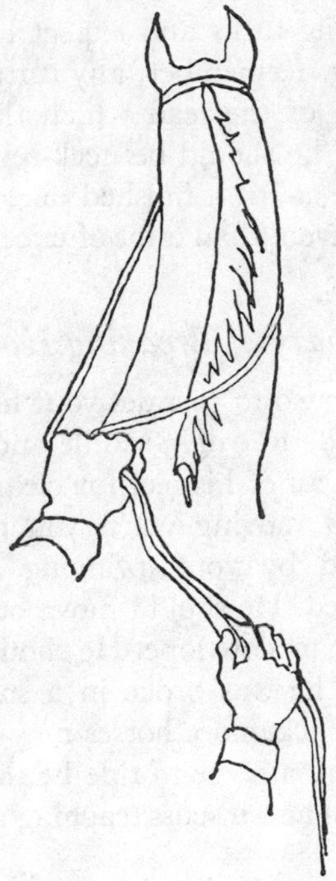

Illus. 176. Reining with one hand. The left little finger leads while right rein bears on neck. To turn right, the right hand must be moved ahead of the left hand on the reins. You also should be using your voice, legs and weight.

and more bearing rein, your hands must always be in position to use only the leading rein if necessary. If a colt gets a little excited and for some reason doesn't want to turn, you must pull him around with the leading rein. Never force him with the bearing rein if you want him light mouthed and not throwing his head. Remember, all this turning is rounding turns at this stage. Let him make nice, easy, rounding turns and use your voice, legs and weight exactly the same way each time. As the horse progresses, use your hands only to reinforce the other cues.

STEP III. NECK-REINING AT THE LOPE

Before neck-reining at the lope, the colt should be completely confirmed at the walk and trot. Speed makes it more difficult for a horse to respond properly, therefore, the rider is more likely to hurt his mouth or pull his head the wrong way with the bearing rein. If you have done the training well at the walk and trot, he should be turning almost entirely with voice, legs and weight and with little or no rein. This is what you are striving for at the lope too. So take it easy, continue making big rounding turns and expect to take considerable time to finish the neck-reining. Remember, any turn at the lope at this stage must be in the direction of the lead which the horse is in. After about 50 rides in the snaffle, he should be neck-reining satisfactorily for a broke horse but not as well as for a finished one. Some trainers can do it much faster, but if you haven't had a lot of experience don't hurry it.

Summary of Breaking Horses to Ride

After 40 to 50 rides your horse should be well broke to ride. He should be gentle to catch, saddle and bridle. You should be able to pick up and handle all of his feet for cleaning, trimming or shoeing. He should stand without moving when you mount or dismount and he should not be spooked by your swinging a rope or putting on your slicker while mounted. He should move out well at walk, jog or trot when asked and be able to slow lope. He should be turning and stopping easily and backing. If he was broke in a snaffle, he should be neck-reining reasonably well. Hackamore horses may take more time to neck-rein. In addition to breaking a horse to ride he should be broke to load and haul in a trailer. We will also discuss teaching a horse to picket.

TRAILER LOADING

As part of the breaking process, all young horses should be taught to load in a trailer. Sooner or later, the horse will be hauled somewhere in a trailer and it certainly makes everything much easier if he has already been loaded. Trailer loading, like all other aspects of horse training, can be accomplished in a number of different ways; what works for one trainer and one horse may not work for the next. So we will discuss a number of different techniques to teach a horse to load and you can take your pick.

In general, there are two basic methods of loading. One involves coaxing the colt into believing that inside the trailer is a good place to be. The other method involves convincing the colt it may be more unpleasant outside than inside the trailer. The first method involves using feed, the second, some method of discipline.

Loading by Feeding

Some horsemen have good luck teaching a colt to load by feeding him in the trailer. The trailer is parked in the corral with the doors open and the colt is fed his hay and grain in the trailer for a period of 2 to 3 weeks. This appears to work well with gentle barn-raised colts which do not have much fear of such things as a trailer.

The big problem with this method is that the day you decide to load up and go somewhere, the colt may decide he isn't hungry. If he isn't hungry, he just may not load and there is nothing much you can do about it, except to wait until his appetite returns. Another problem is that the colt may learn to go in the one trailer you are using but may refuse to load into any other trailer. Another problem would be that you must plan to have several weeks for training before you expect to haul the colt. Not everyone can plan that far ahead.

Loading by Discipline

Many horsemen prefer to teach their horses to load with some method which convinces the horse it is rather unpleasant not to get in the trailer. This involves using a rope or whip as a means of discipline. The following general items should be considered when loading by this method.

1. Teach the horse to load as a part of the regular breaking program. In other words, get it done well before you intend to haul the colt. If some preliminary work with a rope or whip should be done ahead of the day you practice loading, be sure to get this done.
2. Plan to have some help the day you try loading. It is best to have at least two and preferably three people, all of whom know something about horses and who won't be disturbed if you have trouble and must discipline the colt.

3. Park your trailer in the most advantageous position. For example, get the back end as low as possible by dropping the wheels into a shallow ditch or depression if one is available. This makes it easier for the colt to step in. Also park with right side of the trailer close up to a fence or wall. This prevents the colt from running by the trailer on the right side. Some horsemen back up tight to a barn door so the colt has no way to go but in.

4. Do not give the colt the impression he is being trapped in the trailer by closing the tailgate as soon as he steps in. When he gets in the first time, let him stand a minute or two and then back him out without closing the tailgate. The next time close the gate. Load and unload at least three times the first day and preferably do not move the trailer that day. The next day take a short, easy, slow trip of 10 to 15 minutes, being very careful on the turns and start and stop easily.

5. Reward him each time he does something good. For example, when he places one foot in the trailer, pat him on the neck, and again when he places the other one in. If he gets half way in and stops, pat him again. You hope he will go in all the way without backing out, but if he doesn't, start over. When he has loaded easily and you are ready to quit for the day, give him some grain in the trailer. It is a good idea to give the young horse some grain every time you load him for a trip.

6. Do not try to pull him in by brute force. The colt would have to be very small and you and your helpers mighty big and stout to ever pull a colt into a trailer. When you pull on his halter, he is very likely to fight his head and hit it against the trailer. Use the halter only to keep the colt straight.

7. Do not tie the halter rope until the tailgate and safety chain are fastened.

8. Never open the tailgate until the halter rope is untied.

9. You hope the colt will not fight too much, but if he does be prepared to win the battle. In other words, have everything ready for trouble, take all the advantages you can and then get him loaded. Don't give up, because if you do he will be that much harder to load, if and when you try again. If you do give up, he will never forget that he won the battle.

Personally, I would rather a colt did resist being loaded the first time. When he does and you are ready for it and go ahead and make him load, he doesn't forget that you can load him.

He may test you out the next 2 or 3 times you load and even sometime much later, but you can refresh his memory real easy. I am always suspicious of a colt who walks right in the first time. Some time later he may decide not to, and then you may have a battle on your hands when you are not equipped for it.

10. Remember the basic idea is to make it uncomfortable enough outside the trailer that he will want to get away from the discipline by getting into the trailer. In other words, his reward is getting in the trailer, he is punished if he stays out.

LOADING WITH A RUMP ROPE

A common method of the loading is the use of a rump rope, as was discussed in Chapter IV. The idea is basically the same as teaching a colt to lead, except that instead of the colt following you, he should be taught to go by you. When he gets the idea firmly fixed that he is to jump ahead and by you when you give the signal, he should be ready to try to load.

STEP I. TRAILER LOADING, RUMP ROPE—ILLUS. 177.

Have the lead rope in your left hand and the rump rope in your right. You will be standing facing the near side of the colt and should be slightly ahead of him. Take a step to your left as though you were going to lead the colt, use your voice cue for moving ahead, and give a good pull on the rump rope. The colt will be surprised but should jump ahead if you have pulled the rump rope hard enough. When he jumps, give him slack on the lead rope so that he can go by you. Repeat this until he understands that you want him to jump by you when you speak and pull. It would be best but not essential to confirm the colt on this move with a couple of training sessions before the day you plan to load. Many colts will learn what you want in a few minutes work on the day you load.

Illus. 177. Using rump rope to teach colt to jump ahead.

STEP II. TRAILER LOADING, RUMP ROPE—ILLUS. 178.

After the colt is confirmed on jumping ahead, lead him to the trailer and try him. Stand as before, use the same cues and he may jump right in. If not, you or an assistant may have to go in the trailer with him if it is a double one where you can stand on the left side and load him on the right. If he refuses, keep him straight with the halter while you continue to jerk on the rump rope. If he still refuses let him back away, refresh him away from the trailer about jumping ahead and try again. Some colts can't seem to get the idea of picking up their feet to step into the trailer. If this is the case, have one of your assistants pick up each front foot and set them in the trailer.

It may be necessary to have one person holding the halter while another uses the rump rope. Sometimes it might work the best to tie one end of the rope to the trailer and either hold the free end or run it through the other side of the trailer. Sharp slaps with the rope on the rear quarters of the horse should make him jump in. Some horses may kick at a rump rope so always be in a safe position. All of this may sound easy, but it takes considerable patience and understanding. If the horse seems to develop a mental block and just can't understand what you want, try something a little different. Remember to reward him when he does something you want, even though it is only taking one step into the trailer.

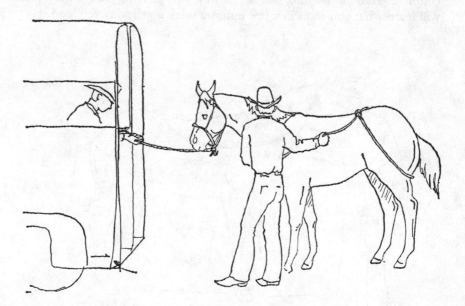

Illus. 178. Using rump rope to load. Helper is inside double trailer on left side.

One advantage to using a rump rope is that after the initial two training sessions it can then be used by one person. If you are alone sometime and the horse refuses to load, you can put a rump rope on to refresh his memory and load him by yourself. Remember the basic ideas of loading discussed at the beginning of this section.

LOADING WITH A WHIP

Some horsemen prefer to use a whip to load horses. The basic idea is the same as with the rump rope, that is, the horse is taught to jump ahead when you ask him.

STEP I. TRAILER LOADING, WHIP—ILLUS. 179.

Stand the horse alongside of a fence or wall and speak to the horse to move ahead. Take a step to your left and at the same time have a helper tap him lightly below the hocks with a long stiff whip. When he moves ahead, be sure to give him enough slack on the lead rope so he can jump past you. Although most horses will not kick if hit below the hocks, you and your helper must be very careful to be in a safe position. It should take only a few minutes to get the horse to jump ahead and by you. It would be best, but not essential, to work the horse a couple of days on this before trying to load him.

Illus. 179. Teaching a colt to jump ahead with a whip.

STEP II. TRAILER LOADING, WHIP—ILLUS. 180, 181.

After the horse is confirmed on jumping ahead, bring him to the trailer. The person holding the lead rope may get in on the left side of the double horse trailer while the other helper stands off to the side to use the

LOADING WITH A WHIP

Illus. 180. Using a helper on the left side of a two-horse trailer.

Illus. 181. One man loading with a whip by running a long rope to the front of the trailer and back to the trainer. *Remember,* horses are naturally afraid of dark, spooky, closed areas. Take your time, give the horse time to learn what you want. Do not overuse the whip. Always stand well to the side to avoid being kicked.

whip. Patience and understanding continue to be important. It may be necessary to lift a front foot in or try other little variations. If a single horse trailer is used or if for some reason you would not want to get in a double trailer, you will need a long lead rope. Run the rope to the tie loop at the front of the trailer and back to you as you stand outside. Keep him straight with the lead rope and take up the slack as he moves forward. After a couple of training sessions with helpers, you could probably load the colt yourself as shown in Illus. 181.

Loading a Foal

If you should need to load a foal, a good method is illustrated in Illus. 182. It would generally be best to have the dam already loaded. Two helpers lock their hands behind the foal and more or less lift him into the trailer. The third person steadies but doesn't pull on his head. Great care must be taken that the foal doesn't hit his head or legs on the trailer.

Illus. 182. Loading a foal. For best results, it takes three people to load a foal safely. Be very careful to avoid injuring the foal. If it struggles it may hit its head on the sides of the trailer or its legs on the back edge of the floor.

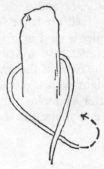

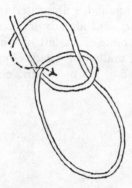

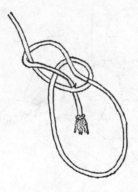

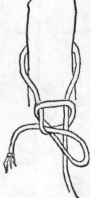

Illus. 183. Tying a bowline. It will not slip but will almost always untie easily when not under a pull. Used for tying a rope around a horse's neck or foot. It will not slip tight and injure or choke the horse.

Illus. 184. Tying a slip knot. This will usually untie with a good jerk on the loose end even when the horse is pulling back. Used for tying a horse to a post or hitch rail. If the horse does pull back, the knot will be easier to untie if a dally (a complete turn around the post) is taken before the knot is tied. Never tie this knot around any part of the horse.

PICKETING HORSES

Some horse trainers may wish to teach a young horse to picket. This means putting the horse on a long rope to allow him to graze without straying off. This method was commonly used in the early days by Indians as well as white people to restrain their horses in open range country. Old timers often taught a range horse to picket by tying him with a long rope to a log placed in a meadow or open area. There was no preliminary training—the colt was haltered and tied to the log. Naturally this was an extremely frightening experience to a wild range horse but a great learning one. After several days of being tied to a log, the colt had developed a great respect for a rope. He was also reasonably well broke to lead and could be handled much easier in a hackamore because his head and neck would be sore. Although such methods were suitable in the early days, there are now better ways to get the job done.

Considerable care should be used in teaching a horse to picket. A horse can injure and even kill himself if he fights or tries to run while picketed. All this can be very dangerous to the trainer too, if he should be in the wrong place when the horse spooks.

STEP I PICKETING—RESTRAINING FEET

The young horse today should be taught not to fear having its feet held. Remember, as we pointed out in Chapter I, most horses have a real fear of any restraint of their feet because it would have meant death to the wild horse. Fortunately, horses can be taught not to fear having their feet held. This is best done by use of a foot rope as discussed earlier in this chapter. It also can be done by using hobbles. Even if a foot rope is used, the horse should be hobbled several times. Such training will reduce considerably the chances of the colt injuring himself by fighting the picket rope when it gets tangled around his feet.

STEP II PICKETING—DRAGGING A ROPE

Another very spooky problem for a horse may be to have the picket rope dragging along behind him. If he spooks at the movement of the rope and tries to run he might be injured when he hits the end of the line. A good way to teach him not to fear a dragging rope is to let him drag one. Buckle a wide leather strap with a metal ring attached around the pastern of a front foot and tie a long rope to the ring. Let the horse drag this around a corral for two or three sessions or until he is not spooked by it in any way. Some trainers let a colt drag a long halter rope for the same reason. However, since we'll be picketing by the foot, it is best to have the rope on a foot. There is more danger of serious injury to a horse if it is picketed by the halter.

Illus. 185. Picketing—horse learning to drag a rope.

Illus. 186. This horse is standing relaxed and quiet after grazing on the picket line.

Illus. 187. Wide strap buckled around fetlock with picket rope attached.

STEP III PICKETING TO A LOG

When the horse no longer fears the dragging rope nor restraint of its feet, it is ready to be picketed. You'll need a strong, soft rope about 30 feet long attached to a wide strap to buckle around the pastern. You'll also need a log or big tire that is heavy enough so that it can't be moved easily by the horse. If a reasonably strong person can just barely drag the log or tire, it will probably be about right. You want the horse to be able to move it a little if he gets tangled or scared, but not to be able to run with it. Picketing to a solid unmovable object is much more apt to injure a horse or break the picket rope because there would be no give.

Place the log in the middle of a big corral or in a pasture about 100 yards from any fence. The horse could be seriously injured if he hits a wire fence while trying to drag the log. Tie the picket rope to the middle of the log. Tying to the end would make it easier for the horse to drag the log. If it began to move, it could scare him much worse.

Lay the rope out full length from the log toward the barn or the direction the horse will most likely want to go. Bring the horse to the end of the rope and face him toward the log with his tail toward the barn. Buckle the strap around the pastern. Remove the halter and try to walk away from the horse without his following you. It is usually best to tell him whoa and move along his side to the rear and then walk directly away. Do not stay close to the horse. If he should spook, he might catch you in the rope or with the log.

It is best to keep an eye on the horse for the first session or two. However, let him learn on his own unless he throws himself and can't get up or has some other serious problem. If it is necessary to untangle the horse, be very careful he does not catch you in any way with the rope or log. Usually a horse can be left on a picket rope for one to three hours the first time. In three or four sessions, he should be reasonably well over any fear and he could be picketed to graze for longer periods.

SUMMARY OF BREAKING HORSES

This chapter has discussed some steps that can be used to develop a gentle, trustworthy, reliable saddle horse. As we have already pointed out, the methods described here are not the only way to break horses. There are many different ways and no one method can be said to be the only way to do something. Any method that teaches the horse to do what you want it to do and produces a safe, reliable horse is a good method. Some of the methods presented here may work well for you. If some don't, then seek advice from other sources and use what is best for you and your horses. If you are breaking a horse, think about and refer to the chapters on horse behavior and learning. An understanding of this material as it applies to breaking horses should improve your chances of doing a good job.

Breaking a horse to lead, ride, picket or load in a trailer may not be the end of his training. You may also wish to finish him to perform a certain job such as pleasure or trail riding, cutting, roping or barrel racing. In the next chapter, we will discuss finishing horses.

CHAPTER VI

Finishing Horses

As we pointed out earlier, horse training can be divided into two major categories: breaking and finishing. We have discussed in some detail the breaking of horses to ride, load in a trailer, etc. In general, a broke horse would be safe and gentle to ride but would not have been trained for a specific purpose such as horse shows, cattle work or rodeo. A finished horse would be trained to do one or more of these special jobs.

We will not attempt to discuss in detail the finishing of horses for specific jobs because of the limitation of time and space. Rather, we will discuss the fundamentals of training a reining horse which then could be finished for special work. Reining, as we will use the term, will mean the horse is collected, light, able to start and stop rapidly and able to change speed and direction easily from any gait. In general this means the horse is completely responsive to the demands of the rider.

Once the basic rein is put on the horse, further finishing for a specific job should progress much easier. Of course, the horse must have natural ability, in addition to a good rein, to become skilled in certain jobs. A cutting horse must have cow sense, a barrel racer, speed. Show horses should be attractive in conformation and way of going. Even though a horse will not be used for anything more than trail or pleasure riding, it is definitely more of a pleasure to ride if it has some reining ability.

The idea that a responsive, highly maneuverable horse could be useful to man is not new. Xenophon, the ancient Greek horseman writing about 2,300 years ago, described some of the attributes of such a horse. His use of the horse was considerably different from our use today; yet he was interested in some of the same responses. Among other things, he described how desirable it was for a horse to flex at the poll and be responsive to the bit, characteristics still considered important by many horsemen today.

Xenophon was a soldier who fought on horseback, apparently mostly with spears. Maneuverability and responsiveness of his horse were a matter of life and death to him. As the centuries passed, men became more and more skillful at training war horses, and cavalry men fought not only with spears but also with swords. About 710 A.D., the Moslems of North Africa invaded Spain and, according to historians, conquered that country rather easily with their superior horsemanship. Apparently, they were mounted on highly trained, agile horses that easily outmaneuvered the Spanish riders. The Moslems stayed in Spain for some 700 years. During that long time, the Spaniards learned horsemanship from them and then improved upon it. As a result, Spain became world famous for its excellent horses and horsemanship from 1200 to 1600 A.D.

However, about the middle of this same period, the decline of the importance of war horses began, finally ending early in World War II when horses were largely replaced by machines. The decline in the need for highly trained cavalry horses began when guns replaced the spear and sword as major weapons. No longer did a man's life depend upon the ability of the horse to position him for the thrust of his sword or to avoid his enemy's sword. The horse continued to be useful in war after guns were introduced but more as a means of transportation and a source of mobility than for actual hand-to-hand combat.

Fortunately, the techniques for training the highly skilled cavalry horse were not lost. In the late 16th century, the rulers of Austria established an Imperial Stud consisting of stallions and mares purchased in Spain. The original purpose of the stud was to perpetuate the Spanish breeding and supply horses for the Austrian nobility. Another reason was to train and educate the young aristocratic horsemen of Austria in the finest techniques of horsemanship developed by the Spanish in the preceding centuries. It also served to perpetuate this type of horsemanship for future generations to enjoy and study. To horsemen around the world it is now known as the Spanish Riding School of Vienna, the home of the famous Lipizzan horses.

The essential moves taught a war horse were: the gallop depart (taking a particular lead), halt and half halt (stopping or slowing down), backing, pirouet (pivots), side pass and half pass (two-track) and rapid transitions (change of gait). The horse also was taught to respond to the rider's cues instantly, without hesitation or resistance. In addition to these moves, the Spanish Riding School teaches a number of spectacular ones to demonstrate the ultimate in horse training. Such things as dancing to the Spanish Waltz, the most unusual and difficult Capriole and the Curvet have no practical value. Nevertheless, they do serve to show what can be done with a highly collected, light, responsive horse. The Curvet, where the horse jumps forward on the hind legs, was taught in Xenophon's time. The basic moves of the war horse have been preserved in another way of special interest to western riders. Not long after the first California missions were established in the 1770's, the Spanish Dons realized they needed expert horsemanship to handle the cattle they had turned loose to multiply on the lush California ranges. These cattle had reverted back to the wild type and it took real horsemanship to gather, brand and sort them.

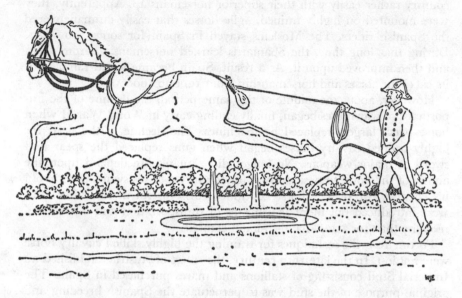

Illus. 188. Capriole—the spectacular jump and kick performed by the Lipizzan horses of Austria is the ultimate in advanced training.

In those early years, it was not unusual for the Spanish Dons to send their young sons to Spain for a year or two to study horsemanship. What they learned, apparently, was how to ride and train a light, collected, highly schooled war horse which turned out to be just what they needed to work the wild range cattle. The fast starts (gallop depart), sudden stops (halts), sudden changes of direction (pirouet) and speed (transitions), so essential to the war horse, proved equally useful to the cow horse. Because the early Californians learned to value lightness and responsiveness in a horse, they learned to use the hackamore for training. They could work cattle while riding green horses without danger of damaging their mouths. Then a spade bit was used to maintain this lightness throughout the useful life of the horse.

The Californians, like the Spanish Riding School, added a little extra performance beyond strictly utilitarian needs. The spin and the long sliding stop have no practical value in working cows but are used to demonstrate that extra bit of finish which can be obtained.

Thus, the California reined cow horse, with its distinctive style and carriage, is carrying on a very old tradition of horsemanship. Originally the life of its rider depended upon the training of the horse. Later, with some modifications, the old time California rider's livelihood depended upon the horse's responsiveness and ability to work cattle. Now in our modern age, when most western horses never see a cow, there is still a place for this type of horsemanship. Not only can it increase the utility of the horse for other types of riding, but it can also give the rider greater satisfaction and pleasure in riding.

This rather lengthy discussion of the history of the California reining horse does not intend to detract in any way from the usefulness and merits of another style of western horsemanship prevalent east of the Rocky Mountains. That style, originating in Texas in the 1800's, is essentially American in origin with only a slight influence from England and Mexico. It developed as the range cattle industry developed in Texas and spread northward. The cowboy wanted a horse that he could use to work and rope cattle and he had little or no concern about such things as headset, collection and lightness. After the horse was broke to ride, the cow became the teacher to finish the horse for its life work. Those conditions produced some of the most expert cow horses the world has ever known.

However, under present day conditions where only a small percentage of western riders can use the cow to finish the horse, training methods have begun to change. We discussed earlier that the use of double reins for finishing is becoming more prevalent. Also many professional trainers and riding instructors now stress the proper use of the natural aids which help the horse learn basic moves learned in the past through the experience of working cattle.

In the remainder of this chapter, we will discuss some of the basic performance characteristics of a western reining horse and how to develop these characteristics without the use of cattle. This will include a discussion of age and condition of horses, headgear, headset, collection, lightness and lateral control as they relate to finishing. In addition, we will discuss training techniques to develop specific moves such as simple and flying changes of leads, sliding stop, pivots, rollbacks and spins.

AGE AND CONDITION

Many of the moves done when finishing a reining horse are difficult, both physically and mentally, for the horse. Working off the hind legs while pivoting, rolling back, starting and stopping requires considerable muscular strength. These types of moves also put a heavy strain on joints, tendons and ligaments of the foot and leg. In addition, the horse has a great deal to learn. Young horses, or ones lacking maturity and strength, could be seriously injured, both in body and in spirit, by such hard physical and mental exertion. They could be hurt physically by the strain on their joints and tendons. Wind puffs, spavins, thoroughpins, bogs and tendon problems can be produced. Mentally the horse may be too young to learn the more difficult moves. Young children are not expected to learn calculus, neither should a mentally immature horse be expected to learn rollbacks, pivots, etc. Also an immature horse is more likely to become what is called sour. This means it loses interest in working and may refuse to perform correctly what it has learned or simply refuse to learn.

In general, a horse should be at least three years old, well developed, strong, mentally alert and willing to work before finishing is started. Four- to five-year-old horses are the most ideal age for finishing. Older horses can be finished, although they often are a problem. The problem is usually one of correcting bad habits they have developed by earlier improper handling.

Anyway, if you want to have good results in finishing a horse, be sure the horse is physically and mentally ready. Be certain the horse is not infected with internal parasites. Make sure its feet are trimmed or shod properly. Some horses can benefit by being shod behind but not in front for certain phases of training. This may help the horse learn to work off the hind feet. Certainly never let a reining horse or any other western horse get tender footed behind. Use skid boots to protect the fetlocks of the hind legs when training for sliding stops. Special hind shoes with longer, slightly turned up heels may help a horse learn to make a sliding stop. Shoes made from half round metal allow a horse to roll over the foot a little easier for pivots and rollbacks. Liberal use of grain is advisable for 3-year-olds and any older horse lacking in condition, strength, stamina or interest.

HEAD GEAR

Most western riders do not consider a horse finished until it can be neck-reined in a curb bit. Neck-reining is essential for a western horse because the rider wants one hand free to swing a rope, hang on to the horn, wave at a friend or some other worthy endeavor. The curb bit may not be quite so essential but is certainly widely used. A few horses can be ridden all their life in a hackamore or snaffle, but most horses tend to get hard and difficult to handle if not transferred to a curb. Hackamore bits can take the place of the curb bit but still must be neck-reined.

As we pointed out in previous chapters, most horses are broke to ride with a snaffle or a hackamore. Then the horse must be finished into a curb. Experienced horse trainers can break a horse to ride, then replace the snaffle or hackamore with a curb and proceed with the finishing. Inexperienced trainers who try this may run into some serious problems.

Head throwing, open mouths and hard mouths frequently result from the improper transfer of a horse to a curb.

Fortunately, there are two methods which can be used to make the transfer in a gradual way. Both methods originated in Europe and both use double reins. One was introduced to the west through Spain, Mexico and Old California. The other came via England and the east coast. The California method involved using a hackamore and curb bit together with two sets of reins. The eastern or English method uses double reins on a snaffle and curb combination either as a pelham or as a true double bridle, the weymouth. The California method was introduced to the West about 200 years ago, the eastern or English method about 25 years ago.

However, we are getting ahead of ourselves discussing double-reined outfits. It may be best to do a part or all of the finishing with the old familiar snaffle or hackamore. Although these two items are usually thought of mostly for breaking, they can be used with excellent results for finishing. This is particularly true of the hackamore. Old time hackamore specialists did not go to double reins until the horse was completely finished in its performance training. Then they taught the horse to carry and respond to the curb by using both the hackamore and bit for a period of 6 months to a year. Finally, the hackamore was removed and the horse was considered finished.

So, unless you are experienced and have good hands, it is advisable to do as much of the finishing as possible with the snaffle or hackamore. The big advantage to this is that you'll be more likely to produce a light-mouthed, responsive, finished horse. Although most of the hard pulling will have been done during breaking, there will be occasions when it will be necessary to double a horse or take hold of him rather firmly during finishing. You can do this with the snaffle or hackamore without hurting his mouth. You cannot, or at least should not, do this with a curb unless you want a hard-mouthed, head-throwing horse.

Another real advantage to the snaffle or hackamore is for lateral control of the horse. You can pull its head around which is very useful for teaching certain moves which we will discuss later. A horse should not be pulled around with one curb rein because it hardens its mouth. Some trainers change back and forth between the snaffle and hackamore. This has the real advantage of preventing the horse from becoming hard in either one.

Anyway, we'll figure on starting the finishing with the snaffle and hackamore. When the horse loses its responsiveness or when its performance training is finished, it can be changed to a double-reined outfit. This will allow a gradual transition from the snaffle or hackamore to curb bit.

Running martingales and German martingales may also be useful in finishing. These would be used on horses that do not carry their heads correctly. Both of these devices can be used to help correct certain problems and after correction, their use can be discontinued. On the other hand, if a tie down or standing martingale is used as a training aid, its use will probably have to be continued even after the horse is finished. Horses learn to depend on the tie down to hold down their heads. Therefore, unless you want to use a tie down permanently, you should not use it during training. Tie downs are commonly used on horses whose usefulness is hindered by being high headed, hard mouthed, or both.

Remember, *it is not the type of equipment that is so important in training, but how it is used. In other words, it is how you use your hands and the other natural aids.*

BASIC PERFORMANCE TRAINING
OF A WESTERN HORSE

There are four basic performance characteristics that are commonly exhibited by a well-finished western horse. These are: a correct head set, a certain amount of collection, instant light response to cues and the ability to readily move forward, backward and laterally (sideways). These characteristics are basic to the performance of most jobs the western horse will be expected to do. However, they are not essential for simple pleasure or trail riding, although they do add considerably to the pleasure and usefulness of such horses. In later sections, we will discuss the specific moves of a finished reining horse.

Remember, *during breaking you're mostly concerned with altering the primary or instinctive behavior patterns of the horse. The most important ones are fear and need for company. When finishing a horse, you're mostly concerned with teaching a horse to respond to secondary stimuli. These stimuli are for the most part the natural and artificial aids. When finishing for a specific job, you may be teaching the horse to respond to a number of other stimuli. These might be cows, barrels, stakes, jumps, etc. You may want to refer back to Chapter II to refresh your memory on teaching secondary stimuli.*

HEAD SET

The development of the correct head set on a western horse is very important. The horse uses his head and neck to balance himself and his eyes to see where he is going. Any serious impairment of these two functions will obviously have very undesirable effects on the performance and safety of the horse. Headset involves two factors, the height the head is carried and the position of the nose in relation to the poll or flexing at the poll.

Height of Head Carriage

A horse that carries its head too high will have problems with balance. If it also carries its nose out and up, it will have a considerable problem seeing the ground. If it cannot see where it is going, it would certainly be dangerous to ride, particularly in rough country. Although opinions differ some on the ideal height of the head, a well balanced reining horse usually carries its head with the eye about on a level with the withers. This is the position that would be maintained when the horse is up on the bit. When he is relaxed or when in an extended walk, trot or run, the

Low

High

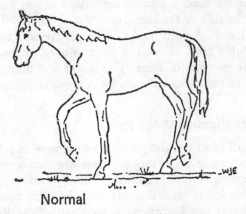

Normal

Illus. 189. Head-carriage—natural head position can be altered by the type of head-gear and how it is used.

head would usually be lower. Not many western riders would want it any higher and some would want it lower. Ropers, in particular, do not want a high-headed horse because it makes it difficult for them to see and rope cattle.

The height the head is carried is determined in part by the natural conformation of the horse. Certain breeds, such as the American Saddlers and some Arabian and Morgans, have a naturally high head carriage. They are bred for it. Quarter Horses have been bred to carry their heads somewhat lower because a high position can interfere with their utility. The height can also be affected considerably by the trainer. A rider, who keeps his hands high and/or tends to be hard and heavy handed, will tend to produce high-headed horses. Riders with this tendency often tie their horses' heads down and thus the high position of their hands is counteracted. However, as we pointed out in the previous section, it will probably be necessary to use a tie-down on such a horse continuously.

It is definitely more of a challenge to correctly position a horse's head with your hands than it is to tie it down. Certainly any student should want to learn the proper use of the hands for accomplishing this. Mostly it is a matter of determining in what position you want a horse to carry its head and then to use your hands accordingly. Hands must be held low on any horse that tends to get its head high. Conversely the hands must be raised on a horse that has its head too low. As important as position of hands is the manner in which the hands are used on the reins. Hard pulls and jerks cause a horse to raise and throw his head to get away from the pain. Therefore, the pulls must be as light and easy as possible to still get the desired response. A pull must be followed immediately by a slack. As training progresses, the horse should respond to lighter and lighter pulls, until the pull and slack are no more than a tremor of the fingers.

The type of headgear used is also an important aid in positioning the height of the head. Snaffle or hackamore action can be used to raise the head by lifting the hands. A curb used with finger tremors tends to lower the head. Using double reins allows the rider to raise or lower the head by proper use of the two sets of reins. The use of a running or German martingale may be necessary on some horses to lower the head.

Position of Nose or Flexing at the Poll

The other aspect of head set, the position of the nose in relation to the poll, is also of considerable importance. There are two acceptable positions and two unacceptable ones. A horse naturally carries its head with the nose slightly extended beyond the vertical. This is an acceptable position for a western horse and is commonly seen east of the Rocky Mountains. The horse can see where it is going and its balance is not disrupted, providing the height is not exaggerated up or down. If the trainer wants the horse to carry its head in this natural position, he must be careful not to hurt the horse's mouth. Pain invariably causes the horse to raise its nose. During early training, it may be helpful to teach the colt to flex slightly at the poll when the reins are pulled. This will encourage the horse to give slightly to the pull rather than resist and extend the nose. This was discussed in Chapter V.

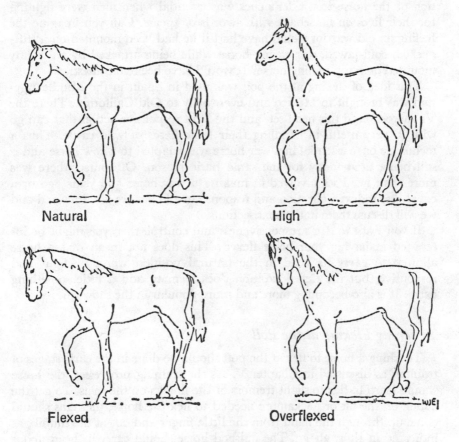

Natural   High

Flexed   Overflexed

Illus. 190. Nose positions. How you use your hands determines the position the horse will carry its nose. The natural and flexed positions are the acceptable ones.

The other acceptable position is to have the horse carry the nose back from the natural position and thus have the forehead and face about perpendicular to the ground. This is called flexing at the poll and is commonly found in the hackamore and spade bit horses west of the Rocky Mountains. It is also the position in which American Saddle Horses, dressage and certain other English horses carry their heads.

The reasons that some western riders prefer this type of head set over the natural one are rather interesting and go back a long time. Xenophon, the ancient Greek horseman, comments on the importance of a horse being responsive to a bit and carrying its head flexed at the poll. He, of course, was referring to war horses. Horses trained to flex at the poll do tend to be lighter and more responsive to the bit. Obviously, instant reaction of the horse to a rider's cues was essential when men were fighting for their lives on horseback with swords or spears. Can you imagine the feeling an old warrior would have had if he had been mounted on a stiff-necked, cold-jawed, star-gazing horse while being attacked by an enemy mounted on a top reining horse? It would have been no contest.

This idea of flexing at the poll was used in Spain in the Middle Ages and was brought to Mexico and eventually to Old California. There the Vaqueros found this head set, and the light responsive action that can go with it, very useful in handling their large herds of wild cattle. Thus a technique once essential in a war horse was adapted to a cow horse and is still being used today for the same basic reason. Of course, there was more than head set involved in making a war horse 500 years ago or a cow horse today. Collection and response to all cues are also involved and we will discuss them in the next sections.

If you want to stress responsiveness and control, then you might be interested in having your horse flexed. This does not mean that a horse allowed to carry its head in the natural position won't be light and responsive, but the flexed position does seem to add a little something extra. It is also becoming more and more popular in the show ring.

Teaching Flexing at the Poll

Teaching a horse to flex at the poll should be done in the early stages of training as discussed in Chapter V. As the training progresses, the horse should learn to flex to slight tremors of the fingers on the reins. To get the action on the bit or hackamore needed to flex the horse, the reins should come up through the hand from the little finger and out at the thumb, as indicated in Illus. 26–29. The finished horse should carry its head about perpendicular anytime the rider has the slightest pressure on the reins. It may, however, extend its nose slightly at the extended walk and trot. At the extended run, the nose must be out in the natural manner to allow it to reach the length of stride needed to run. Some trainers who want a horse flexed at the poll prefer a heavy bit. The extra weight encourages the horse to carry its head perpendicular. This position will be more comfortable to the horse because the weight of the bit is placed on the poll through the headstall. If the horse extends its head, the weight is more on the mouth and can be more uncomfortable.

At the start of this section, we said there were two undesirable positions of the nose. The obvious one would be with the nose too high or, as some say, the horse is ahead of the bit. Not only is it very difficult for the horse to see where it is going but the horse is completely out of balance for stopping and turning. Also the horse is usually difficult to control. With its nose extended, the rider has considerably less leverage because the horse can use all of its neck muscles to resist. Martingales and draw reins are useful in overcoming this problem. A tie-down can be used as the last resort on a horse that refuses to get its nose down. This undesirable position usually starts in the early breaking of the horse by improper use of the hands. It may also result when a horse is changed too early into a curb or when neck-reining is started too soon and done improperly. A bit that does not fit the horse's mouth can cause the problem.

The other undesirable, but far less common, nose position is being overflexed or behind the bit. Some horses will bring their chins completely back to their chests. In this position, it is very difficult to control the horse. It is also very difficult to correct the problem. Changing curb bits, using a snaffle or hackamore with high hand action may help. Some trainers advocate using a gag snaffle. An overcheck rein run from the bit up to rings placed high on the headstall and back to hands can be tried as a last resort.

In summary, it is very important to have the correct head set if you want a useful western horse that is a pleasure to ride. Head position is determined largely by how you use your hands. In general, you should keep your hands low, always use pulls and slacks and eventually only tremors of the fingers. It's not easy to develop a correct headset, but it's well worth the effort.

COLLECTION

Collection in a western horse means the hind legs are collected or kept under the body as the horse moves. In other words, it is working off its hind legs. Collection in other horses may also include a high way of going with considerable animation and flashiness. Working off the hind legs allows the western horse to start, stop or change direction and speed easily at the rider's command. A horse can be collected at the walk, trot or lope but not the run. When a horse is really running, the hind legs must extend out behind in one part of each stride. The front legs also reach out as far as they can in front. In this case the horse is said to be extended or the opposite of collected. A horse can also be extended at the walk and trot.

Collection is not found in all western horses but is essential for certain show classes and for cow horses. It also makes a horse more of a pleasure for just ordinary riding. A collected slow lope is a real pleasure for me to ride. Western horses would seldom be expected to do a collected walk, but should be taught to show some collection at the trot or at least have a slow trot or jog.

NOTE: Highly trained English dressage horses are taught so much collection that they can trot and even lope in place without moving forward. (Trotting in place is called the piaffe.)

Cutting horses work off their hind legs more than any other western horse and thus are exhibiting collection. The only time a cutting horse is not collected, (without its hind legs under it), is when it must run across the arena to head a fast-moving cow. Even then the good horses are careful not to extend the hind legs too much because they would then be out of position to stop and change directions rapidly.

Teaching Collection

The techniques for teaching a horse to work off its hind legs were developed a long time ago with war horses. When combined with lightness and flexing at the poll, it gave the warrior the control and maneuverability he needed to fight effectively with swords and spears. Under our modern conditions, a certain amount of collection allows the horse to perform more successfully in the arena, on the ranch, or for pleasure riding.

A basic idea in teaching collection is to urge the horse forward with voice and leg cues and at the same time hold him back, or at least slow him down, with the hands. It usually is best to teach a horse some collection at the trot before working on the lope. Urge the horse into an extended trot, using your voice and leg squeezes. Then start using light finger movements on the reins to slow him down. Keep on squeezing and releasing with the calf of your leg and urging him with your voice. As he slows, he will probably drop to a walk, then release your hands and let him extend into a trot. Repeat the process until you can maintain a slow collected trot. This will take a week or longer to develop.

Although there is no need for a collected walk, you can do some work on it if you wish. This gives a little variety for the horse and may be particularly useful if you want the horse flexed at the poll. As a matter of fact, if the horse is not giving to the bit as well as he might, you may want to work him from an extended trot to a collected trot, to a collected walk, to a stop and finally make him back a few steps. All the time you would be using light finger movements on the reins to flex and collect him. Thus you may be teaching collection and flexing at the poll at the same time.

Once the horse will collect into a slow jog and is carrying his head to suit you, then he can be taught to go collected at the lope. The sequence here is about the same. That is, the horse will be extended into a gallop

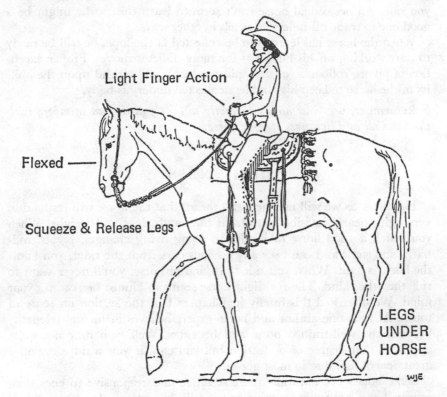

Light Finger Action

Flexed ——

Squeeze & Release Legs

LEGS
UNDER
HORSE

Illus. 191. Teaching collection—light finger action and alternate squeezing and releasing of legs will teach the horse to keep the hind legs collected under him.

and gradually slowed to a slow lope by finger action on the reins. It will
take some time because the lope is not a natural gait for the horse. Baby
foals will slow lope alongside of their mothers, but when they get older
they use an extended trot and go directly into a gallop.

Anyway, your horse will want to trot when you slow down from the
gallop. Some horses, who can't seem to get their legs collected under
them to a slow lope, may be helped by the tap of a stiff whip at the root
of the tail. This gives them some extra forward impulsion, which, if accompanied by careful use of the hands, may get them collected enough to
slow lope. Don't expect too much, too fast. Remember a slow lope is not
a natural gait and so it may take from 10 to 15 sessions before the horse
will execute it properly. However, as I pointed out earlier, it is essential
that a western horse slow lope, so keep trying until it is perfected. Once
you have ridden an easy, collected lope, you will want it on every horse

you ride. An occasional horse can't seem to learn this, so he might be a good one to trade off unless he excels in other ways.

When the horse has learned to be collected at the lope, he will be ready to start working off his hind legs for more difficult moves. Proper execution of pivots, rollbacks, offsets, spins and stops all depend upon the ability of the horse to keep his hind legs collected under his body.

Remember, *use your hands correctly so that you do not interfere with the head set and lightness of your horse.*

LIGHTNESS

Lightness, as we will use the term, means that the horse will respond to very light, nearly invisible cues from the hands, legs and weight. When you watch a good horse taking leads, doing flying changes, pivots, rollbacks and stops and can't see any obvious cues from the rider, you know the horse is light. When you ride that kind of horse, you'll never want to ride the other kind. The real light horse seems to almost be reading your mind. We discussed this briefly in Chapter I in the section on sense of touch. At least one author and horse expert believes in mental telepathy between the well-trained horse and his rider. Well, you may not quite approach that degree of perfection but you can, if you want, develop a great deal of lightness in most horses.

Some horses are naturally more sensitive and responsive to cues than others. These naturally sensitive horses will, in general, develop lightness more easily than the others. However, being more sensitive they will also learn bad habits faster, such as throwing their heads or switching their tails. On the other hand, it is surprising how light and responsive an apparently unresponsive horse can become by careful training. Even older, somewhat-spoiled horses can often be lightened up considerably. Naturally it takes time, patience, understanding and careful thought to work out the correct approach on different horses. On some horses, a change of headgear will make considerable progress in softening their mouths. We discussed the various headgear in Chapter III.

Teaching Lightness

Not too many years ago it was a common thought in some areas that the term reining horse meant the only cue used was the reins. However, it is a rare horse that can learn to perform satisfactorily and remain light responding only to the reins and we might add, a rare trainer who can teach a horse all the moves with only his hands. Most all experienced riders, riding in balance with the horse, will consciously or unconsciously use their weight, legs and voice to a certain extent. For example, a person might think he is not using weight as a cue; yet he unconsciously sits down in the saddle as he stops the horse. When this is done consistently, the horse soon learns to respond to the change in the weight distribution of the rider. Anyway, for our purposes we will assume we will be using all the cues needed for a certain response, consistently and in the same sequence.

Now, to develop lightness, the trainer must use each cue more and more lightly. For example, in the first rides of a green colt, we said in Chapter V, it may be necessary to use your legs strongly, even kicking with your heels to get some colts to move. At the same time, you would be using your voice and leaning your weight slightly forward. In a few rides, the colt should be responding to less leg pressure. Before too long you should be able to start him with your voice, a slight shift of weight up and ahead, and a very light squeeze with your legs. Thus the colt is learn-

Illus. 192. Lightness. A light, responsive, athletic horse is hard to beat. Note how this horse has one ear back, listening and watching for the slightest cue.

ing to respond to light leg pressure. The same basic idea applies to the use of the hands, weight and voice. In the early training, the cues must be obvious, distinct and clear. But as training progresses, you should be able to use lighter and softer cues and get the desired response.

Some horses, as the training goes along, may get harder rather than lighter. When this happens, several factors could be the cause. Perhaps the horse is being worked too much and is getting sour and needs a rest. Maybe he is getting sick or maybe you are confusing him by inconsistent use of the cues. Maybe he is just getting ornery and lazy. If you're certain the last one is the problem, it will probably be necessary to wake him up a little with a whip or spurs. These artificial aids can be very useful at such times but must be used with considerable discretion. We discussed their use in Chapter II in the section on motivation and learning.

One more thought about your hands and developing lightness. One of the most common problems with western horses is their hard mouths and incorrect head carriage. This type of problem can be traced almost entirely to improper use of the hands during breaking and finishing. So, if you want to avoid these problems and develop a light soft mouth, you must do as much of your training as possible with the other cues. Obviously you'll need to use your hands, but try to be very careful. It is a real challenge to develop lightness, but as I've said before, well worth the effort.

LATERAL MOVEMENTS

A finished horse should move easily and without resistance in three different directions, forward, backward and laterally (sideways). The forward and backward movements are obvious; the lateral movements are often overlooked or their importance not understood. When a horse is being broke to ride, one of the first things he is taught is to move forward. Except for some refinements, such as taking a lead on demand from a standing start, not much finishing time will need to be spent on forward motion. If the horse is being finished for some job that requires a fast start, like a rope horse, then some more work will need to be done. About the same is true for backing. As part of breaking, the horse would be taught to back. Some refinement of backing during finishing may be done to speed the horse up and to be certain he backs straight. Also some backing may be done as part of the training on headset and lightness.

On the other hand, lateral movements are not taught until the horse is being finished. Their proper execution is the mark of a well-trained horse. Lateral movements take two basic forms, the sideways movement of the entire body of the horse or the sideways movement of fore- or rearhand separately. The lateral movement of the whole body is called the side pass. The two-track is a modification of the side pass where the horse moves forward and laterally at the same time. The lateral movement of the forehand, while the rearhand stays in place, is called the pivot (pirouette to dressage riders) or offset. If this move is done while in motion without a complete stop, it is called a rollback. If the horse goes completely around on its hind legs making a 360° circle, it would be called a spin. All of these lateral moves, except the spin, were essential to a war horse used for sword and spear fighting and are still very useful in western riding today.

The side pass has a number of practical uses. Some of these are opening and shutting gates, positioning a horse in a roping or steer wrestling chute and maintaining position while sorting cattle in a corral or alley. Cutting horses are taught to side pass when blocking cattle against a fence. Most trail horse classes at shows require side passing. The two-track is a useful exercise while training and may, on some horses, be taught as a preliminary to the side pass. Once a horse will two-track easily, it is usually quite easy to teach it to take either lead on demand.

The pivot, offset and rollback are moves used for working cattle. They may also be part of a reining pattern at a horse show. Barrel racers often teach their horses to pivot and rollback as part of the basic training for turning the barrels. The spin has no practical use, that I know of, except in the show ring where it may be part of a reining pattern. When properly done, it does show the handiness and agility of a horse.

Teaching Lateral Movements

The hands, assisted by the legs, weight and voice, control the forward and backward movements of the horse. As the horse progresses in its finishing, each of the cues becomes lighter and lighter, particularly the hands, if a soft mouth is wanted. The hands, assisted by the three other natural aids, also control the lateral movement of the forehand. In the early training, the hands are used to lead the front end laterally. The finished horse should move laterally with a light touch of the indirect or neck-rein.

Now, that leaves the rearhand (rear quarters) to be controlled and this control is the one most often overlooked or misunderstood. From the earliest rides, the horse is taught to move ahead with leg pressure. Thus the rider's legs provide what is called impulsion or forward movement. The legs also provide the principal source of impulsion for the lateral movement of the rearhand. In other words, leg pressure can move the horse sideways as well as forward. Also leg pressure can be used to hold, and thus prevent, the rearhand from moving laterally. That action would be needed in pivots and offsets.

Thus to teach lateral movements, the horse must be taught to move the

Illus. 193. Pull the head to the left and apply pressure on ribs about where your leg hangs. Push and release with your thumb, fist or blunt object. Use a voice cue (clucking). Reward with a pat on the neck when he takes a step or two. Repeat on the right side.

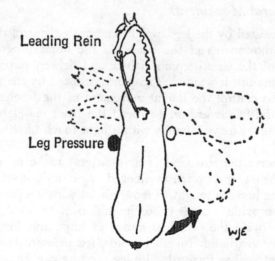

Leading Rein

Leg Pressure

Illus. 194. Apply same basic cues when mounted. Some kicking with the heel may be necessary at first, but as soon as possible reduce this to light pressure from the calf of your leg.

hind quarters away from, or in some cases, not into leg pressure. Moving the rearhand away from pressure can be taught on the ground. After several sessions on the ground with good response, the same cues should be used while mounted. That is, the leading rein and pressure (in this case from the leg), is used to produce a lateral step or two with the rearhand. This is the beginning of what is called a pivot on the forehand.

The forehand pivot is not used with western horses, except as a training aid to teach lateral control. It is an awkward, unnatural movement that is never made by the free moving, unridden horse. Cows never turn on the forehand either but always on the rearhand. A cow horse must turn the same way or lose the cow. Unfortunately many horses acquire the habit of turning on the forehand during training. The weight of the rider and improper use of the hands and legs apparently produce this unnatural and undesirable turn. For this reason, some trainers do not like to teach lateral control in this manner. The horse may get the idea that turning on the forehand is the correct way to turn. However, it should cause no problems if it is done only enough to give the horse the idea of moving a few steps away from leg pressure. Many of my students have used it successfully.

When the horse responds properly to leg pressure by moving the rearhand laterally, training can be started for the side pass and two-track. Illustration 195 indicates how the horse is being moved one end at a time. He is positioned facing the fence to keep him from moving forward. Left leg pressure is used to move the hindquarters a couple of steps to the right. Then the left leg is used to hold the rearhand in place while the right leading rein leads the forehand to the right. Remember to reward him with a pat on the neck and a kind word. The process is repeated several times each direction. It will be difficult for the horse to respond correctly. Take your time, do it all very slowly. Give the horse time to think about each cue and each step. Moving the entire body sideways is not a natural move for the horse. He will have trouble stepping on himself until he learns how to place his feet. Expect to use at least 4 to 6 sessions along the fence before moving back away from it.

If the horse has trouble getting the idea, skip the side pass for a while and work on the two-track. Some horses will learn it easier and then you can return to perfect the side pass. The two-track is easier for some horses to learn first because they have less trouble placing their feet. The forward movement allows them to place the moving foot ahead of the foot that is on the ground.

To teach a two-track to the right, the horse should be positioned facing the fence at about 45° angle. Start the horse moving along the fence and try to maintain the 45° position. Use your left leg strongly to push the hindquarters away from the fence. Use the left leading rein (snaffle or hackamore) to bend his head toward the same side as your leg pres-

STEP ONE

Move Rear Hand

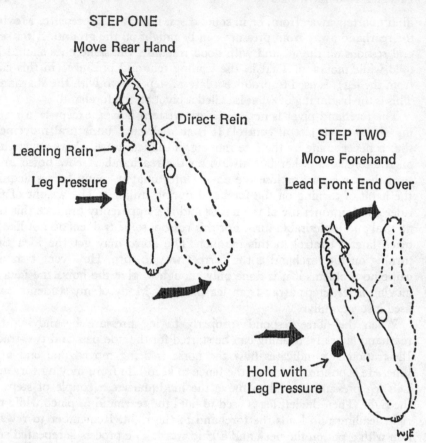

Direct Rein

Leading Rein→

Leg Pressure

STEP TWO

Move Forehand

Lead Front End Over

Hold with
Leg Pressure

Illus. 195. Teaching side pass to the right. To move the rearhand use exactly the same cues you used for a forehand pivot to the right. Then hold the rearhand in place with left leg pressure while you lead the forehand to the right.

sure. When the horse makes a few correct steps, reward him with a pat on the neck. Do this 3 or 4 times each direction each time going a little further. Then quit for the day on this lesson. In several days he should be two-tracking freely along the fence. Next move back from the fence about 10 feet and eventually completely away from the fence. Once the horse is responding to leg pressure on the two-track, it is usually fairly easy to straighten out the two-track to a side pass. This means the horse would be moving at a right angle to the fence rather than 45°.

All of this will take some time, maybe 10 to 15 sessions. The horse must learn not only to respond to your cues but to execute an unnatural move. In particular, he must learn the correct placement of his feet. On

Fence

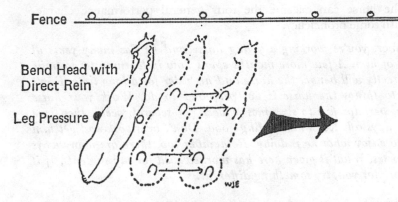

Bend Head with
Direct Rein

Leg Pressure

Illus. 196. Two-track to the right. With some horses it may be necessary to start almost parallel with the fence. Then use more of a left leading rein and strong left leg pressure.

your part it will take some careful thinking and planning. You must use your cues carefully and consistently. If the horse is not responding, try a slightly different approach.

Remember, *in these early lessons, to take advantage of the horse's need for horse company. Work toward the barn or toward horses, the first few times. He'll probably learn easier. Of course, after he gets the idea of what is wanted, you must make him go away from where he wants to go.*

If a horse refuses to yield to leg pressure, it may be necessary to use spurs or a whip. If you do, use them only to punish for not yielding. As soon as the horse yields, reward him by using only the legs. Remember you're trying to develop lightness. Continued use of spurs or whip will develop hardness instead.

Up to this point, we have discussed the general characteristics of a finished western horse. These have been head set, collection, lightness and lateral movements. You could be working on all of these during the same training sessions. The correct execution of one is not dependent upon, or basic to, the performance of another one.

However, the remaining subjects we will discuss are dependent upon the horse's understanding and reasonable execution of the above four items. In particular, the horse must be doing the lateral movements without difficulty. Pivots, offsets, rollbacks and taking leads are all dependent upon the horse yielding laterally to leg pressure. It would also be difficult for a horse to perform any of these specific moves unless he is balanced (this means a correct head set) with a certain amount of collection and lightness. Therefore, do not start on the next part until you're satisfied the horse can execute the four general performance characteristics with some proficiency.

Remember, *you're working a young horse and he has many years of use ahead of him. A few more months spent now in learning to do basic things correctly will benefit the horse and his rider for a long time. Don't hurry on to things the horse is not prepared to do. Work your horse frequently, perhaps five to six times a week for several weeks, then give him a few days off. Keep him feeling good. Don't overwork and get him too tired to enjoy what he is doing. Remember too, there are many ways to train horses. What is given here has worked well for my students. If it doesn't work for you, try something different.*

SPECIFIC PERFORMANCE TRAINING
OF A REINING HORSE

Before we proceed, we should point out that many western riders may not want to go further with the finishing of their horses. Riders who ride only for pleasure will have little use for a horse that will take leads on demand, make flying changes, pivots, spins, etc. These moves are primarily for horses that will be worked on cattle, barrel or stake raced, or entered in reining classes at horse shows. If you are going to compete in pleasure classes in the show ring, your horse should take leads easily but the other moves would not be necessary. What follows is for those who have some special use for their horse or would like to try their hand at developing a finished reining horse.

LEADS

It is essential that a horse used in the show ring take a lead on demand and execute correct flying changes of leads in reining classes. It is useful to have a horse do these things outside the show ring too under certain conditions. For example, if you are going to turn to the left at a lope, it makes it easier for the horse if you put him in a left lead when you start. There is also a certain amount of satisfaction in having enough control of your horse to do these things as you want to and not to be dependent upon your horse's doing them if and when he wants to.

The preliminary step in teaching leads to be certain the horse is willing and able to take both leads. Taking either lead is natural for a horse. Some people say a horse may naturally be left or right leaded like a person is left- or right-handed. I do not agree. It would have been a distinct disadvantage for a wild horse to have preferred one lead. If he preferred the left lead, for example, he would have been at a disadvantage turning to the right. When a predator attacked him and he needed to go right in a hurry, he probably wouldn't have done it fast enough to stay alive. Also, preferring one lead would have produced greater fatigue and chance of injury to the lead foot.

Now this doesn't mean that a broke horse may not prefer a certain lead. During breaking or finishing, a horse may learn, or be forced to use, one lead more than the other. Some riders who do not understand leads may unconsciously encourage a horse to take a certain one. Perhaps the rider feels a little more comfortable in that lead. Thus he is inclined to favor this lead and train the horse accordingly. For example, many people ride with the reins in the left hand. Because of the way a horse moves, they may feel a little more comfortable in the left lead and unconsciously encourage the horse to take this lead. Horses may also use one lead more because of an injury which hurts when they use the other lead. Some horses appear to develop a mental block against taking a certain lead. So, although horses, in my opinion, naturally have no lead preference, they can acquire one. When they do develop a preference, it can be a real problem to get them to use both leads freely.

Simple Changes of Lead

One way to insure that the horse does not develop a lead preference in the early training period is to be certain he is using both leads. This may have been done during the breaking, but if not, here is a suggested procedure.

The following steps can be used to get a left lead from a trot.

STEP I.
Trot the horse in a large circle to the left.

STEP II.
Use a slight leading left rein.

STEP III.
Step lightly in the left stirrup and move it slightly ahead.

STEP IV.
Apply pressure with your right leg.

STEP V.
Cue for a lope.

Unless the horse is sour or is hurting, he should take a left lead. Obviously the cues for a right lead would use the right rein, left leg pressure, etc.

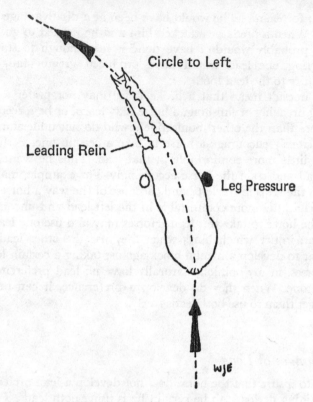

Illus. 197. Taking a left lead. Note natural bend in horse's body.

If the horse will not take one lead, make certain he is not hurting in some way. Then try some variations such as circling with another horse, or turning toward the barn or other horses. You can trot into the corner of a corral and, as the horse starts to turn, make him lope. Sometimes it helps to be posting on the correct diagonal as you trot the circle. (The correct one is the outside diagonal.) This keeps the weight off his inside lead foot and may make it easier for him to take the lead. Some horses will be helped if you pull their head to the outside away from the lead wanted. This tends to push the hindquarters into the circle. Sometimes it helps to stop working on leads for several weeks or longer. This would be particularly true of an injury such as a pulled muscle. This could be difficult to detect if it is in the quarters or shoulders. If all else fails, quit working on this and proceed to the part on taking leads from a standing start.

Perhaps an explanation of the cues listed above for a left lead would be helpful. The left leading rein bends the body of the horse slightly to the left. This is the natural position of the body to turn left. The slight weight to the left stirrup also cues the horse to turn to the left. The horse will learn that the movement of the rider's left foot ahead is a cue for that lead. The right leg pressure encourages the rear quarters of the horse to move to the left.

Now would be a good time to analyze how a horse moves at the lope. The natural moving horse does not travel with his body exactly in line with the direction of travel. There will be a slight slant, as illustrated in Illus. 198. Even a race horse in a dead run will have a very slight slant, depending on the lead he is in.

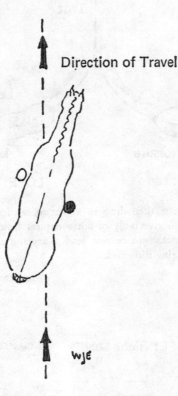

Direction of Travel

WJE

Illus. 198. Left lead—natural position of horse and rider's legs, slightly exaggerated.

The natural rider in balance with his horse in a left lead will also have this same slant to his body. The left foot will be slightly ahead, as will his left shoulder. In a show ring equitation class, this slant should not be obvious. Now, in order for a horse to take a left lead, he must put his body into this slight slant. The rearhand must move slightly to the left of the straight line of direction the horse is going. This is what the right leg pressure is meant to accomplish.

SIMPLE CHANGES OF LEAD

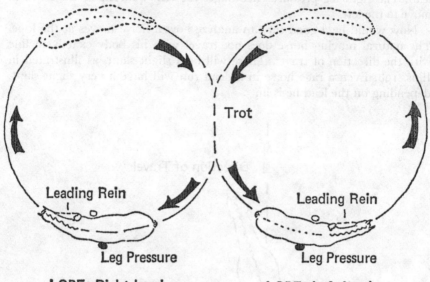

Illus. 199. Lope large circles then drop to a trot to change directions and leads. Note use of leading rein to give body of horse natural bend for the lead. Outside leg pressure encourages horse into correct lead. Vary the number of circles from one to several before changing direction.

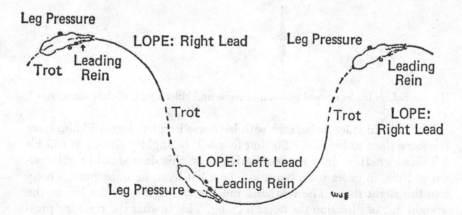

Illus. 200. Doing simple changes in a serpentine provides variety for the horse.

Getting back to taking leads, the horse should be worked at a trot until he is taking both of them easily. Usually you can work in a large figure eight, dropping to a trot and changing leads where you cross the eight. You can also, for variety, do serpentines, dropping to a trot each time you change directions. The action of dropping to a trot is called a simple change of leads. As the training progresses, the amount of trotting between changes should gradually be reduced. The horse should only trot two or three strides and then go on into the next lead.

Taking a Lead on Demand

Once a horse will take the leads in a simple change by dropping to a trot, he is ready to advance to flying changes, or to taking a lead on demand. It depends on the horse and your judgment which should be done next. We will discuss taking leads on demand first. This means that the horse is taught to take a lead from a standing start, or with only one or two steps. Before this can be taught easily, the horse must execute these basic moves: lope directly from a walk, or preferably, from a standing start; move the rearhand laterally with slight leg pressure; and two-track easily without noticeable use of a leading rein. When he performs these basic moves correctly, the following steps can be used to get a right lead:

STEP I.
Start a two-track to the right.

STEP II.
Maintain the pressure of the left leg and the left direct rein* as you cue for a lope.

The cues for a lope in the right lead should be:

1. Movement of the right stirrup slightly ahead.
2. A lifting or inclining of your weight forward and slightly to the right stirrup.
3. Pressure of your left leg.
4. Your voice.

If the body of the horse is moving laterally to the right, and if you can hold his body in this position as he starts to lope, he should take a right lead. Your left leg pushes and holds the rearhand to the right. The left direct rein acts as an aid to your leg. Use the opposite leg and rein for a left lead.

You will notice that one of the cues for loping in the right lead is the movement of the right stirrup ahead. As we pointed out earlier, this is the natural way you will sit once the horse is in the right lead. Therefore, it

* The horse should be two-tracking freely enough so that it is not necessary to bend his head to the left; thus only a direct left rein is needed.

serves as a natural, in-balance cue for the horse. Some English riders touch the horse on the shoulder with their foot as a cue for a lead.

Within a few sessions (maybe 6 to 8), your horse should be two-tracking into either lead with some ease. When he does, you can begin to reduce the amount of two-tracking. Gradually reduce it until, from a standing position, he'll move the rearhand one step laterally and lope into the correct lead. When the horse approaches this stage, you should get a lead from a standing start with cues that are essentially undetectable, except to the horse. In other words, you're developing lightness.

Remember, *once a horse has learned to do something, do not do it too often. Reward him with rest.*

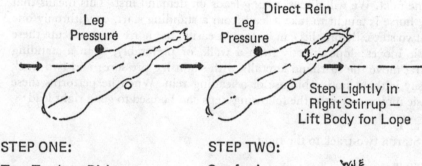

Leg Pressure

Direct Rein

Leg Pressure

Step Lightly in Right Stirrup — Lift Body for Lope

STEP ONE:

Two-Track to Right

STEP TWO:

Cue for Lope

WJE

Illus. 201. Taking a right lead on demand. You must maintain the two-track as you cue for the lope.

Flying Changes

The correct execution of a change of leads at a slow collected lope is a real pleasure to watch or ride. It takes some training and it takes a horse with some natural coordination. Unfortunately, there are a lot of horses that cannot execute a good one. They either cross up (disunite), go too fast or don't change at all. Part of the problem is the training and part is the lack of athletic ability of a horse. Changing leads at the gallop or run is natural for the horse; changing at the lope is not. The free horse will almost always drop to a trot to change leads if he is galloping slowly.

It is essential for a horse to change leads when he changes direction. If he doesn't, he just can't make the turn. There is nothing more awkward in appearance and feel than a horse trying to turn left in a right lead. Not only is it awkward, it can be dangerous because a horse is much more apt to slip and fall. If he crosses up his leads and changes in front and not behind, he is even more dangerous and difficult to ride.

Horses used in the show ring or for working cattle are the ones that need to make the flying change. Cutting horses often need to be able to make the change at a slow lope, while rope horses will change at the run. It is very interesting to watch a wise old rope horse change as he runs to the calf. The smart ones will anticipate the slightest change in direction of the calf and will change leads to gain ground and position on the calf. Horses working cattle outside in big areas must make the flying changes to head and turn back the strays.

Teaching the Flying Change

For the best results, the horse should be making simple changes with only a couple of strides at the trot. It may be helpful if he is also taking either lead on demand. Now, the two biggest problems most inexperienced riders have with flying changes are improper use of their weight and not enough speed with the horse. If the rider's weight is used to turn the horse and "throw" him into the change, it very often results in crossing up the lead. That is, the horse is forced to change in front to compensate for the rider's sudden shift in weight but he doesn't change behind.

As to the problem of speed, we pointed out earlier, it is not natural for a horse to change leads at the lope. Therefore, it will be much easier for the horse if he is allowed to gallop or run to make the change. When he has learned what is expected, he can gradually be slowed down to a lope. This is the one exercise that needs to be done with speed. All the others will be easier for the horse to learn if he goes slow.

Another problem in making the flying change is the timing needed as the change is made. There is only a split second to give the cues for changing. This is difficult to describe and more difficult to execute. The time is that point in the stride when the horse pushes off with his hind feet and his front end starts up. If you learn to feel this, it will help considerably.

Here is one series of steps that may work for you in changing to the right lead from the left. One word of caution: be sure you're working on good ground where there is no danger of the horse slipping because you'll be using some speed.

STEP I.
Start a good sized circle to the left at the gallop and approach the place where you will hopefully make the change with good speed.

STEP II.
Stand up in the stirrups and lean ahead slightly. This gets your weight out of the saddle seat and well over the center of balance, making it

easier for the horse to change behind (his hindquarters must come up a little as he changes).

STEP III.

When you stand up, let him increase his speed a little more.

STEP IV.

Step lightly in the right stirrup and squeeze with the left leg. If the horse is responsive, he'll respond by turning to the right. It may take a light rein too in the early stages. These last cues are most effective if given in that split second as the horse drives off the hind legs.

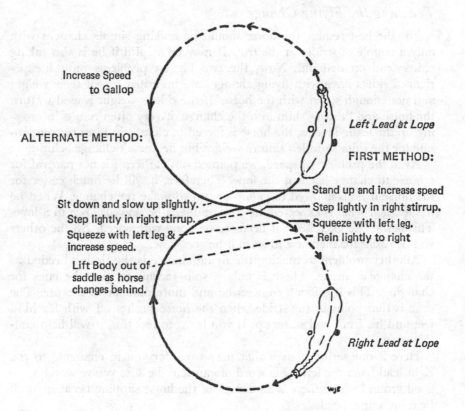

Increase Speed
to Gallop

Left Lead at Lope

ALTERNATE METHOD:

FIRST METHOD:

Sit down and slow up slightly.
Step lightly in right stirrup.
Squeeze with left leg &
increase speed.

Stand up and increase speed
Step lightly in right stirrup.
Squeeze with left leg.
Rein lightly to right

Lift Body out of
saddle as horse
changes behind.

Right Lead at Lope

Illus. 202. Flying change from left to right lead. First method described is on the right.

If the horse is handy, if you have enough speed, have not turned too sharply and don't cross him up by using too much weight, he should make a flying change. If he doesn't, here is an alternate method.

STEP I.

Same as first method.

STEP II.

Do not stand up but stay sitting in the saddle and slow the horse slightly.

STEP III.

Step down lightly in the right stirrup as you move it ahead slightly.

STEP IV.

Allow or make the horse speed up as you squeeze with the left leg.

STEP V.

Rise from the saddle seat as the horse starts to change behind.

This alternate method requires a little more timing because of slowing down and rising out of the saddle as the horse starts to change. However, it does allow for stronger use of the left leg cue and does tend to gather or collect the horse when you slow down slightly. You use the leg squeeze with the first method too, but it is more difficult to do when you are standing up.

Third Method—This method would allow the horse to make a simple change but reduces the trot to merely a hesitation. Eventually the trot is eliminated and a flying change is made.

STEP I.

Lope in a circle to the left.

STEP II.

Where the eight crosses, sit down as a cue to slow down.

STEP III.

As the horse hesitates to a trot, use a strong left leg.

STEP IV.

Step lightly in the right stirrup as you move it ahead and cue for a lope.

Regardless of the method used, you must recognize which lead you're in and, in particular, you must know if your horse is crossed up. As soon as a horse crosses, he should be corrected, usually by dropping to a trot. If you allow a horse to go crossed up very much, he may get the idea that is the correct way. If you have doubts as to leads, have someone watch your horse as you work and tell you if your horse is wrong or crossed up.

If you're still having problems, stop and think about it all and try to figure out if it is your fault or the horse's. Maybe a little change in speed, timing or amount of leg pressure will make the difference. Perhaps changing the location where you're working, or turning toward the direction the horse naturally wants to go will help. Try serpentines instead of figure eights. Anyway, give it some careful thought. You might find a solution.

There are some other methods that can be tried, too, such as going over a low jump and using your weight and leg cue to change in midair. Although an unnatural way to ride, you can also try shifting your weight just the opposite of what we have described. That is, if you're coming around in a left lead and want to change to the right, you shift your weight to the left stirrup, not to the right. This will help some horses change. The theory is that it lightens the right side of the horse, allowing him to get his right legs ahead into the desired lead.

Remember, *there is no one perfect way that will work for all horses. Also, there are some horses which lack the coordination necessary to make a flying change. Some of these can do almost everything else you want, but can't change. If you have one like this, enjoy and use his good moves and forget about the flying change.*

Changing Leads on the Straightaway

When you have perfected the flying change and want to go further with leads, changing in the straight line is the ultimate. Dressage horses are taught this, and it is certainly most impressive, particularly on those highly trained ones that can change at every stride, but those are exceptional horses. If you can get a change every 3 or 4 strides, it will be quite an accomplishment. You'll see some rope horses or cow horses do this with great ease and perfection. It is entirely natural, of course, for them.

Changing leads on the straightaway can be taught in at least two different ways. One is dropping to a trot to get the change. It would be similar to the third method described for making flying changes, except you would be going in a straight line instead of a figure eight. The hesitation to a trot becomes only a hesitation as the horse learns to change without dropping to a trot. The other method is to use a serpentine, gradually straightening it out until the horse is changing on essentially a straight line. This sounds easy, but takes some careful thought and some very careful riding. However, it is great fun when your horse learns it properly. It will also impress your friends.

SLIDING STOP

In the previous chapter, we discussed teaching a horse to stop from a lope in 3 or 4 strides. The finished horse may be taught to make a sliding stop from a run. There are two uses for which a horse should be taught this and two different styles of stopping. The two uses are for calf roping and reining classes. The two styles are the long, California sliding stop and the "stick their tails in the ground" sliding stop used by calf ropers and in some reining classes. We will call the latter a short sliding stop and the former the long sliding stop.

In a short sliding stop, the horse stops as quickly as possible, usually in two or three strides. The horse stops mostly on the hind legs with the front legs acting as brakes. The practical value of this stop is that it can increase the speed with which calf ropers can tie down calves. The long sliding stop differs in that the horse slides on the hind legs for as much as 15 feet or more without coming off the ground. The horse does not use the front legs to brake but to help extend the slide. There is no practical use for this stop that I know of. It is, however, a spectacular show ring feature of the California reined horse. Both stops require soft ground and, therefore, are used almost exclusively in rodeo or horse show arenas.

Much practice in stopping can be done at the walk, trot and slow lope to teach the horse to respond to the cues. Stopping at the run should be done very seldom. Some professional trainers stop at the run only when

I. Say "Whoa"

IV. Hands low

II. Sit down

III. Squeeze

Illus. 203. Sliding stop at the run. Teach your horse to stop easily at the slower gaits before attempting a sliding stop. Be very careful to use your hands as light as possible.

actually competing. It is difficult and apparently unpleasant for the horse to slide from a run and, therefore, it should not be done often.

Chapter V discusses the cues for stopping at slower gaits and these same cues would be used at the run. However, because of the speed, the timing becomes more critical and more difficult. The best stops are made when the horse stops on leg, weight, and voice cues with a minimum use of the hands. The cues for stopping at the run may be as follows:

STEP I.

Say "whoa."

STEP II.

Sit down, or if you ride sitting tight in the saddle, roll up on your knees and then sit down as the horse stops.

STEP III.

Squeeze with your knees and upper leg.

STEP IV.

Use your reins with a pull and slack or in an easy steady pull with your hands low.

Review—Before we continue on to turns on the rearhand, it would be a good idea to review some of the basic principles of teaching cues that were discussed in Chapter II. If a horse is going to learn to respond in a certain way to a cue, the cue must be given in exactly the same way each time. Not only should a cue be given in the same way, a series of cues should be given in the same sequence each time. In the early stages of teaching a cue, the stimuli for the cue must be definite and obvious. As the horse learns what is expected, the cue can become more subtle and thus lightness is produced. You cannot expect your horse to learn cues readily unless he is feeling good physically. Neither will he learn unless you have his undivided attention. If he is worried about being away from other horses or the barn, it will be very difficult for him to learn the correct responses.

Remember, *too, the cues we're using are not something I've developed myself. They have been used by horsemen for a long time, in some cases for several thousand years. They're all basic, tried and true methods based on the natural responses of the horse and rider. They apply to English as well as western riding.*

TURNING ON THE REARHAND
PIVOTS, ROLLBACKS, OFFSETS, SPINS

Xenophon wrote about how important it was for a war horse to turn and run. He pointed out that on active service, one turns in order to pursue or in order to retreat. So, he added, it is a good thing to practice going fast after turning. Although it was not clearly stated, we assume he was talking about a turn on the rearhand. That is the only way a horse can turn and run easily. We want our western horses to be able to do the same and we have specific terms to describe this.

We will use the term pivot for a horse turning on the hind legs from essentially a standing position. The pivot might be preceded and followed by a run. That is, the horse would be stopped from a run, pivoted 180° and run back in the opposite direction. In another exercise, the horse may be pivoted 90° or 180° in one direction and then 90° or 180° in the other direction, without moving forward. For purposes of clarity, we will call this exercise an offset. Both of these moves are used in working cattle and for reining classes. They are moves that cattle and horses do naturally.

Another type of natural turn on the rearhand is the rollback. This is similar to the pivot and run, but is done in motion without a complete stop. Cutting horses excel at making the rollback. The spin is a turn in which the horse goes completely around (360°) without stopping and without moving the hind feet from a very small area. It is a flashy eye-catching move when executed properly. It is not something a horse or cow would do naturally. At least, I can't recall ever observing it being performed by a loose horse.

Teaching the Pivot

It is usually not too difficult to teach a pivot on the rearhand if the horse has properly learned the lateral moves. If a horse will side pass and two-track freely, he should be ready to pivot. We will discuss the pivot first because it can be done slowly and carefully. The offset is more difficult and the rollback and spin are done with speed.

The following cues would be for a pivot to the right:

STEP I.
Stand the horse alongside and about a horse's length away from a high fence on your right side. The high fence is needed to prevent the horse moving ahead in the process of turning and/or getting his head over it as he turns. For the first few sessions, it is best to stand facing away

from the barn or other horses. Your horse's natural desire to turn toward the barn will help him learn to pivot.

STEP II.

Back the horse a step or two, or until it feels as if he has his hind legs slightly under him.

STEP III.

Shift your weight slightly back to the right side of the saddle. This places your weight over the off hind leg which is the leg the horse should pivot on.

STEP IV.

Move your right stirrup slightly ahead as you shift your weight. This will be the natural position of your foot later on when the horse is jumping out of the pivot in the right lead.

STEP V.

Squeeze strongly with the left leg. This should prevent the horse pivoting on the forehand.

STEP VI.

Start your voice cue for turning as you squeeze. This may be a clucking sound.

STEP VII.

Use the right leading rein to lead the forehand to the right a step at a time. Use the left direct rein to prevent the horse from moving ahead. The fence will also help on this.

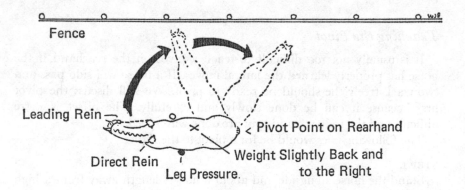

Illus. 204. Pivot on the rearhand to the right. The right rein leads the front end over while your left leg prevents the rearhand moving to the left.

STEP VIII.

When he moves the forehand a step or two, stop and reward him with a pat on the neck. Continue walking around until he has pivoted 180°. Allow the horse plenty of time to move the forehand a step or two at a time. Not only must he learn to move the forehand, he must learn the proper placement on the hind legs.

Continue to walk the front end around until the horse will do it easily and is placing his hind legs correctly. Of course, you'll practice pivoting in both directions. In a few sessions you will want to walk the horse down the fence, stop and back if necessary and then pivot and walk out of the pivot in the opposite direction. Be sure to keep your hand low and well out to the side as you lead the front end around. As soon as you can, stop using the fence.

As the horse learns, you will use the leading rein less and less, eventually using only a light indirect rein on the finished horse. Your goal, if you want lightness and a correct head set, will be to teach the horse to do this move almost entirely on leg, weight and voice cues with very little need for reining. However, it will take many sessions before you'll attain this perfection. He won't start getting light until more speed is used.

Speeding up the Pivot

When the horse has learned to walk the front end around, it is time to speed him up. The idea will be to get him to swing the front end around a full 180° without touching the ground with the front feet. It is usually best to teach this at the trot to provide momentum without the excitement and possible confusion which might be caused by loping.

To speed up the pivot:

STEP I.

Trot down the fence.

STEP II.

Stop and back, if necessary, to get the hind feet collected under the horse. The back should be eliminated in a few sessions. The stop should be followed by a slight but distinct hesitation.

STEP III.

Cue for a pivot—Your cues for pivoting should be the same as you have been using.

STEP IV.

Pivot and Trot Out—With the added speed, the horse should start picking the front end up to swing around. As he does this, you will want to get in balance and swing your body with him. Be sure to trot out of the pivot to help give him momentum. It may be best to change your voice cue as you pivot from a turning sound (cluck) to your go ahead sound (lip smacking). This gives the horse the cue for jumping out after the turn.

Jumping out of the Pivot

As soon as he gets the idea of swinging around and trotting out, it is time to urge him into a lope as he completes the pivot. Eventually he should pivot and jump out all in one smooth motion. If a horse doesn't want to make the 180° pivot in the air, it may be necessary to use a light, stiff whip on his neck or shoulder. This should be done with mostly wrist action to sting the horse, not to scare him into ducking away from your arm swinging the whip. Obviously you would use the whip on the same side as your leg pressure, that is, left leg and whip on left side for a right pivot. Some horses may respond best if whipped on the hip rather than on the front end. If he does not want to jump out after the pivot, a sting with a whip on the hip or over the tail will wake him up. Spurs could be used in place of the whip for these two purposes but it is more difficult to use them properly.

Run, Stop, Pivot and Run

The final finishing for this move will be to lope along, stop, hesitate, pivot 180° and lope out. When this is done smoothly and in balance, the horse will pivot and take the lead in the direction he pivots. That is if he pivots to the left, he should jump out in the left lead. About this time, you will need to use a considerable amount of variety to prevent the horse from anticipating what you are going to do. For example, part of the time you will want to stop, back and then ride on without pivoting, or stop and lope on in a different lead. The final step will be to gradually increase the speed until the horse can run, stop, pivot and run. When the horse can do this, he will be finished on this move.

Teaching Rollbacks

Some trainers will teach the rollback before the pivot and run. However, since this move requires speed, your horse might learn it easier after he learns to pivot properly. Also, it may be more difficult to teach the horse to stop in a pivot and run if he has learned to rollback first. It is usually best to teach the rollback at the trot, turning back alongside a fence. The following steps would be for a rollback to the left.

STEP I.

Trot down a fence about a horse's length away from it.

STEP II.

Slow slightly but do not stop. (Sitting down in Step III may be sufficient cue to slow slightly.)

STEP III.

Give the cues for a left pivot.

These cues are:

a. Sit down with weight slightly to left side of the saddle.
b. Move your left foot slightly ahead.
c. Use a strong right leg.
d. Use enough leading left rein to pull his head around. You should be using a snaffle rein or hackamore at this stage. Use of an indirect (neck-rein) on a green horse will turn his head the wrong way. It may also cause him to throw his head.
e. Use some direct right rein to slow and prevent him from going ahead into the fence.
f. Use your move out voice cue (smacking).

Try to keep about the same momentum as you make the rollback, that is, do not allow the horse to slow down too much as he turns. Use a whip if necessary as you would in a pivot to encourage him to come around. When he will do it properly at the trot, you can work him at a lope and eventually a gallop. When you lope down the fence for a left rollback, put your horse in a left lead. This will make it easier for him to rollback to the left. It is also good practice in taking leads. Many horses learn to rollback on a fence rather easily. They appear to enjoy doing it. Of course, you should not do too much of it. Also, your horse will not be finished on this move until he will do it when not near a fence.

A good way to practice rollbacks is turning back another horse. This works particularly well if someone has a finished horse and you use your green horse to turn him back. Start this at the trot along a fence with your green horse on the outside. As the other rider turns the inside horse back toward the fence, use the cues listed above to rollback with him. He'll soon learn to cue on the inside horse but he will also be learning your cues.

Teaching the Offset

When the horse will stop, pivot and run properly, he should be ready to learn the offset. This is a difficult move for a horse and few horses appear to enjoy doing it. It must be done carefully to avoid developing cer-

302 WESTERN HORSE BEHAVIOR AND TRAINING

tain undesirable habits. There is a temptation to overuse the hands and this can destroy a good head set and produce a hard mouth. Some horses want to come off the ground too high in front and some move the hind legs too much. It is not a move that can be taught by slow stages because a lack of momentum makes it more difficult for the horse. So—be careful!

The cues would be the same as for the pivot with one important difference. There is no cue for the horse to jump out after he turns. This means you will need a different voice cue and you must not shift your weight ahead as a cue to jump out. These different cues must be carefully exaggerated at first because the horse is going to want to jump out as you have taught him to do in the pivot and run. The cues for an offset to the right and then left would be:

STEP I.

Alert the horse. Pick up the reins, squeeze lightly with your legs and back a step or two if the hind feet do not feel under the horse. To give the horse momentum you may want to be walking the horse, then stop and start immediately to make the offset.

STEP II.

Move your right foot slightly ahead and sit back to the right.

STEP III.

Squeeze with your left leg, use the right leading rein and give your voice cue for turning (clucking) but not for jumping out. Use the left direct rein to prevent the horse moving ahead. Later when the horse is finished on this move, you should need only a light neck rein.

STEP IV.

Swing your body with the horse as he comes up in front and turns in the air.

STEP V.

When the front feet hit the ground after the offset to the right, use both direct reins to prevent him from jumping out, but do allow him to walk a few steps after the pivot. This will give him some momentum for the next offset and will not be a complete drastic change from the pivot and run. Gradually reduce the steps to none with only a hesitation after the first offset. The hesitation will be eliminated on the finished horse.

STEP VI.

To start the second offset move your left foot slightly ahead and shift your weight to the left.

STEP VII.

Squeeze with the right leg, use the left leading rein and give your voice cue. Use the right direct rein.

STEP VIII.

Swing your body with the horse.

After the second offset, walk the horse around a minute or two before repeating. As we mentioned before, while teaching the offset be very careful with your hands. The horse should be far enough along to be responding mostly to the other cues with little rein needed. If you must use a strong rein, you will probably have some problems. It would be best to finish the horse more on pivots and rollbacks and come back to the offset later.

When the walking steps between pivots and the hesitation are eliminated, the cues must be given in rapid succession to maintain momentum and avoid a noticeable hesitation. By this stage, the horse should be working almost entirely off your leg pressure and your voice. You will not have time to shift your weight and you should not be using much rein, or head and mouth problems will result. In the show ring, horses are usually expected to make a 90° offset one way, followed by one or two 180° offsets.

Teaching the Spin

As we pointed out earlier, the spin does not have any practical use except to show the handiness of a reining horse in the show ring. Therefore, unless you expect to show your horse or want to try this as a learning experience for yourself, you may want to skip this part.

Since this is a difficult, unnatural move for a horse, it is not easy to teach. Certainly the basics of pivots, rollbacks and offsets should be well understood by the horse. In addition, it may be beneficial to teach the horse to lope into and out of a very tight circle. This will help the horse learn to handle its hind feet properly. This can be started early at about the same time you are working on figure eights. The idea is to gradually decrease the diameter of a circle until the horse is loping around without moving the hind legs out of a very small circle. To maintain momentum and to discourage the horse from expecting to stop when the circle gets tight, you should always lope out into a larger circle before stopping. This same exercise will help prepare a horse for a 360° rollback.

When the horse is performing all the rearhand turns correctly and is doing it mostly from leg cues, he can be started in the spins. If it is necessary to use the hands very much, the horse is probably not ready. As you would expect, his head position as well as his balance will be adversely effected if it is necessary to do much reining.

The cues for the spin will be essentially the same as for the offset. The voice can be used as the principal motivation for speed and maintaining the spin. On some horses, it may be helpful to trot the horse into a small circle and from this lead into a spin. On others, you may want to start from a standing or walking start as you did in the offsets.

For a spin to the left, the cues could be as follows:

STEP I.
Shift your weight slightly to the left side of saddle.

STEP II.
Move the left foot ahead slightly.

STEP III.
Squeeze strongly with the right leg.

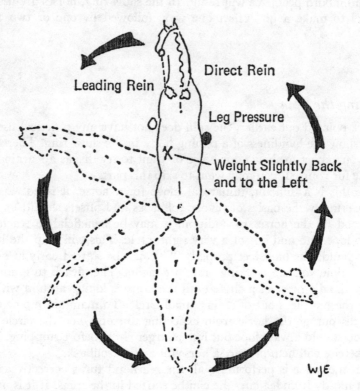

Illus. 205. Spin to the left.

STEP IV.

Use a strong, rapid voice cue for turning.

STEP V.

Use the left leading rein to start the horse to the left and a light, direct, right rein to hold him from moving ahead.

As the horse comes around, the cues must be repeated each time the front end hits the ground until he has spun around 360°. Now, if the horse is really coming around, there is not enough time to repeat all of the above cues. Therefore, to prevent confusing the horse and, in particular, destroying its head set and balance with too much rein, you will need to rely primarily on leg pressure and voice. To spin to the right, obviously all cues would be reversed.

Remember, *we said at the beginning of this chapter your horse must be feeling good with plenty of energy, to learn all these finishing moves. This is especially true of the spin. A tired, slow horse will not perform this one correctly and may quickly develop some bad habits.*

CONCLUSION

If you teach your horse most of the moves discussed in this chapter, you'll be riding a good horse. If you don't get them all taught, don't be discouraged, particularly if this is the first horse you've tried to finish. It is very difficult to teach yourself and the horse all at the same time. However, as you gain more experience and if you really try to think out solutions, your techniques and results will improve with each horse you train.

Remember, we said at the beginning, this material has been written for those who, regardless of age and regardless of experience, want to learn more about training horses. It is a basis that you can use, add to and/or alter to fit your needs. Keep an open mind, continue to think, continue to learn and you'll always ride a good horse.